Penda, Mercia's First King

*Josee, Rowan, Violet and Willow; the family that inspires me.
My mum, sister, grandparents, aunts, uncles, and cousins;
the family that raised me.
The ancestors, wights, and Gods who guide me.
Gæþ a wyrd swa hio scel*

Penda, Mercia's First King

The Last Great Heathen Warlord of *Anglo-Saxon England*

Paul Barrett

Pen & Sword
MILITARY

First published in Great Britain in 2024 by
Pen & Sword Military
An imprint of Pen & Sword Books Limited
Yorkshire – Philadelphia

Copyright © Paul Barrett 2024

ISBN 978 1 03610 256 2

The right of Paul Barrett to be identified as
Author of this Work has been asserted by him in accordance
with the Copyright, Designs and Patents Act 1988.

A CIP catalogue record for this book is
available from the British Library

All rights reserved. No part of this book may be reproduced or transmitted in any form or by any means, electronic or mechanical including photocopying, recording or by any information storage and retrieval system, without permission from the Publisher in writing.

Typeset by Mac Style
Printed in the UK by CPI Group (UK) Ltd, Croydon, CR0 4YY.

Pen & Sword Books Limited incorporates the imprints of After the Battle, Atlas, Archaeology, Aviation, Discovery, Family History, Fiction, History, Maritime, Military, Military Classics, Politics, Select, Transport, True Crime, Air World, Frontline Publishing, Leo Cooper, Remember When, Seaforth Publishing, The Praetorian Press, Wharncliffe Local History, Wharncliffe Transport, Wharncliffe True Crime and White Owl.

For a complete list of Pen & Sword titles please contact

PEN & SWORD BOOKS LIMITED
47 Church Street, Barnsley, South Yorkshire, S70 2AS, England
E-mail: enquiries@pen-and-sword.co.uk
Website: www.pen-and-sword.co.uk
or
PEN AND SWORD BOOKS
1950 Lawrence Rd, Havertown, PA 19083, USA
E-mail: uspen-and-sword@casematepublishers.com
Website: www.penandswordbooks.com

Contents

Prologue		ix
Chapter 1	Origins	1
Chapter 2	Iclingas	15
Chapter 3	The Land, the People, the King	29
Chapter 4	Mercia's Rise	45
Chapter 5	To the South	60
Chapter 6	Cadwallon	73
Chapter 7	Hatfield Chase	87
Chapter 8	North of the Humber	101
Chapter 9	Eastward	115
Chapter 10	Oswald's Tree	128
Chapter 11	Cenwalh	141
Chapter 12	Cnobheresburg	154
Chapter 13	Bebbanburg	167
Chapter 14	Pendingas	180
Chapter 15	Winwaed	191
Epilogue		205
Notes		210
Bibliography		224
Index		233

The battles of King Penda.

Etymological look at migration and settlement.

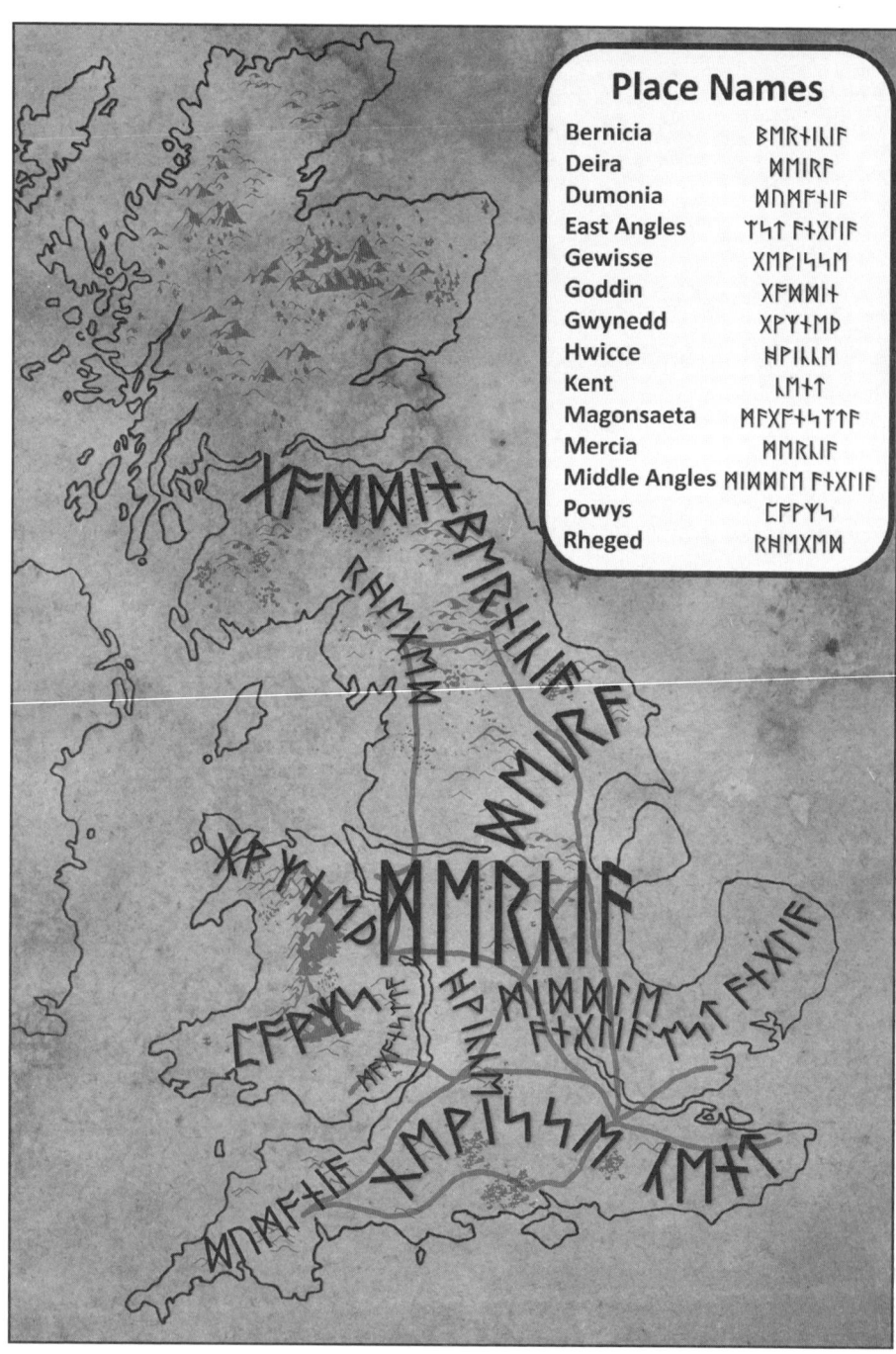

The Kingdoms of Britain in the seventh century.

Prologue

He had known this place for many years, visiting it frequently enough when the pace of events allowed him to. For most people, this was just a spot to pass as you moved east or west along the old road. For him, this was a quiet corner of the world where he could slip away, find peace and hunt. His connection to this land was personal, and born from the effort and experience of his ancestors. Riding from the west the open fields gave way to this forest, not gradually but suddenly, a dark and foreboding wall. In the eyes of many, this area represented danger; wild animals, wild spirits, and most concerning, wild men, hidden from the laws and oaths of kings. Typically, none of these fears were of great concern to him as he usually rode with a band of heavily armed men, and only a fool would take a chance at confronting them. This morning though, he was alone, a rarity for him, and so the concerns of what lay ahead in the woods occupied some of his focus as the open fields ended at the edge of the forest.

He pacified his concerns by feeling the spear in his right hand and glancing down to his left hip where a sword and seax hung, bouncing rhythmically on his hip as his horse trotted along the pathway. The sword had been his closest companion since he first ventured into the world as a warrior. It had been with him in countless conflicts and seen the vastness of this land. The rider wore no mail, no helmet, and didn't carry a shield; the lack of protection was liberating. Without the weight, heat and noise that inevitably accompanies these items, the rider found he was better able to absorb the natural world around him as he entered the woods. Within only a few minutes the open fields were behind him and he was encased by the woods. As he proceeded deeper into the woods the road began to summit a small ridgeline, where, on the downward slope, he turned south off the road and into the wild landscape.

This corner of the wood had always been a great spot for hunting boar; an animal renowned for being intelligent, protective, aggressive, brave, and above all, dangerous. A fitting adversary for a man with all of those same qualities. For the boar, those qualities ensured its own survival and the continuation of a line of descendants that would carry the same characteristics, and roam the woods for generations. For the man, those qualities could build a kingdom, protect a people and echo across an age. He lowered himself from his horse, drew a deep breath and stretched out his back. In those few quiet moments he watched the fresh sun push through the morning gloom, and smelled the wet earth; the only sound was his breathing and that of the horse. He untied the satchel and shovel from the back of his horse and began walking up the gentle rise which overlooked the road. At the top of the ridge was the mound. The mound seemed to be shaped as if it was the boss of a giant's shield left behind following some great clash. The morning dew glistened in the low sun showering the entire scene with a warm orange glow.

Atop the mound stood a noble yew tree, with branches spreading in all directions sheltering this place from the sky under a thick awning of green thatch. It was the singleness of this tree in particular which he always remembered. There were other yews in the wood, but none of them stood so separate from the rest. There were other mounds near here, Mucca's hlaw and Catte's hlaw, both had yew trees but neither were half the size of this one. No one he could recall had been to this place in years, though he had always told himself he would bring his children here, perhaps ask them to place him near this spot when the sisters who weave the wyrd of all men came to collect the debt he, like all people, owed to them. The sisters had weaved him a rather mixed lot if truth be told, but what was the point in complaining? He had heard the churchmen say that their god was all-knowing, that he alone controlled the future, but that didn't make much sense to him. The gods themselves couldn't avoid wyrd; Gæþ a wyrd swa hio scel (Fate goes ever as fate must). He walked to the top and placed his hand on the yew tree, paused and made an offering. He spoke directly to the dwellers of the woods and those that inhabited the mound, seeking their protection and reminding them that they were not forgotten. He grabbed the offering of food and placed it under the yew tree. He knew some people had long processes for the blot, the sacrifice offered from one to another, but he preferred a simple gift and a kind word. He descended to the far side of the mound; he was now at its south edge.

He unfastened his cloak, placed it on the ground and ensured it was as flat and spread as large as he could make it. His sword and seax remained firmly on his waist, but he tossed the spear he was carrying to the side of the cloak. After cutting a small section of sod away and placing this off to the side, he began removing soil and throwing it onto the cloak. Within minutes he could feel the sweat beading down his back and dripping down his brow. At war, in the middle of a fight, he never noticed the sweat, but in this task he noticed it, in fact it was so utterly annoying that it was all he could focus on. He tried to fight off the drops but was outnumbered. Each one piled onto the preceding one like a steadily rising river. He took a break from digging, wiped his brow, cooled his temper and went back to digging. He had thought about bringing one of his sons to help with the hard work of digging, but in the end he decided that this was firmly his burden and something he should do himself. It made him smile to think of the men of other nations who sat in high halls doing this type of work. He found it hard to believe they would have the fortitude or will to put black earth under their fingernails. His mind wandered from one thing to the next, as minds tend to do when they are less engaged than they ought to be. His horse let out a soft sound, but it was enough to bring his senses back to a finely honed point. His horse had always been a good gauge of threats, a guard dog with hooves. He reached down and grabbed his spear. He had a sword with him, but in this spot the likely threat was not a person but a boar, and the spear would provide better protection in that scenario. He opened his mouth slightly to clear his ears and pick up any new sounds while his eyes methodically scanned the undergrowth for movement. He was concerned about his grip on the spear's ash shaft; his hands were covered in mud. He was acutely aware of the advantage he had positioned on the top of the rise, but also knew he could achieve more of an advantage if he gained some elevation. Slowly he stepped rearward keeping his back to the yew tree, gradually rising up the mound. When he was within a spear's length from the tree, he slowly steadied his feet, tested his grip and continued to scan the woods for the threat. His senses were now focused. He was calm, ready to strike, and then, nothing.

He could hear the horse moving slowly somewhere off to his right, it didn't seem too concerned any longer and had returned to foraging for green shoots and grass to nibble on. With one more exhale he relaxed his grip on the spear, stood up right, relaxed his shoulders and walked back to the hole. By now the depth of the hole was as deep as his arms would allow him without carving out more space and climbing in himself. Here, he poured ale into the bottom of the hole and tossed in some dried rowan berries before lifting up the bag. The satchel was heavy enough, it was certainly heavier than his shield. Holding the weight in his hands reminded him that amongst the trials and hard times he had achieved success, great success, and victory in every direction. He was a ring-giver, a protector, a warrior, a father, a king that people sought to defeat but couldn't; he was a memory of the past and a constant reminder to all of the old ways. He had given freely to those loyal to him but he knew he also had to give beyond those who swore an oath to him, which brought him here. This place near an old mound, and old tree, and old road.

The satchel was laden with remnants of battles he had won over the years. Parts of this treasure he was intimately familiar with for they were trophies taken from some of his fiercest rivals, but the majority were just bits and pieces of gold and silver recovered from one battle or another. Some of the treasure he had amassed over the past twenty or more years had been given as gifts to his warriors. Some of it he kept, but some of it he needed to return to the land, an offering. Clearing his mind of thoughts of treasure and gold, he gently lowered the satchel into the hole, carefully buried it, replaced the sod and scattered the remaining soil into the woods. He closed his eyes, inhaled deeply and paused, feeling the burden of the hoard leaving him. Reciting something he had often heard said, he whispered to himself 'Draca sceal on hlæwe, frod, frætwum wlanc'.[1] The burden of taking care of it now lay with whatever dragon called the mound home. He reached down and lifted his cloak up, it was filthy with earth. He shook it off, threw it over his left shoulder and clasped it on his right side; he picked up the spear and walked to the left of the mound toward his horse. Before he left the spot, he checked to make sure he returned the place to the same state he had found it, leaving no mark that would suggest anything was here, and turned away.

Chapter One

Origins

On 5 July 2009, some 1,300 years after the man had deposited the material near the mound, another man named Terry Herbert entered the exact same location. The field is as non-descript as any other field and nothing about it seems particularly special. It is located just south of the village of Hammerwich in Staffordshire, right alongside a major motorway. The place has been completely altered and would have been unrecognizable to the man who dug the hole; the road was enlarged, the wood replaced by houses, and the mound itself is missing. The effort of generations of people pushing and pulling ploughs had levelled the mound over the years. The farmer who works this field now had just completed ploughing and turning the soil, preparing it for future plantings. Terry Herbert was an out-of-work coffin builder. On this particular day, he carried with him a second-hand metal detector that cost him £2.50p, and written permission from the land owner to search the freshly-ploughed field. Within minutes he was finding gold under the surface of the freshly tilled soil. As he worked back and forth he continued to pull gold from the earth; some of it was even right on the surface, glinting in the sun. Over the next few days Terry recovered hundreds of gold and silver pieces.[1] The size of the find was enormous, and it quickly became clear that whatever was in this field it was of national significance. Terry notified the land owner and then the local authorities, as required under the Portable Antiquities Scheme. Within a short period of time the local representative of Her Majesty's Coroner was dispatched as required under the Treasure Act 1996.

An archaeological team was deployed by the Staffordshire County Council to undertake an immediate excavation of the site. This excavation was conducted under the cloak of secrecy to protect it from looters. The archaeological dig and cataloguing of the find identified over 4,000 items, with the vast majority coming from weapons and armour; sword fittings alone made up 80 per cent of the total findings.[2] All told, there were 5lbs of silver and 11lbs of gold found strewn across the site. The archaeologists returned to the site where Terry had found the 'Staffordshire Hoard' in the following years and continued to turn up additional finds, most of them small gold items, likely scattered over the generations as men worked the field.

Further research on the hoard's location was conducted through a geophysical survey in both 2009 and 2010. These surveys detected some interesting anomalies near the likely location of the hoard's burial spot. In particular, there is an underlying circular ditch at the location, along with the remains of a bank in the same spot. The bank is semi-circular running along the west side of the ditch. While it is pure conjecture, these features can be interpreted as a sign of a tumulus in this location, which could create the link between the location and the burial of the hoard. During a geophysical survey, a field boundary was also identified moving in a north-west and south-east line near the centre of the current field. What is interesting is that the field boundary veers to a north direction near the ditch feature. This could be another sign of a tumulus at the site when that field boundary was established.

In the final episode of Beowulf's life, a slave finds a great treasure hoard buried in a mound guarded by a dragon. The slave is overcome by the vast quantity of treasure in the hoard and elects to remove a gold goblet from the treasure. As he removes the goblet he is relieved that the dragon doesn't stir. Eventually, the dragon does awaken, and with his intimate knowledge of the treasure he quickly recognizes that the goblet is missing. The dragon, angered by the theft, immediately begins to range far across the land killing anyone he finds and destroying anything he can. An aged Beowulf is forced to confront the dragon, and ultimately dies defeating it. For Terry and the landowner, the dragon protecting this treasure hoard dragged the two of them through a protracted legal fight, eventually ending with an equal share of £3.3 million for the find.

The Staffordshire hoard, as it is known, is the single largest treasure hoard ever found in England. While it appears that the majority of the hoard has been located, many mysteries still swirl around it, not least of all the date of deposit. Initial estimates placed the hoard in the eighth, and even ninth centuries, but since its discovery in July 2009 that date has slowly slipped deeper in time and is now believed to be in the mid-seventh century, sometime between 630 and 650.[3] What really stands this hoard out amongst many other fabulous finds is its make-up. The Staffordshire hoard contains only the spoils of war, swords, armour, saddle fittings and church regalia. The Staffordshire hoard is fascinating because of what it contains, and equally interesting because of what it lacks: no coins, no brooches, no rings, no arm rings. The trouble with this hoard in particular is that it is devoid of coins, which means no definitive earliest data of deposition can be made. There are many theories about the hoard, and the acceptation of one or another is tied up with an individual's interpretation of when it was deposited, their academic and professional view point, cultural reference point, and perhaps their desire to link it to one event or another. What the research efforts by historians, archaeologists, paleobotanists, theologians, jewellers, art historians, gemologists, geographers, geologists, geo-technicians, coroners, priests and lay persons have provided all of us with, is an opportunity to interpret the hoard through our own lens. Who, and why, remain the crucial missing pieces to the mystery. But with the enduring mystery there is an opportunity for all of us to contemplate the reason and story of the hoard.

Perhaps the easiest assumption to make is that the hoard was placed with the expressed purpose of recovering it, but this view is tainted by our modern ideals of treasure and value, and fails to explore the hoard through the eyes and culture of the period. It is cultural bias at its most damaging, something that our understanding of the era in which it was deposited is plagued by. The Staffordshire hoard is a direct connection to people almost 1,400 years in the past, during a time of extreme turbulence, social change, and cultural competition. The people of the seventh century did not simply occur at a particular space and time; they were the product of thousands of years of history and the outcome of both small and large turns of wyrd.

Migration has been a regular feature of human existence in Britain with successive waves of people arriving one after another. The first people arrived in Britain some 44,000 years ago and were followed by subsequent groups; some we can name, others we can't. Pivotal to this story, the people that would one day be called 'Britons' arrived sometime around 600 BC as part of a great Celtic migration. The Celtic movement was followed in the first century by a military invasion of Britain by the Romans, who would draw Britain into the Roman Empire for the next 400 years. Following a period of sustained warfare, a general peace was achieved under Roman governance driving relative stability across Britain. The Romans did as future invaders would do and effectively decapitated the existing polities, replacing and subjugating indigenous leaders with their own. Many of the traditional tribal identities of the Celtic Britons condensed with the new Roman culture into a Romano-Britonic culture, losing some but not all of tribal affiliations. In the broadest of generalities it appears that the Roman Empire stopped operating as a functioning political entity in Britain around AD 410.

From this point, the devolution of authorities and increasing movement of people began to fundamentally alter the social make-up of Britain. If you are searching for a contemporary record of events, then the term 'Dark Ages' is quite accurate for this period. There are a host of records before AD 400, and a steady increase of records from the mid-seventh century, but that period in-between is difficult to see and challenging to understand. The limited records from and even near to this period provide a wide range of dates and many of them do not seem to align with the evidence left behind for archaeologists to find and interpret.

The 250 years following the constriction of the Roman Empire and its withdrawal from Britain left in its wake a fractured social order. The immediate reaction to the legions leaving was the decentralization and redistribution of power from a central singular government to a host of localized polities. These local authorities were being constructed on a variety of bases, some of them were shaped around Roman governance models, and centred on traditional seats of Roman power, the civitas. At the same time, other groups were looking to more distant foundations for authority, the Brittonic tribal affiliations, and yet a third group was arriving and establishing their own power centres and geographical boundaries.

The upheaval and political instability had a significant impact on the internal economic system as well. During the Roman period market towns were established across the island at locations such as York, Cirencester, Wroxeter and Exeter. Exeter, for example began its life as a Roman fort between AD 55 and AD 60.[4] The legion assigned to Exeter departed in AD 75 and by the end of the second century the town had grown and achieved the status of a civitas. The market at Exeter drew in goods from the rural environs, some of which was tribute and tax, and then processed it for consumption by the local community, and further afield through an established trade network. In the case of livestock the process included stockades, butchering and waste facilities. Between 1970 and 1975 a number of archaeological digs were conducted to examine Exeter's waste piles which resulted from animal butchery. These surveys identified over 18,317 bone fragments from the Roman period of the first to the fifth centuries.[5] These same surveys recovered 40,555 bone fragments from the eleventh to the fourteenth centuries.[6] What the archaeological digs didn't find was anything between those periods. The market place had ceased to function, with no animals brought for sale, no butchering and no waste. The exchange of goods and wealth had apparently ceased. The economy in the interceding period had resorted to a localized and subsistence-based economy bound to smaller polities. It can be inferred that similar economic changes were occurring across Britain in the wake of the Roman withdrawal and the regionalization of power.

Alongside the geo-political and economic changes, cultural diversity began to flourish in all corners of Britain. When a farm field is abandoned it doesn't continue to grow a singular crop; nature begins a process of wilding, where new species arrive and biological diversity thrives. Initially the crop may still be present in the abandoned field, but as new species begin to populate and grow, the local ecology will change even further. This alteration allows for yet more species to arrive and drive ever increasing variance in the local population. This is the same cultural process that occurred between the fifth and seventh centuries. As the Roman cultivation ended, traditional cultures began to sprout again, and new cultures arrived from distant places. From a cultural standpoint this era wasn't dark, but it was vibrant and diverse, an explosion of languages, religions, cultures and identities. Throughout the fifth century the cultural mosaic of the British Isles continued to expand as new peoples arrived from the continent.

Several sources speak of AD 449 as the date the Germanic peoples arrived in Britain, at the request of a King Vortigern. Prior to this date though a range of Roman forts were set upon the 'Saxon shore' not to protect the owners of the coasts, but to prevent others from arriving on that shore. Clearly the threat from Saxons and Angles was present long before these people from across the sea arrived as this defensive system was being constructed and commanded in the fourth century by Roman legions and auxiliaries. The term 'Saxon Shore' is quite an astounding etymology, the only way to understand the threat is to assess it in our own time. This is paramount to naming Dover as the French coast, or Australia's Victoria, the Tasman coast. The etymology says 'this is their coast, and they are coming, but we hold it for now'. It's as if the builders, the soldiers, and leaders had accepted the inevitable failure of the defences and fatality of the future.

Much of our understanding of the arrival of the Angles, Jutes, and Saxons is a recording of oral history and folk memory captured by Christian monks, in particular Gildas Sapiens in the sixth century and the Venerable Bede in the eighth century. Gildas was from Strathclyde, a Brittonic monk, and Bede was a Bernician Angle monk. These men did not share the same religion, nor did they identify as the same nationality, but they do both record a similar story of the arrival of Germanic warriors. These similarities could be due to Bede using Gildas as a primary source, or they could record an event based on the generally accepted narrative which occurred following the arrival of the Angles, Saxons, and Jutes from modern Saxony, Denmark, and the Netherlands. Gildas' account is found in his work, 'The Ruin of Britain', a catchy title with an ominous bit of foreshadowing, which shows precisely how he interpreted the period of time. Gildas focuses on the depravity of the barbarians from the north, the Picts and Scots, and Germanic peoples from the eastern sea. Gildas tells us that the Picts and Scots began raiding once the Romans abandoned Hadrian's Wall. King Vortigern, chief amongst the rulers in Britain, decreed 'that, as a protection to their country, they sealed its doom by inviting in among them like wolves into the sheep fold, the fierce and impious Saxons, a race hateful both to God and men, to repel the invasions of the northern nations'.[7]

From this point on, Gildas tells us that Saxons were successful but wanted more, and inevitably turned on their poorly-advised master King Vortigern, thus ending the Romano Celtic world of the Britons through death, enslavement, and migration. 'Some therefore, of the miserable remnant, being taken in the mountains, were murdered in great numbers; others, constrained by famine, came and yielded themselves to be slaves for ever to their foes...some others passed beyond the seas.'[8]

For Gildas, the arrival of the Germanic tribes was the end times.

Bede's telling is slightly different and focuses on who the people from across the sea are. He goes on to provide detail of origin of the Angle, Saxon, and Jutish kingdoms which had developed in the two centuries following Gildas:

> From the Jutes are descended the people of Kent, and of the Isle of Wight, including those in the province of the West-Saxons who are to this day called Jutes, seated opposite to the Isle of Wight. From the Saxons, that is, the country which is now called Old Saxony, came the East-Saxons, the South-Saxons, and the West Saxons. From the Angles, that is, the country which is called Angln, and which is said, from that time, to have remained desert to this day, between the provinces of the Jutes and the Saxons, are descended the East-Angles, the Midland-Angles, the Mercians, all the race of the Northumbrians, that is, of those nations that dwell on the north side of the River Humber, and the other nations of the Angles.[9]

Bede's comment that Angln became deserted during this period is likely more than just artistic license and seems to be backed up by fact. Based on archaeological evidence it does appear that the population of Angln decreased by about half in the fourth century, and was further reduced through the fifth century leaving only a quarter of the population that had been there in the third century.[10] This decrease in population was not entirely owing to the draw of settling in Britain, but was likely the product of numerous push and pull factors including the movement of other continental people, climatic change, and a decline in agricultural output.[11]

From Bede we also get the names of the first Dryhten or warlords to arrive from the continent as Hengist and Horsa. These two men are said to have arrived at Ebbsfleet with their Angle and Saxon warriors and begin the dominance of the Germanic tribes over the Britons. Bede's record goes on to echo Gildas in the disposition of the Britons in the immediate aftermath of the invasion:

> Some of the miserable remnant, being taken in the mountains, were butchered in heaps. Others, spent with hunger, came forth and submitted themselves to the enemy, to undergo for the sake of food perpetual servitude, if they were not killed upon the spot. Some, with sorrowful hearts, fled beyond the seas.[12]

Bede's telling of events related to the Britons seems to be directly lifted from Gildas, so it doesn't stand as a second verification of events on the ground. The truth behind the migration is likely best built from pieces of the recorded narrative and items we can discern from modern science including DNA analysis. What likely happened is that the Angles and Saxons settled in a piecemeal way, with no overall invasion plan, and that the alteration from a dominant Romano Celtic culture to that of a Germanic one occurred through conflict, contact, further migration and all the other social contexts people can devise. Put simply, this invasion was 'patchy and opportunistic.'[13] While some areas would have seen more migration from the continent, other areas were lightly impacted, generating diverse results. The migration was not only one from across the sea, but also within Britain as people moved west in some cases, and others came from Ireland, moving east and eventually populating parts of the Welsh coast.

The migration of peoples in the fifth and sixth centuries had a lasting impact on modern Britain, Ireland, Denmark, and the north of France. In France, people fleeing from the instability in Britain and the withdrawal of the Roman Legions settled in modern day Brittany, bringing with them the Brittonic language and their culture, tying them directly to modern Cornwall and Wales. Denmark, which had been the home of the Jutes, Danes and Angles is transformed by the mass migration of the Angles, which the sources tell us wholeheartedly abandoned their home lands on continental Europe for Britain, perhaps allowing the Danes and Jutes to slowly begin to dominate the peninsula and eventually leading to the nation of Denmark.

For Britain in particular it is in this period where the modern ideas of nationhood are born; Wales, England, Scotland as ideas are all formed in this period of time. The Britons move west into the hilly western country, and the Angles term them 'wælsc', meaning foreigner or slave. This term alters over time eventually becoming the modern 'Welsh' and Wales. The Scoti, a tribe from Ireland, begin to settle in the lowlands of modern Scotland, eventually coming to dominate that nation's other people, the Picts, and attaching their name to the land. In the south the Angles and Saxons become the dominate force, and the language and culture develop into English and England, words which descend from Angle.

In the period of migration, the Saxons, Angles, Jutes, and Frisians divide their warbands by ceols (Keels or ships). There are two Germanic ceols known to archaeology currently which provide examples of these vessels. The first is a pattern in the sand at Sutton Hoo, and the second is a sacrificed ceol in Nydam, Denmark. Both vessels were clinker built, nearly ninety feet long with fifteen pairs of oars on the Nydam ship and twenty pairs on the Sutton Hoo ship. Based on the Sutton Hoo ship and the Nydam ship, it can be estimated that each of the ceols contained around thirty to forty warriors. These vessels were streamlined, shallow drafted, and very capable in coastal and riverine environments. They had a long fore and aft curve which formed a prominent sweeping bow and stern. Both of these vessels were the product of great craftsmen, and the vessels show many of the elements which would lead to the development of the Danish and Norseman longboats 300 years later.

Gildas Sapiens wrote in the sixth century on the arrival of the Angles and Saxons that, 'A multitude of whelps came forth from the lair of this barbaric lioness, in three ceols, as they call them, that is, in their ships of war, with their sails wafted by the wind.'[14]

Both of the preserved vessels lack the true keel and apparent fittings to carry a mast, rigging and sails, leading to the conclusion that they were rowed vessels, in spite of what Gildas provides us with. Pulled by men, at worst from Jutland, and at best from the Frisian coast. The lack of canvas and need to row consistently would make a blue sea crossing difficult in the extreme. But, the men in the ceol were neither new to the sea, nor perturbed by the activities of sea faring. A letter written in AD 480 by the Gallic poet Sidonius Apollinaris describes the sea-going Saxons:

> look out for curved ships, the ships of the Saxons, in whose every oarsman you think to detect an arch-pirate… His is no mere acquaintance with the perils of the sea; he knows them as he knows himself. A storm puts his enemies off their guard, preventing his preparations from being seen; the chance of taking the foe by surprise makes him gladly face every hazard of rough waters and broken rocks.[15]

It is still widely debated whether or not the northern tribes powered their vessels by oars alone, or if they had sailing technology. However, it is generally accepted that sailing technology did not arrive in Scandinavia until the seventh century based on known rock art in Tjängvide, Gotland.[16] Evidence of oar propulsion only rests with the two known vessels of the era, the Nydam ship and the Sutton Hoo ship. While clear distinguishing rigging features can't be discerned to support a sail on these two vessels, it could be that these two vessels, or this class of vessel simply didn't have sails, but other types did. The Sutton Hoo ship was distorted when it was interred, including the addition of a house works amidships to entomb the king. This tomb would cover any of the fittings on the keel including the mast-step designed to hold a mast and rigging. With the vessel fitted for burial, key clues to its rigging may have been undetectable by the archaeologists who uncovered the vessel.

On the opposing side of the discussion, the lack of evidence of a sail is not necessarily proof that sails weren't being used. Sails were being used in the Mediterranean Sea by the Bronze Age, and are known to be in use by the Britons by at least the sixth century. Contact and trade alone may have exposed the northern tribes to this technology by the time Caesar attacked Britain in the first century. Moreover, there appears to be anecdotal evidence in contemporary writing by Roman sources which provides support to the notion that northern tribes operated vessels with sails. However, these accounts may just be assumptions made by second-hand writers and not eye witnesses. For example, Sidonius Apollinaris says of the Saxons, 'when the Saxons are setting sail from the continent…'[17]

On the other hand Tacitus states that in the first century these northern tribes did not sail. 'The form of their vessels is peculiar in this respect, that a prow at either extremity acts as a forepart, always ready for running into shore. They are not worked by sails.'[18] These observations are supported by a later Roman author. In the sixth century, the Roman Procopius wrote down the story of the Angles and the Varni engaged in a conflict. This conflict included a large fleet of ships, 'And there were no supernumeraries in this fleet, for all the men rowed with their own hands. Nor do these islanders have sails, as it happens, but they always navigate by rowing alone.'[19]

With a sail it is possible that the northern Germanic tribes could raid and invade anywhere in Britain in the exact same way as the Vikings would do in the eighth century, but under oars alone it would seem that Britain's near shore, the modern counties of Kent and East Anglia, would be the most obvious targets. At the moment it is impossible to prove the use of sails by the Angles and Saxons, but without question they were still very capable mariners using oars alone. Globally there are examples of people travelling great distances without the use of sails including the great seafaring traditions of the Haida on Canada's pacific coast. The Haida are known to have conducted slaving raids as far south as Washington State, a distance of over 700 kilometres.

It could be that raiding was conducted using ships with only oars, and that some other merchant vessels carried canvas. In the North Sea, the prevailing winds are from the west and north-west, meaning raiders would likely be forced to row towards their target more often than not, except on their homeward leg which could be downwind and thus allow the use of a square-rigged sail. Those being raided would only ever witness the arrival of these ships and so would primarily see vessels without sails as the raiders approached. As to the lack of rigging on the Sutton Hoo ship, if warships were under oar when attacking, and only under sail when headed home, there may be cultural reasons to burying the king's ship rigged for war and not for transit. Sidonius Apollinaris' observations of the Saxons and their use of sail does state that they are under sail when they leave enemies' shores and return home.

The sails eventually used by the cousins of the Angles and Saxons, who we now call Vikings, in the eight century were made of wool. It is estimated that it would take almost 8,000 hours, or about four years, to produce a single sail for a Viking longboat.[20] This time investment was likely available to the Angles and Saxons, but were the raw materials accessible? With certainty the Germanic tribes were engaged in husbandry, but the focus seems to have been on cattle and not sheep, though sheep were around and their wool used for textiles. In the later Viking example, sheep became the prime domestic animal due to the limitations of pasture, something the continental Angles and Saxons didn't face, allowing for a greater focus on cattle. In Norway, heathland was used very successfully to graze sheep. During the age of migration, and into the Viking era, climatic changes led to the rapid expansion of heathlands.[21] The increase of lands which were available for grazing provided a greater quantity of raw materials, supporting the development of sail technology and material. These same conditions were not occurring at the time of migration for the Angles and Saxons.

It is likely that the first three ceols to arrive in Britain, and all the following vessels departed their traditional homes and moved south-west along the Jutish, Angle, Saxon, Frisian, and Frankish shore to Caletum (Roman Calais). The men would work the oars in two watches and could likely achieve a speed of seven kilometres per hour. Under purely oar power this is a ten day trip along the coast before crossing the Channel. The position of the Saxon shore forts seem to support the lack of Germanic sailing vessels as the forts are largely grouped in Kent and the East Anglian south coast directly opposing Caletum. The density of forts drastically reduces both to the north along the North Sea coast, and to the east along the English Channel. The crossing from Caletum to the island is thirty kilometres, for the seasoned oarsmen this was a four hour pull to the safety of coastal waters.

Before attempting the crossing the men of the ceols would have sacrificed and sought favour from Wade, father of Wayland-The-Smith to carry them upon his back and provide a safe crossing. Sacrifices to Wade are even recorded in the Roman era by Sidonius Apollinaris, though they should be taken with a grain of salt:

> When the Saxons are setting sail from the continent, and are about to drag their firm-holding anchors from an enemy's shore, it is their usage, thus homeward bound, to abandon every tenth captive to the slow agony of a watery end, casting lots with perfect equity among the doomed crowd

in execution of this iniquitous sentence of death. This custom is all the more deplorable in that it is prompted by honest superstition. These men are bound by vows which have to be paid in victims, they conceive it a religious act to perpetrate this horrible slaughter, and to take anguish from the prisoner in place of ransom; this polluting sacrilege is in their eyes an absolving sacrifice.[22]

Once the three ceols arrived, the brothers Hengist and Horsa lead their ceols in support of a failing Romano Celtic king, before eventually establishing their own communities. The story of this first arrival goes on to tell us that word was sent back to the homelands of the Angles, Saxons, and Jutes about the glory of the land, and the weakness of its inhabitants and over time they were joined by more of their countrymen. It seems fair to suppose that some of the men from the ceols died in combat, some sought to establish a home on the island and others returned to ancestral lands with tales and riches, prompting more adventurous people to make the journey. As more ceols arrived they began to land along the undefended coastal areas and gradually moved north and east from Ebbsfleet, fighting and colonizing as they went.

The archaeology on the other hand tells a slightly different story, in which gradual migration to the island and settlement by Germanic peoples was likely occurring before the total Roman withdrawal. The distance in time from these events makes it hard to verify or eliminate the story of the arrival of the first ceols of warriors hired by a desperate king in a turbulent time. It seems safe to suggest that there was likely employment of warriors by some remaining political Romano-Celtic organization, and there was also the establishment of remote Germanic coastal communities occurring at the same time.

The *Gallic Chronicle*, recorded in Gaul in the fifth century, certainly disputes the Gildas and Bede version of events and seems to be more supported by the archaeological record. There are two entries in this chronicle related to Britain, and it can be assumed that the author was aware of the events due to some form of Romano-Celtic migrating from the island. The first occurs in AD 410, and simply states that, 'The British provinces were devasted by an incursion of the Saxons.'[23] The second entry occurs for AD 452, 'The British provinces, which to this time had suffered various defeats and misfortunes are reduced to a Saxon rule.'[24] These two entries paint a broad picture of the interaction between the Germanic migrants and the island of Britain. In AD 410 there is raiding along the coast not dissimilar to the Viking raids which would occur 300 years later, and by AD 452 wholesale dominance of geographic areas, not unlike the Danelaw which followed in the wake of the Viking raids in northern Britain. Though it is worth noting that the *Gallic Chronicle* chronology is not far off the date Bede gives us of AD 449 for the arrival of Hengist and Horsa. Clearly, the specific date of when the Angles, Saxons and Jutes arrived is somewhere between the fourth and fifth century and in all likelihood their arrival spans that entire period.

There is one more point to assess with Germanic migration. As the Roman Empire struggled to maintain control and field its legions, it turned to the establishment of Foederati for protection of the empire's border lands. The Foederati were people and groups bound by treaties to serve the Roman Empire. There is no doubt that Germanic tribes, including the Saxons, participated in campaigns and military duties for the empire as part of a Foederati. It is a reasonable jump to assume that some Foederati of Saxon and Angle descent were deployed to the coast of Britain to dissuade the invasion and raiding by their brethren. This would help align the story of Vortigern and the employment of the Angles and Saxons and could explain the earlier presence of Germanic people in Britain. The story of the arrival of Germanic peoples into Britain is ultimately a messy, complicated, cloudy and perhaps dark origin story. The arrival of the Saxons and Angles was likely a combination of many factors, with some arriving as part of the Foederati and others arriving as raiders, and yet others arriving in search of land to work. This was not an invasion of one nation by another nation, but rather a migration of individuals.

From the moment that the Roman Empire started to contract, a process of political devolution began on the island of Britain. Beyond Hadrian's Wall there was little change, but in all other parts, regional and local leaders jockeyed for authority and supremacy. With the influx of Germanic migrants, another layer of pressure and complexity was added. By the mid-sixth century, a level of stability had occurred north of the Humber estuary, where two Angle kingdoms, Deira and Bernicia, competed for supremacy. The *Anglo-Saxon Chronicles* gives us the date of AD 547 as the founding of the Northumbrian dynasty and the establishment of the centre of power at Bebbanburg Castle. This entry does need to be interpreted slightly as the very idea of 'Northumbria' doesn't occur until the ninth century; but that aside, by the mid-point of the sixth century there is a power structure in place north of the River Humber. The northern kingdoms of Bernicia and Deira shared land borders with Brittonic kingdoms including Catraeth, Gododdin, Rheged, Strathclyde, and some wilder areas which may have been controlled by smaller warlords or been outside the control of lords and kings altogether. Mapping these places out is a difficult process, as there were no stable borders and, in the case of Rheged, limited historical accounts. However, in general these kingdoms can be estimated to cover 4,000–5,000 square kilometres. The similar sizes of nations north of the Humber estuary and the River Mersey seems to have created a balance of power and regional stability.

In the Saxon and Jute lands far to the south, political equilibrium had formed by the first quarter of the sixth century. The chroniclers in this period were heavily focused on activities of the Gewisse, a southern kingdom, and the lack of mention of other nations may be down to the fact that the sources within the known chronicles were from Gewisse. The political stability of the south may have been born out of dominance of the Saxon nations which was achieved through success on the battlefield against the Britons. So dominant had the Saxon nations become that direct conflict with the Britons and neighboring Germanic kingdoms was reduced. South Saxons, East Saxons, Kent and Wihtwara were all confined by their Germanic neighbours, and seemingly comfortable with the established borders. East Anglia, the largest of the southern nations, was the power house for large periods of time. This nation was nearly twice the size of its neighbours and had the benefit of naturally defensible location.

Far to the west, the hills and coast were firmly under the control of Britons who became the bastion of the Brittonic language, religion and culture. These areas would eventually become Wales and Cornwall and the Brittonic language would develop over the ensuring centuries into both Cornish and Welsh. That's not to say that the Britons, their culture, and even their power were restrained to these places. The Kingdom of Elmet, near the Humber estuary was still a Brittonic kingdom in the seventh century. North of the Humber and Mersey rivers Brittonic kingdoms still survived. Beyond the Firth of Forth the Pict and Scoti people remained unmolested by the incoming Germanic peoples. The Scoti in this period were migrating east from Ireland and establishing control in Lowland Scotland and in pockets of the Welsh coast. At the mid-point of the fifth century the archipelago of Britain was populated by people modern academics would identify as Brittonic, Roman, Scoti, Pict, Angle, Saxon, Jute, Frisians and perhaps others.

In the fifth century, the linguistic palate of Britain included Latin, Brittonic, Pict, Scoti, Saxon, Angle, Jute, and Frisian dialects. These people certainly communicated with one another and the languages overlapped as groups attempt to trade, wage war, and establish peace with one another. Latin very well may have been the lingua franca in the fifth century, as many Germanic warriors had long contact with the Romans, including service for the empire as Foederati. Over generations Latin eventually became isolated to the church, and the dialects that would evolve into Old English filled the gap in most scenarios.

The changes continued through the fifth, sixth and seventh centuries as new people and new ideas continued to arrive. The *Anglo-Saxon Chronicles* contains several entries which show that migration didn't start and stop in AD 449. A warlord called Ella arrived in AD 477 with his ceols, from him would descend the kings of Sussex. In AD 495 Cerdic and Cynric arrived and eventually established the West-Saxon Kingdom, and in AD 501 Porta arrived with his ceols and two of his sons at the place we now call Portsmouth. The story of King Penda starts in this period of migration and change, with the arrival of people from Angln, either as Foederati, invader or settler. Somewhere in this great movement of humanity, a man named Eomer and his son Icel arrive on Britain's eastern shore in the future kingdom of East Anglia.

Chapter Two

Iclingas

The first recorded mention of the Angles comes by way of a Roman author, Tacitus, in the first century. Tacitus travelled widely throughout his known world, including north of the Roman border and into Germania, recording an ethnography of the Germanic people, including the Angles. The Angles receive limited specific attention from Tacitus and the reader is left to accept the implication that Tacitus' general observations are applicable in broad strokes to the many Germanic nations. What we do learn from Tacitus is that the Angles, along with their neighbours including the Lombards, Aviones, and Varinians, have a special accord with Nerthus, that is Mother Earth. This passage in 'Germania' stands out as it runs counter to the general narrative of the Germanic nations 'warlike nature'. According to Tacitus the Angles and their neighbours:

> universally join in the worship of Nerthus; that is to say, the Mother Earth. Her they believe to interpose in the affairs of man, and to visit countries. In an island of the ocean stands the wood Castum: in it is a chariot dedicated to the Goddess, covered over with a curtain, and permitted to be touched by none but the Priest. Whenever the Goddess enters this her holy vehicle, he perceives her; and with profound veneration attends the motion of the chariot, which is always drawn by yoked cows. Then it is that days of rejoicing always ensue, and in all places whatsoever which she descends to honour with a visit and her company, feasts and recreation abound. They go not to war; they touch no arms; fast laid up is every hostile weapon; peace and repose are then only known.[1]

In the eighth century Bede provides us with a few more details about the Angles and specifically their land of origin, Angln. Bede tells us that the Angles were bordered to the north by the Jutes and to the South by the Saxons, this is roughly the border region between modern Germany and Denmark. This area is centred on the Schlei estuary, which seems to corroborate the origin of the name Angles. The root word 'Ang' means either narrow, or bend, but both could be applied to this geographic area. There is still an area in modern Germany called Angeln, however, there are limited other place names which tie the land directly to the

Angles. This could be due to the fact that the area was depopulated, and then repopulated by Danes and other people who replaced early name forms. Bede provides a clue to the Angle exodus by mentioning that the migration was so large that it virtually emptied their traditional homelands. 'Angln which is said, from that time, to have remained deserted to this day.'[2]

The primary early Angle-based settlements in Britain were East Anglia, Lindsey, Deira, and Bernicia. The Angles would eventually move west as well, founding new dynasty. Based on a combination of archaeology and some limited historic records we have established that between AD 410 and at least AD 501 (but likely longer), Germanic migrants began arriving and settling in Britain. King Penda's dynasty was named the Iclingas. Throughout this period powerful families took dynastic names which were formed to create linkages to some ancient or powerful individual. The inclusion of the suffix '-ingas' created a patronymic name showing the line of decent. 'Ing' on its own can be interpreted as direct line of descent, perhaps similar to modern Scandinavian names ending in 'son' such as Larson, or Ericson. The addition of '-as' creates a pluralized form of 'ing'.[3] In its pluralized form 'ingas' can be read as meaning 'the people, the dwellers'.[4] The pluralization of the patronymic name implying a larger kin group and perhaps a tribal identity. While we tie the '-ingas' names primarily to kings, it could very well be that these were tribal names which all members of the extended kinship group used as an identifier of the clan.

Penda's line was named the Iclingas, in honour of someone named Icel. It could be that Icel was the first of the line to arrive in Britain, or the first born in Britain, or the first of the line to establish his own dominion. All we can tell from this detail is that Icel was held in great regard by a group of people, and that his name was carried forward for generations. Aside from the name Iclingas, the only other connection to the dynastic past is from regnal lists, most of which were written long after the events they reportedly recorded. Developing a timeline of events is difficult in this period, but can be extrapolated by working backwards from known dates captured in documents such as the *Anglo-Saxon Chronicles*.

The death of Penda can provide a suitable point to work back from; the *Anglo-Saxon Chronicles* tells us that Penda died in AD 655. Another entry for AD 626 provides us with details on Penda's ancestors, how long he reigned, and his age,

> This year Penda began to reign; and reigned thirty winters. He had seen fifty winters when he began to reign. Penda was the son of Pybba, Pybba of Creoda, Creoda of Cynewald, Cynewald of Cnebba, Cnebba of Icel, Icel of Eomer, Eomer of Angelthew, Angelthew of Offa, Offa of Wearmund, Wearmund of Whitley, Whitley of Woden.[5]

This entry is not as clear cut as it may initially appear. If this entry is correct then we would have to believe that when King Penda dies in battle in AD 655 he was eighty years old! While that may be possible in our time for a leader to be an octogenarian, in the seventh century that simply wasn't possible. In this era, kings and warlords fought at the very front of their warbands and armies. Tacitus mentioned about the Germanic tribes that,

> They choose their kings by birth, their generals for merit. These kings have not unlimited or arbitrary power, and the generals do more by example than by authority. If they are energetic, if they are conspicuous, if they fight in the front, they lead because they are admired.[6] (Tacitus translated by Church 1877).

In all likelihood the entry for AD 626 is an error and should read, 'Penda began to reign; and reigned thirty winters. He had seen fifty winters when his reign ended.' Accepting that interpretation of the AD 626 entry, and the AD 655 entry which records Penda's death, we can extrapolate his birth year as roughly AD 606.

Using the year AD 606 as a starting point, we can backtrack and make some conclusion on a likely timeline of the Iclingas. To do this is simply a matter of subtracting intergenerational years and working backwards. Intergenerational years fluctuate a great deal, but in general terms thirty years between generations is a safe estimation.[7] Studies have shown that the variation in intergenerational years also has a gender component, with women tending to have shorter, and men tending to have longer generational gaps. This is even attested to by Tacitus who says of the Germanic tribes, 'The young men marry late, and their vigour is thus unimpaired.'[8] This makes sense during this era, as a young man in the warrior classes would need to be gaining wealth through combat before he could look towards gaining a bride and supporting children. Using a thirty year intergenerational gap gives a date of birth for Eomer at AD 426, and his son Icel at AD 456. These dates fit within the known timelines of Angle arrival in Britain. While there are many ways to interpret the Iclingas story based on these dates, it seems feasible that Eomer came ashore in a ceol, perhaps as a young warrior around 450. However, the generational gap could be much less, perhaps twenty years; it could also be highly variable year to year. The difference between a twenty and thirty year average could put Eomer's birth in a range between AD 426 and AD 486. It is important to remember that the *Anglo-Saxon Chronicles* records 449 as the critical date, the date when the Angles arrived in Britain, 'And in their days Vortigern invited the Angles thither, and they came to Britain in three ceols, at the place called Wippidsfleet.'[9] As mentioned previously it does appear that there were Germanic settlers already present in Britain, and that they had started to arrive after 410, but the proximity of the dates is tantalizing to consider. An entry in a Gallic chronicle for the year AD 452 states 'Britain abandoned by the Romans, passed into the power of the Saxons.'[10] If a significant invasion did occur around AD 450, and landed in Kent or East Anglia, it would appear entirely possible that Eomer, Penda's distant ancestor, could have played a role in it.

The traditional narrative of this event is that three ceols came ashore at Ebbsfleet under the command of brothers and warlords Hengist and Horsa. Hengist and Horsa are a challenge in the story of the migration period as there is simply no way of validating their existence and there are many who think they may have been a mythical addition to the narrative at a later date. Regardless of that debate it seems appropriate to consider that a raid or invasion of some magnitude did occur around AD 450 and led to a string of battles between the Angles and the Britons through Kent and along the Thames estuary. In the year AD 455 the *Anglo-Saxon Chronicles* tells us, 'This year Hengest and Horsa fought with Vortigern the king on the spot that is called Aylesford.'[11] In AD 457 the *Anglo-Saxon Chronicles* records that, 'Hengest and Esc fought with the Britons on the spot that is called Crayford, and there slew four thousand men. The Britons then forsook the land of Kent, and in great consternation fled to London.'[12]

Aylesford and Crayford are easily plotted on a map, and show a north-west direction heading inland. If the chroniclers were accurate there is a period of relative peace for the next eight years, with no recorded significant battles until the year AD 465. In all likelihood there were continuous skirmishes and raids occurring in these ensuing years, but they either weren't significant or the memory of them was lost over time.

During this interlude, Eomer settled in East Anglia, perhaps between Felixstowe and Dunwich and had a son, Icel, in the latter half of the fifth century. In the following decades this area would see the rise of a significant seat of power at Rendlesham. Archaeological activities in the vicinity of Rendlesham between 2008 and 2014 found a total of 568 objects which can be confidently dated between the fifth and seventh centuries.[13] The fieldwork showed one other intriguing factor; this site was seemingly in use before the Romans arrived, during the Roman period, and then through the migration period. Rendlesham, it would appear, has been an attractive settlement location for a multitude of peoples dating back to the Mesolithic period, and the Angles would continue to use the area.

The area around Rendlesham and modern-day Suffolk had been the home of a Celtic tribe called the Iceni during the Roman occupation. The Iceni came to prominence in AD 60 when they rose in revolt against the Romans. Tacitus provides the earliest discussion on this revolt, and even had firsthand accounts of the events in his *Annals*. Tacitus tells us that the Icenian King Prasutagus named the Emperor and his two daughters as his heirs upon his death. This was done to placate Rome and to ensure the future welfare of his family. However, when Prasutagus died the Roman centurions ignored his wishes and,

> his kingdom was pillaged by centurions, his household by slaves; as though they had been prizes of war. As a beginning, his wife Boudicca was subjected to the lash and his daughters violated: all the chief men of the Icenians were stripped of their family estates, and the relatives of the king were treated as slaves.[14]

The Iceni, led by Boudicca, rallied other British tribes to their call and began a campaign of revenge to destroy Roman control within Britain. Boudicca and her revolt would attack Camulodunum, modern-day Colchester, where the city was methodically demolished. Boudicca then advanced on Londinium where the city was largely abandoned to her by the Romans. Just like Camulodunum the city of Londinium was destroyed and any Roman who remained behind was slaughtered. Verulamium, modern St Albans, was next to be attacked and destroyed by the revolt. The revolt came to an end when Boudicca and her army were defeated after the destruction of Verulamium. The Romans delivered an extremely punitive reaction to the revolt, doing their best to destroy all traces of the Iceni, which Tacitus writes, 'The troops gave no quarter even to the women: the baggage animals themselves had been speared and added to the pile of bodies.'[15] Tacitus closes the story of Boudicca by providing the reader with a bit of an understatement about the outcome of the revolt: 'Still, hatred of Rome was persistent.'[16]

The Iceni may have a role to play in the story of the Iclingas. Icel's name is unusual with a challenging etymology and a largely unknown origin. It could be that Icel was named for the Iceni. This argument is constructed out of the similarity of the words, along with the overlap of geography. The Iceni were likely called the Icen, but the word was latinized by the Romans to read as Iceni. The etymology of the Icen is still debated and could be a form meaning Oxen, or the name of a river. The Iceni themselves did record their name on some minted coins as 'Ecen' in the first century.[17] Modern Welsh is a direct descendent of the Brittonic language and contains the word 'Echen' which is defined as 'Stock, Lineage, Family, Tribe, Source, Origin.'[18] The link between modern 'Echen' and the Iceni coins 'Ecen' seems a logical connection, and likely provides the etymology for the Iceni. In later generations of the Iclingas there are many theories about connections to Britons based on the unusual, and apparently un-Angle names such as Pybba, Penda, and Peada. The link to Britons through marriage could date back to the beginning of the Iclingas dynasty, with the name Icel being given to create the linkage to historic Iceni power on the island. This type of process occurs even in the modern world where a dynasty uses assumed or given names to tie their power to ancient sources. One has to look no further than the modern house of Windsor to see this. Perhaps Eomer was wed to an Iceni woman, and Icel is the first of the dynasty born in Britain, the first generation with no direct connection to Angln. Tying this young Icel to the traditions of the land he now inhabited would allow him to lay claims to the authority of the Iceni.

Icel is also the first of the dynasty to leave an impression on the landscape through place names. As is the case with so much of this era there are only limited clues available to piece together a story. With Icel and the Iclingas, most of those clues are hidden within place names as the dynasty doesn't receive mention in any document until the rise of Penda in the seventh century. However, the place name evidence is interesting as it fundamentally differs from the traditional narrative about the Iclingas dynastic establishment.

The traditional view on migration of Mercian people was that they entered the island through Lindsey or the Humber estuary. From there Angles, and perhaps some Saxons used the river systems as their highways inland settling along its shores. Portions of this group eventually set up a small dominion called the Tomsæta, meaning 'People of the River Tame'. Examining the position of Angle and Saxon cemeteries shows three general migration routes from the eastern shores moving west.[19] The first seems to centre round the Humber estuary before moving in a south-west direction towards modern-day Birmingham. The defining feature of this route is the Trent River. The second route originates in the Wash and moves in a westerly direction towards Birmingham. This route appears to follow the Welland River, before deviating to the north-west near Market Harborough and then following the low-laying country west towards Birmingham. While the Welland River plays some part in the second route, it becomes clear that this route would rely on overland travel and not on vessels alone. This route is interesting as it isn't supported by Roman roads until it reaches High Cross. This creates a scenario where groups would be travelling by foot track, or cross-country, both of which are not ideal. At High Cross, the Roman road known as Watling Street does provide a direct route to Tamworth, one of the key seats of future Mercian power.

Both the Humber and the Wash migration routes are devoid of any place names associated with the Iclingas. This perhaps wouldn't stand out if the third option also lacked etymological evidence, but that isn't the case. The third route which is demonstrated by the presence of cemeteries, similar to the other two routes, includes a wealth of place-name evidence for several generations of the Iclingas. There are four place names which show an etymology directly linked to Icel. From east to west they are, Icklingham, Ickleton, Ickleford and finally Ickford.[20] These four towns follow a south-west course, running on a general heading between Norwich and Oxford. This general course is the same as the collection of Angle cemeteries running from Thetford to Oxford. The distribution of both place names related to Icel and the cemetery locations does seem to show a migration corridor out of East Anglia. To the south of this Angle migration route there are Saxon migration routes out of Kent and headed west into what would become Gewisse lands and eventually Wessex. Finally there is another apparent Saxon route coming out of Portsmouth and heading due north which appears to terminate south of Swindon. That point of termination is important as it may imply some impassable point, likely created by the presence of the Angle migration out of East Anglia.

Ickford is thirteen kilometres east of Oxford and it appears to be the terminus of Icel-based place names. There are no more clues to work with, but we can infer from this that Icel and his warband were moving rapidly south-west out of East Anglia. This migration was likely the result of a number of push and pull factors. The push could be coming from an increase in arrivals in East Anglia, and increasing competition, the pull forces could have been the desire for new land to settle or the need for wealth through raiding. Internal to Eomer's family, Icel could have been forced out by older siblings who were taking power from Eomer. This pattern plays out in other Angle kingdoms, particularly north of the Humber where Æthelings go into exile for long periods of time.

If the primary factor in migration for Icel was the acquisition of new land to settle and farm, one would imagine those could be found in East Anglia in the late fifth century; so while this may have been a factor, it was likely not the key driver. Raiding and the acquisition of wealth on the other hand could explain the distance. As an area is raided, the wealth is depleted forcing the band to go farther to acquire greater wealth. It seems that Icel must have been fairly highly regarded for so many sites to be named for him. In a Heathen Angle culture, few things were as highly revered as the warrior culture. The poem *Beowulf*, along with archaeological finds of grave goods left with the deceased, demonstrate the value placed on warriors by the Angles and their Saxon cousins. When examining a map with the Icel-based place names plotted, what jumps out is the appearance of generally balanced spacing between the locations named after Icel. Moving east to west it is forty kilometres from Icklingham to Ickleton; it is thirty-two kilometres from Ickleton to Ickleford; and then it is fifty-seven kilometres from Ickleford to Ickford. Three of the four 'Icel' locations Icklingham, Ickleton, and Ickleford are linked together on the Icknield Way.

The Icknield Way is an ancient byway which links East Anglia to Dorset. This road is a series of interlinked footpaths which traverse the high ground and was in use starting in the Neolithic period.[21]

The consistent distribution of place names is intriguing and could be a reference to campaigning seasons, with each one achieving similar results, while building on the success of the previous expedition. For this to be viable Icel would require new warriors to replace those lost in battle. Young warriors seeking wealth and reputation could have been attracted to his banner, and thus each success drew in more men and led to greater success on the campaign trail. It would be likely that some men settled along the way, taking over existing Brittonic settlements as they moved along the Icknield Way until they reached Ickleford. From this point the warband moved toward Oxford, likely on another ancient road way. This is the longest distance between any of the Icel place names, a total of fifty-seven kilometres. Perhaps this is a sign of weaker resistance or greater strength in Icel's warband.

It's worth noting the order of place names from west to east as well. The first site is Icklingham, which means 'The village of the followers of Icel';[22] this would be an appropriate name for the home base of the Icel Warband. The second location is Ickleton, meaning 'Farm/Settlement called after Icel'.[23] This could show a movement and settlement by a significant portion of the warband here. The third and fourth locations are both fords named for Icel.

Ickford remains a bit of a question on the trail of Icel. It does show discrepancies when compared to the other three locations: it is missing an 'L'. It is not on the Icknield Way, it is the longest distance between Icel place names, but it also seems to fit the general pattern and direction of locations. Unfortunately the trail of Icel-based place names runs cold at Ickford. There are many questions left unanswered here: Did Icel die at Ickford? Did the warband settle here? Did the warband and Icel continue on from Ickford, but didn't continue naming locations? And what qualified a location to name it after Icel?

Judging by the place names and the general distribution of those names along the Icknield Way, it would seem appropriate to suggest that Icel was a dryhten of some renown, leading a warband deep into Britain. As a young man Icel would have been driven to establish fame and wealth by joining his father's warband, or other allied warbands. Eventually, Icel would have been granted his own estate to protect with a small warband. The push and pull forces forced Icel and his band to follow the Icknield Way establishing some control, and possibly a small settlement at Ickleton, before moving on to Ickleford. The ford could have been named for Icel, with settlement coming much later, or a small settlement could have been established here. It is also very possible that an existing settlement was simply renamed after being captured. Throughout this period, fords held a high strategic and tactical value. The destruction of whole armies in the time of Penda occur at fording locations. Perhaps Ickleford warranted a new name because of battle at the site that was either a victory for Icel, or the place where he died. Either way, Ickleford was important enough to warrant a name.

Both Eomer and Icel were actively moving through Britain at a time when the Saxon Gewisse were starting to gain territory and power along the upper Thames river valley and west towards the Severn valley. This was the birth of what would become the Kingdom of Wessex. The entry in the *Anglo-Saxon Chronicles* for AD 508 states, 'This year Cerdic and Cynric slew a British king, whose name was Natanleod, and five thousand men with him. After this was the land named Netley, from him, as far as Charford.'[24] Henry of Huntingdon goes on to say 'Cerdic and his son entreated aid from Esc, the king of Kent, and from Ælla, the great king of the South-Saxons and from Port and his sons.'[25] Although Icel, or Eomer and his Iclingas warband are not mentioned, it seems they could have been drawn in to the fight, possibly enticed with an alliance sealed by a marriage between the families. Around AD 526 Icel had a son named Cnebba; the exact date is unknown. Cnebba is almost invisible in records and even in place name etymology. While he no doubt followed in the warrior footsteps of his father, there is very little left behind him to pick up the story. Some thirteen kilometres south of Ickleford is a village called Knebworth. Knebworth's distance means it is a three-hour walk, or a ninety-minute horse ride, from Ickleford. Most importantly the etymology of Knebworth is 'Cnebba's Enclosure'.[26] Unfortunately there are no other clues hidden in the place names related to Cnebba.

Cnebba had a son named Cynewald at some point around the year AD 546. Cynewald is extremely interesting as his name seems to show distinctly Gewissan or West Saxon tones. The Gewisse and future Wessex kings maintained a fairly steady pattern of alliteration in naming conventions. Both alliteration and variation were two of the most important naming conventions in Angle and Saxon communities until the Normans arrived in 1066.[27] The use of 'Cyne' as part of a name is fairly common in the Gewisse and Wessex aristocracy for generations. While a direct connection cannot be made, the use by a member of the Iclingas could be a sign that there was a marriage between a Gewissan daughter and Cnebba. In future generations Penda married Cynewise, who it appears is also of a Gewissan line, and they had two daughters, Cyneburh and Cyneswith, providing an excellent example of the alliteration and variation processes.

The continued growth of Gewissan, South Saxon, and East Saxon authority and military success may help to explain why the Iclingas stop moving south-west. As these Saxon peoples pushed north, they were adding a migratory push for the Iclingas. Competition, alliances and conflict with the Saxons and Britons may have forced them to turn to the north as there was nowhere else to move to the south. Fortunately at Knebworth and Ickleford there was an open route to the north, the Roman Watling Street. Watling Street is an ancient path which begins in Dover and moves north-west across England to High Cross before turning in a more westerly route past Tamworth and on to Shrewsbury. This path, or sections of it were used by Neolithic people, and Celtic Britons, before the Romans arrived and began paving Watling Street. Although it would have fallen into disrepair by the sixth century it still would have provided an effective route to traverse Britain. Roman roads retained their value in the migration period as is attested to be the congregation of Angle, Saxon, and Brittonic battle sites immediately adjacent to these thoroughfares.

Henry of Huntingdon's *Historium Anglorum* states that in AD 527, 'large bodies of men came successively from Germany, and took possession of East Anglia and Mercia.'[28] These new arrivals could have pushed existing people out of lands, or they could have augmented the warbands already in Britain and supported greater success against the Britons. Unfortunately the *Anglo-Saxon Chronicles* focus almost entirely on the Gewisse or West Saxons for all the entries until AD 547, leaving large gaps in the historic record across Britain. Similarly, Bede has a bit of a blind spot between AD 456 and AD 596. What Bede does tell us without dates is that, 'In the meantime, in Britain, there was some respite from foreign, but not from civil war. The cities destroyed by the enemy and abandoned remained in ruins; and the natives, who had escaped the enemy, now fought against each other.'[29]

Before Cynewald can take over the mantle of the Iclingas, his father Cnebba seems to be mentioned in the *Anglo-Saxon Chronicles* for the year AD 568 which states, 'This year Ceawlin, and Cutha the brother of Ceawlin, fought with Ethelbert, and pursued him into Kent. And they slew two aldermen at Wimbledon, Oslake and Cnebba'.[30] This battle is important, as it certainly occurs in the vicinity of the Iclingas' migration route and aligns with the theoretical chronology of Iclingas births. It is also interesting as it seems to be the first record in the chronicle of conflict between the Germanic people in Britain. Prior to this point violence was occurring between the Britons defending their home and the invading Angles and Saxons.

Henry of Huntingdon does have some further details for this period but it's primarily focused on the Gewisse, North of the Humber, and to a lesser extent on East Anglia. If any period can be called dark, then it is surely the sixth century.

The next etymological connection with the Iclingas occurs at a place called Kinwalsey Farm. This location is about thirteen kilometres south-west of Watling Street, and eighteen kilometres south of Tamworth. Kinwalsey is important to the migration route as this is the first occasion where there may be a connection between a member of the Iclingas and what will one day be the focal point of Mercian supremacy. Kinwalsey has been interpreted as meaning 'Cynewald's Enclosure'.[31] Just ten kilometres north-west of Kinwalsey is Curdworth. Curdworth means 'Creoda's Enclosure', which is important to the story as Creoda was Cynewald's son. Creoda may have been born around AD 566, so it's a fitting assumption that Curdworth was founded twenty to thirty years after, sometime between AD 586 and AD 596. Between Kinwalsey and Curdworth is a location called Coleshill. It is almost in the centre between the two Iclingas locations. What makes Coleshill special is that it has a long heritage as a spot for a þing or a mæthel, that is regional government and court. A charter from AD 799 refers to decisions made at Colles Hyl, but it is likely that this spot had a long heritage as a place for governance and court business.[32]

It is clear that the mæthel, its procedures, and methods, predated the rise of kingdoms in what would become England.[33] The mæthel must have occurred at pre-established periods to ensure all of the local people could attend to press decisions on legal matters, conduct business, and meet amongst the local communities. In fact Tactitus gives us a reference to the process that would evolve into the mæthel when he says,

> They assemble, except in the case of a sudden emergency, on certain fixed days, either at new or at full moon; for this they consider the most auspicious season for the transaction of business. Instead of reckoning by days as we do, they reckon by nights, and in this manner fix both their ordinary and their legal appointments.[34]

The mæthel is most certainly the Angle inheritance of these assemblages which Tacitus observed in the first century. As power and authority was slowly centred round a king, the mæthel would have lost some of their influence over local decisions, but they were certainly still occurring well into the ninth century.

Coleshill is named for a river, the Colle River and 'river names are frequently used by metonymy to name the district through which the river runs.'[35] Perhaps Coleshill was the site of the mæthel for the Collesæta. That sæta name is not recorded anywhere, but in theory it could have existed, similar to the Tomsæta or Pecsæta. There is one more location in this area that needs to be examined, and that is Peddimore. Peddimore can be interpreted as 'Peadas Moor' or perhaps 'Pybbas Moor', in both cases it supports a multi-generational focus for the Iclingas in the vicinity of Coleshill. It is widely accepted that Tamworth and its environs became the seat of power for the future Kingdom of Mercia, and the Iclingas connections around Coleshill put their dynasty very close to the heart of the forthcoming Mercian state.

The year AD 591 is the first concrete mention in any record about Creoda. Sometime before that date Creoda is implicated in action far to the south-west near modern Hereford where we find Credenhill or 'Creoda's Hill'. Credenhill is the second largest Iron Age fort in Britain covering fifty acres and ringed by earth works constructed of a series of ditches and ramparts. Why this ancient site was renamed for Creoda is a mystery, but the obvious conclusion would be that the site was used by Creoda on a campaign against the Britons. After this southerly campaign, Creoda likely returned to the Coleshill. Following Creoda, the Iclingas pick up names of Brittonic origin, in particular his son Pybba and grandson Penda. Creoda's push west may have ended with a treaty between Powys, and sealed with a marriage to a suitable Briton.

Henry of Huntingdon records, almost as a sidenote, that in the year AD 584, 'Creoda, as far as we learn from old records was the first king of Mercia'.[36] In AD 591 there was a battle at Wodensburh, between the Britons and the Saxons. Henry of Huntingdon provides some interesting detail on the fight: 'The British army advanced in close order, after the Roman Fashion, but the Saxons rushed forward with desperate, but disorderly, courage, and the conflict was very severe'.[37]

While we could be seeing some artistic flourish from the author, we could also be viewing some of the cultural hold overs from the Roman era, in particular some of their advanced battle tactics. If the latter is the case then the system could have been the maniple system. In this type of positioning combat groups are staggered to allow the line to flex and provide freedom of movement for each group. This tactic is quite advanced and would require training at all levels of the combat team to be successful. The Britons we are told carry the day and the Saxons in retreat are severely mauled. The scene of the battle is followed with 'after these times Creoda, King of Mercia, departed this life and his son Pybba succeeded him'.[38] The *Anglo-Saxon Chronicles* records these events as well, though there is a full two years between the battle and the death of Creoda. The naming of Creoda as king seemingly implicates him in the battle. The biggest unanswered question is whether his death was directly caused by the battle or not.

As Henry of Huntingdon mentioned, Pybba was the successor to Creoda's kingdom, though we can't be certain what that kingdom entailed. Based on the thirty-year generational gap it is likely that Pybba was born around AD 576, though it may be slightly before this to allow him time to mature and take over his father's role; a fair estimate would be around AD 570. This timeline would make him about thirty-six years old when Penda was born, most certainly implying that Penda was not the eldest son, which does align with future events. Pybba is mentioned in the ninth-century *Historia Brittonum* written by Nennius which states 'Pybba had twelve sons'.[39] Coleshill continues to be the focal point for the Iclingas, but there is no contemporary place name, other than the possibility of

Peddimore which ties Pybba to this location. Perhaps Pybba inherited his father's estate at Curdworth, or he began to utilize a site near Tamworth, spreading his control through the establishment of other estates. On the other hand he may have been pressured by internal strife to move his entire estate to a different location within only a few years of succeeding his father.

There is a sign of a settlement that fills both of the above scenarios, and that is Pebworth, a small country village forty kilometres south of Coleshill, and firmly in what would become the Kingdom of Hwicce. The etymology for Pebworth is 'Pybba's Enclosure'.[40] What is interesting about Pebworth is how far it is from the Inclingas centre of power, as if Pybba had been pushed out. A rather interesting pattern is forming with the Iclingas, all of the descendants of Icel had a settlement named for them, and involving an enclosure: Knebworth, Kinwalsey, Curdworth and Pebworth. This tells us something of their wealth. In this period of time wealth was shown by way of gold and silver, but also livestock, and in particular cattle. The use of the term enclosure underlies the keeping of livestock, and in particular cattle.

Pybba is mentioned in an entry by Henry of Huntingdon for AD 597: 'Pybba was succeeded by Ceorl, who was not his son but his Kinsman'.[41] This line, along with a similarly minor mention in Bede begins the mysterious tale of Ceorl. Pybba did not hold power for long, which suggests that the lands of the Iclingas were embroiled in some form of an internal power struggle. This could make sense if Pybba wasn't able to establish his authority following Creoda's defeat in AD 591, adding credence to the theory that Pybba was forced south to new lands. It is telling that Henry of Huntingdon does not provide a date for Pybba's death, only that Ceorl has taken up the reigns of authority. Leadership instability is quite alien in the twenty-first century, but common enough in the Iclingas time. Ceorl could have been a brother, uncle, or even an in-law of Pybba who was able to establish authority, perhaps with the backing of a foreign power such as Deira or Bernicia. This pattern of subservience to other nations was extremely common across Britain, and was held together by oaths, support in exile, fostering, and marriages.

Pybba, with his sons and loyal warband, was forced to set up a home in Pebworth, removed from the centre of power. The warband still raided and perhaps participated with larger armies when the opportunities presented themselves. It seems likely that Pybba had at least two wives: the first wife at the turn of the century may have been a Briton, and she gave birth to a son named Penda around AD 606, perhaps at Pebworth in the land of the Hwicce. The migration south must have been driven by competition to the north, and some relative safety to the south. Pybba may have been relying on connections to the Gewisse which were formed between his father and the Gewissian kings and the Battle of Wodensburh in AD 591. At some point, Pybba takes a second wife, perhaps on the death of his first wife.

Geoffrey of Monmouth says that this second wife of Pybba was 'descended from the noble race of the Gewissians'.[42] This marriage reflects Pybba's move to the south and a shifting of allegiance southward to the Gewisse for protection. The marriage to a Gewissan wife was most assuredly done by Pybba in an effort to counter the domination of Ceorl to the north. There may be a link between Pybba and the small village of Publow, or 'Pubba's Burial Mound'[43] which is eight kilometres south-east of Bristol. A direct connection cannot be made between Pubba, and Pybba, but the etymological similarities are worth considering.

Details for this period, even those that end up in recorded histories are very difficult, if not impossible to corroborate until archaeological findings can verify them. Examining Pybba's private life, the only thing we perhaps know is that he had twelve sons according to Henry of Huntingdon. We can estimate an average of eighteen months between each child, giving us a spread of eighteen years from the first and the last child. Assuming that Pybba had his first child at around twenty-five years of age, this would mean the last was born when he was forty-three years old, perhaps around AD 619. A significant battle occurs around this time in AD 616 on the River Idle between East Anglia and the Northumbrian nations. We are told by Henry of Huntingdon that both sides brought numerous armies to the location on the Mercian border. Pybba and his warband may have played a role, if they were now subjects of Ceorl, or they may have not played a role if they were closer linked to the Gewisse; it is yet another mystery. This battle would have big implications across the kingdoms, as it dealt a significant blow to the dominance of Deira and Bernicia following East Anglia's victory, and effectively created opportunity for other nations to rise into the power vacuum, including Mercia under the governance of the Iclingas.

Chapter Three

The Land, the People, the King

The seventh century was not an easy time for people across Britain. The entire island was in a near perpetual state of instability. Conflict existed at every level, between cultures, religions, neighbours, nations, brothers and kings. The young Penda would be in a better position than most being a member of the warrior class, and a member of distinguished dynasty, even one that was seemingly usurped. In sixth- and seventh-century Britain, survival was firmly attached to the kinship group, and the ability of a locality to generate and produce food from crops, livestock, and natural foodstuffs. In the Roman era, the reliance on market locations allowed for the longer distance trade of food items, providing a layer of protection against localized crop failures or the loss of livestock. The fragmentation of authority and localization of community and the economy following the constriction of the Roman Empire removed these safety nets.

In the sixth and seventh centuries, food insecurity may have been increasing across northern Europe due to acute natural events which drove chronic climatic changes. Between AD 536 and AD 547, a series of volcanic eruptions led to a period of climatic cooling and the establishment of the late antiquity Little Ice Age. The outcome of this period of rapid cooling led to crop failure, famine, and disease.[1] The Little Ice Age was layered over another climatic cooling period called the 'Dark Ages Cooling Period' (DACP) which occurred between the fifth and tenth centuries.[2] These climatic changes played a part in the political and economic stability across the ancient world, and may in part have driven the migration of continental Germanic peoples to Britain and the constriction of the Roman Empire.

In Britain specifically, these climatic impacts shortened the growing season available for staple crops such as wheat and barley. Studies of peat stratigraphy showed a general trend towards colder and wetter weather in Britain beginning in AD 550.[3] Throughout this period, fords provided the main crossing solution for waterways, but as volumes of rivers increased so too did isolation of settlements driving greater localization. Less collaboration led to the further isolation of small kinship groups through flooding and the danger of river fording, leading to the localized focus of food generation and inward focusing of power. Food security was thus tied directly to the local environment, which in turn incentivized the raiding of livestock from other kinship groups, to offset the risk to a kinship group's food sources. In turn, these raids drove up the frequency of conflict throughout the period.

As a child and young man, Penda would have lived in a communal long house with his father, mother and siblings, along with transient members of his father's warband and other members of the community. The building itself was constructed from timber, wattle and daub, and thatch. Heating was provided by a central hearth; the smoke from the hearth would rise up to the high ceiling and filter through the thatch without the use of a chimney. The settlement would have had smaller buildings scattered about providing housing, workshops, and shelter for livestock. Unlike the early Britons, the Angles did not ring their settlements in defensive earthworks, instead relying on the power of the local warband or dryhten to protect the settlement and confronting raids from hostile groups. While the dryhten would have formed the offensive force during the campaign season, it is fair to assume that all of the freemen in an area may be called upon to defend a settlement and form what would later be called the fyrd. The fyrd was a local militia pulled together from the local population for the purpose of defence. In most cases the fyrd would be armed with spears, axes, and shields. A fyrd would be no match for a dryhten, but could have augmented the local warriors to support the defence of a settlement.

If Henry of Huntingdon was correct, than Penda was one of twelve sons. It is a reasonable assumption that they were all brought up to be leaders and more importantly warriors. As an adolescent, Penda would have been expected to begin training in the weapons of a warrior and the tactics of a leader. Weapon handling was straightforward enough. With ranged weapons he would have participated in small game hunts and perhaps even a boar hunt. The true measure of a warrior was his ability to hold a shield and confront the enemy as a part of a rigid tactical system and ultimately alone as a bringer of fear and death to his enemy. As Penda grew in age and strength he would be loaded down with a shield, spear, and perhaps a sword. Eventually he would join the dryhten and work collaboratively as part of that warband, with locked shields in the scyldburh, that is the 'Shield-Fortress'.[4]

The Angle shield was traditionally made of linden, maple, alder, willow and any other suitable and available wood. The wood was cut into planks and then shaped into a circle between one to three feet in diameter. A central boss was added to protect the hand when the shield was being used. Shields could also be covered with leather and occasionally have an iron rim. It is unknown if they were painted, though it seems highly likely that they were as is attested to in *Beowulf*, and before that by Tacitus in the first century. Though the shield is an often forgotten component of war gear in comparison to the beautifully smithed swords of the period, it formed a crucial piece of equipment that was common to all on the battlefield. Tacitus tells of earlier Germanic people that 'To abandon your shield is the basest of crimes; nor may a man thus disgraced be present at the sacred rites, or enter their council; many, indeed, after escaping from battle.'[5] For most warriors in the early seventh century, particularly younger men, the shield was the primary armour of a warrior and crucial to his survival, and the survival of the man next to him in the shield-wall. While all men likely had access to spears as a general hunting implement and day-to-day tool, and some men had swords as weapons and status markers, it is the shield that sets apart the warrior.

To be an effective warrior, Penda must have spent countless hours training with the spear and a sword. The spear could be used as a projectile in the early stages of combat, but then formed the medium range weapon as the shield-walls came together. Learning to strike over the shield, and under the shield with the spear, while maintaining a grip on his own shield required strength, balance and skill. Penda, being born the son of royal line, was likely given a sword as a sign of his rank. This was the ultimate tool for single combat, but also for the tail-end of a shield battle when the enemies' defences became ragged and a motivated warrior with skills and sharp blade could sow mayhem and cause terror amongst the enemy, scything them down and forcing a rout from the battlefield.

As a warrior with no other tasks, he would have trained daily with weapons, or contests against others such as running and wrestling. As the warrior aged, he would begin learning the tactical movements of the shield-wall. This was not a matter of standing in a solid wall and moving forward; there were multiple arrangements and techniques to be learned. Many of the Angles and Saxons had operated as Roman Foederati in the later Roman Empire, exposing them to Roman tactics. Tacitus, looking more distant in the past, tells us that Germanic tribes would commonly form their lines 'in a wedge like formation'.[6] This is the formation that would become known as the boar head, used to punch a hole through the opponent's shield-wall.[7] When used in later Scandinavian generations, this formation was led by two champions at the pinnacle of the formation. It's fair to suggest this was a long-held tradition across the Germanic tribes. Additionally the Germanic tribes would commonly disengage, re-establish their line and then charge forward again which Tacitus says was 'considered prudence rather than cowardice'.[8]

Henry of Huntingdon records the nickname of 'Penda the Strong' throughout the *Historia Anglorum*. This stands out because none of the other kings are offered such a title throughout the entire work. As a simple descriptor it may give the briefest glimpse of Penda, a strong powerful man. His strength must have made him stand out against his competitors enough to warrant mentioning it. As a young man, it's easy to imagine Penda excelling at martial activities and sports. As his skills and strength increased, Penda, along with other young men, would finally be recognized amongst the people as a warrior, and a member of the dryhten. Although the process likely changed and adapted, it could have been similar to Tacitus' observations in the first century:

> in the presence of the council one of the chiefs, or the young man's father, or some kinsman, equips him with a shield and a spear...the first honour with which youth is invested. Up to this time he is regarded as a member of a household, afterwards as a member of the commonwealth.[9]

In his mid to late teenage years, Penda joined his father's warband along with other young men his age, in the magodriht – that is, a 'troop of youths'.[10]

Examining recorded conflicts between the seventh and eighth century, it becomes clear that there was a defined campaigning season. Within the *Anglo-Saxon Chronicles* there are ten battles recorded which include the month the battle occurred, all but two of these battles fell between March and August. Based on these limited figures, it is clear that spring and summer provided the annual campaigning season. For the warbands travelling by horseback and foot, the need to ford rivers forced them to observe the campaigning seasons. The risk of fording rivers in the wetter months was a gamble most would be unwilling to take. Those who didn't listen to the natural cycle of the world paid a steep price on the banks of rivers across Britain.

Penda, like most of his contemporaries, was raised in an ancient ancestral religious setting which formed a close bond between people, the land, and their ancestors. The religion had no name to Penda, but outside influences would eventually call it Heathen. The word Heathen descends from the term hearth, and is similar to the Latin use of the term Pagan. While the term took a negative connotation over time, the original interpretation was in relation to the rural setting of the people, the opposite of the metropolitan setting of the city. It is not likely that the term Heathen would have been used by Penda, as he would have no use for the word. His culture was intrinsically linked to the spiritual belief system and was likely inseparable for many people. The Angle's belief system was closely connected to the people; it was polytheistic, and focused on the natural environment and the ancestors.

Our understanding of the religious beliefs of the Angles is plagued with religious intolerance and cultural bias underpinned by 'notions of hierarchies of religions and the supposedly superior rationality and intellectual coherence of world religions in general and Christianity in particular'.[11] Cultural bias surfaces throughout the historic records and centuries of research where the belief system has been, 'dismissed by historians as "superstitions", "primitive", "dark ages" – an embarrassing interlude of history between the Romans and the Normans'.[12] Penda, it will turn out, was one of the final bastions of this ancient belief system, and is also treated with much of the same general disregard as the entire belief system. The narrative of the story of Penda and the conversion period in general approaches this era with an accepted opinion that Christianity was ordained to succeed and that the traditional belief systems were of a lesser value and doomed to be overcome. This is the opinion of Bede, and one that has been picked up by historians for the better part of the following 1,400 years, but it is not an accurate way to look at the period. Christianity at the time of the Angle and Saxon conversion was cultural imperialism, recognizable in more recent history when compared to European colonialism of the nineteenth century.

Understanding the belief systems of the Angles is hampered by a lack of records and a near total destruction of the culture through the aggressive conversion where 'evangelists used every method available: trickery, bribery and armed force'.[13] What limited detail is known has been pulled from scattered references, inferences from later records, and interpretation of archaeological findings and the landscape.

Angle spirituality shared many common elements with earlier Germanic peoples which they brought with them to Britain and which would largely continue in Scandinavia until the eleventh century. The belief system was formed around an evolving and flexible Polytheism which saw the rise and fall of gods over time depending on the direct needs of the people. At its earliest form, these gods were likely ancestors, 'in the early tribal days the divine ancestor of the king was the deity of the tribe'.[14] Many of these gods are known to the modern world through Scandinavian sources such as Woden, Thunor, Frigg, Tiw, and Freya. These gods and goddesses were commonly known across the Germanic world, even in the time of Tacitus where he equates Roman gods with those of the Germanic deities. 'Mercury is the deity whom they chiefly worship, and on certain days they deem it right to sacrifice to him even with human victims. Hercules and Mars they appease with more lawful offerings.'[15]

Mercury is synonymous with Woden, Hercules with Thunor, and Mars with Tiw. Alongside this shared pantheon the Angles and Saxons brought other tribal gods with them including Eostre, Wade, Seaxnat, Nerthus and likely many others who are now lost. On Nerthus, Tacitus tells us that the Angles believed that, 'She was interested in men's affairs and drives about amongst them.'[16] For the Angles this was a living religion, which was constantly adapting and happening in the world around them.

Woden in particular took a great interest in Middle Earth and the activities of people. He was also renowned for travelling the world himself as a wanderer to interact with people. Woden is recalled in all of the ancestral lists for the Angle and Saxon kings of sixth and seventh century. This has often been seen as a tie to war and a need for kings to have success on the battlefield. The warrior was one of the aspects of Woden, but it must not be forgotten that he was also a god of knowledge, wisdom, poetry, and even shamanic rites. All of these would be of equal value to a king. It is worth acknowledging that the stories which have survived intact about Woden are often focused on him travelling in search of greater knowledge and not specific battles. This may show that his value to a king was knowledge more than war.

While Woden had a special attachment amongst the warriors and leaders, other people would have looked towards other gods and goddesses to support them. The afterlife for the Angles was as complex as real life; gods and goddesses kept their own halls where they could select the dead to join them. Hel was a goddess with a particular focus on the dead. Her name has been tarnished since Christian conversion began in the Germanic lands, but she has no link to the Christian understanding of hell. Hel takes the dead to her great hall, a place that is said to be a realm of knowledge as it contains the majority of human experience. The word Hel is often interpreted throughout Indo-European languages to mean 'concealed'. It seems a logical jump to assume that she was a particularly important goddess for her name to have been picked up by the Christian world at some point. The term hell doesn't appear in the original Christian texts, instead Greek terms such as Tartarus and Hades are used. This process of replacing older terms and concepts with newer ones was a tactical method used throughout the period of conversion.

The Angles believed that all things, people, gods, wights, and ancestors lived in a complex cosmology of interlinked realms. Shamans such as Woden were able to see and sometimes travel in these realms. The use of shamans and seers was common and likely in many cases the only specialist in spirituality. While there was some priestly class, the majority of the religion was bound entirely within the people, and was largely presided over by the king or local leader. The king or chief was likely seen as the mediator between the gods and the people.[17] The religion was maintained by the people and there were no written records to fall back on. This allowed for an ever-developing system which acclimatized to the needs of the community. For example, Tacitus tells us in the first century that the Angles are believed to have worshipped Nerthus, Mother Earth, as a first amongst gods. By the fifth century, Woden seems to have taken precedence, at least amongst the warrior class. None of this should register as a surprise as the belief system allowed for this level of flexibility.

Alongside the gods, the people left offerings to wights or spirits on the land, at wells, groves, standing stones and other locations. Polytheism allowed for a range of theological beliefs to be combined in an entirely personalized manner, this was not religion for the masses, but rather religion for the individual. Each person and household could honour a myriad of known gods and spirits to best meet their own spiritual demands. The choice was likely driven by the necessity of the person, their ancestry, and the local environment. This was a deeply personal connection to spirituality where the boundaries between the physical world and the spiritual world were very limited. The lack of central authority and the imbedding of spiritual power in areas that were commonly accessible, was one of the key conflict points with Christianity at the time of conversion. Christianity saw spirituality very differently: 'Treating elements of the landscape as spiritual forces went against the idea of the Christian God as the sole source of spiritual and heavenly intervention.'[18]

Wyrd was a central concept to the northern European belief systems, and while it is often interpreted as fate, it is a more complex idea. Wyrd is not a standalone start-and-end as fate may be interpreted, but is rather the intertwined nature of all things. The concept of Wyrd was seen as a complex fabric formed by the weaving of individual strands linking all things and time together. Each strand in the weaving process was the life and experience of a single individual, which interacted with other strands; Wyrd is 'the intricate linking between everything that was the very grounding of existence'.[19] Although each thread of Wyrd may have a start and an end, what was more important was the interaction of the weave and the lacing together of people, events, places, decisions and experiences. Viewed through this lens, Wyrd eliminates the concepts of coincidences and accidents, and instead builds sequences and inter-related components.

Following a sequence backwards allowed a person to understand how they arrived at a particular point. Wyrd could also be mapped in the other direction by those who could read the patterns which were present in the world. Brian Bates' fictional shaman Wulf provides the clearest understanding of this:

> Imagine you were to witness a raven swooping from the sky to peck out the eye of a warrior…You would say that the flight of the bird was connected directly to the wound. But if you observed the flight of the same raven a half day before the attack you would see no connection with the warrior's injury. Nevertheless the pattern of a raven's flight at noon is bound to the pattern of its flight at dusk, just as surely as the progression of day and night. One can read the pattern and thus see what future has in store.[20]

Wyrd linked not only the people, events, and things together, but also provided a pathway between time itself. To the Angles and Saxons, time occurred in two opposing directions: the past and the future. There was no concept for the present as it was only a fleeting moment. The past was to be remembered, and the future thought of, and Wyrd provides a pathway to explore both. Woden is often depicted in Norse sources with two ravens as companions; these are Huginn and Muninn. While there isn't a historic attestation to Huginn and Muninn by the Angles, it is likely they formed part of their spiritual world as the concept of birds, 'visiting distant places and returning, is a commonplace of Germanic and Celtic verse.'[21] The translation of the two names Huginn and Muninn is interpreted as 'thought' and 'memory'.[22] Memory symbolizing the past, and thought the projection of the future. Each day Woden sends Huginn and Muninn out to gather news and return it to him, giving the all-father knowledge of the past and the future on a global scale. The *Grimnismal*, a thirteenth century poem, records Woden's words as: 'Huginn and Muninn fly each day over the spacious earth. I fear for Huginn that he come not back, yet more anxious am I for Muninn.'[23]

For Woden, understanding the future was built on the knowledge of the past, that is where the clues and signs of Wyrd could be seen and interpreted, and thus his concern over the daily return of Muninn. Wyrd was so powerful that even the chief amongst gods considered it as part of his daily routine and was also governed by the weaving of Wyrd. Beowulf says to the people in Heorot while they wait for Grendal 'Gæþ a Wyrd swa hio scel', 'Wyrd goes ever as it must'. Wyrd was a force that drove all of the forces in the world and could be neither sheltered from nor altered.

Wyrd was created and maintained by the Norns, who weave the tapestry of all things together, including the gods. One of the often recited reasons for a king's conversion to Christianity related to the competition between the new god and the old gods, that they would choose the one which gave them success on the battlefield. However, this is a reading from a culturally biased position and doesn't take into account the deep understanding of Wyrd. No king in the pre-conversion age believed that Woden would change the outcome of a battle, for the Wyrd was already woven, and even Woden himself could not change that. It is clear that the concept of Wyrd continued on well into the conversion period, so it is hard to imagine newly-converted kings believing the new god was not also tied to Wyrd. Wyrd in its original meaning can best be summed up as 'a deep, unimaginably complex interaction of forces beyond our understanding'.[24]

The modern English word 'weird' is a direct descendent of Wyrd, yet its meaning is in complete opposition to how the word and concept was understood before the period of conversion. Today we attribute 'weird' to strange, unusual, or unexpected things. Yet the original concept was characterized by interconnectedness, and it was most certainly normal. Accounting for this change in understanding is difficult, but can likely be tied to the very act of conversion.

The importance of Wyrd as a primary force in the world, which expanded beyond the control of any god, was in opposition to the Christian ideals of creation and an all-powerful, all-knowing, singular deity. As was the case with physical representations of the indigenous belief systems and terminology, the term 'weird' was repurposed rather than erased.

Sometime in the seventh or eighth century a monk recorded a number of cultural teachings, which were in turn transcribed in the tenth century into the *Exeter Book* and what is now called 'Maxims I'. Maxims I shows that the knowledge of Wyrd continued on through the conversion period for it mentions Wyrd in two different passages. The first says 'ne wendaō hine wyrda', which translates to 'the fates do not change him.'[25] The 'him' in this sentence is the Christian god. This passage is interesting as it is being transcribed in the tenth century and recording the conflict between the indigenous concept of Wyrd and the imported religion. The transcription of this single line suggests that some knowledge of Wyrd was still commonly held for decades after the conversion period. A second passage in Maxims 1 lines 173 and 174 states, 'Earm biþ se þe sceal ana lifgan, wineleas wunian hafaþ him wyrd geteod'.[26] Or as modern English would present it, 'Wretched is he who must live alone; fate has ordained him to remain friendless'.[27] The modern translated use of fate in place of Wyrd in this passage is largely inaccurate. A more accurate reading of the latter part would be 'Wyrd has ordained him to remain friendless'. Leaving the word Wyrd in place in the modern English translation creates a distinct contradiction with the earlier passage which sought to decrease to power of Wyrd. The contradiction is interesting enough as it once again continues to show some form of understanding of Wyrd in later years and that it still played a role in people's lives.

As a group belief system, the community was tied together by a cyclical calendar of events, which was formed by the natural world. Bede provides us with some detail on this through selections of the Angle and Saxon calendar:

> The months of Giuli derive their name from the day when the Sun turns back [and begins] to increase, because one of [these months] precedes [this day] and the other follows. Solmonath can be called 'month of cakes', which they offered to their gods in that month. Hrethmonath is named for their goddess Hretha, to whom they sacrificed at this time. Eosturmonath has a name… was once called after a goddess of theirs named Eostre, in whose honour feasts were celebrated in that month… Halegmonath means 'month of sacred rites'. Blodmonath is 'month of immolations', for then the cattle which were to be slaughtered were consecrated to their gods.[28]

Hretha is likely the same as Nerthus, showing the continued importance on the celebration of Mother Earth. It is possible that the processions of a cart with an effigy of the great mother may have still occurred, as they were witnessed by Tacitus in the first century. Eostre was a goddess of spring and the return of life. Her name was eventually subsumed by the Christian celebrations around Lent and the resurrection of Christ, giving us 'Easter'. Many of the modern celebrations at Easter seem to tie directly to more ancient rites including eggs, rabbits, and flowers. This would have been a time of celebration having made it out of the lean winters.

Blotmonath likely started with the end of the year, something like Halloween, or the Celtic Samhain, the celebration of the dead and the ancestors, and the closing of the year. At this time animals that were not likely going to survive the winter were slaughtered and offerings were made. The year's campaigning season would come to an end at this point as well, with warriors returning home.

Between these specifically named months, the people would have held feasts and celebrations at Geola (the winter solstice) and the Liþa (summer solstice). Both of these points would have seen communal celebration. These two days are recorded in the monthly calendar by the establishment of a named month on either side of the observance. For Geola we have Ærra Geola or before Yule, followed by the next month which was Æfterra Geola, after Yule. Similarly, the midsummer solstice we have Ærra Liþa followed by Æfterra Liþa, which is before midsummer and after midsummer. The fact that these celebrations had both pre and post periods shows the importance of them; they were key turning points of time.

The Angle calendar was deeply connected to the natural rhythms, and was clearly structured around the importance of agriculture and husbandry with þrimilce-monaþ, the month of three milkings, and Weod-monaþ, the month of weeds. While the calendar provides some clues to the belief system based on scheduled celebrations, it also shows the deep understanding and importance of the natural world.

The flexible nature of the belief system allowed for the integration of new gods and local spirits. When the Angles reached Britain, they were exposed to traditional Celtic belief systems similar to their own but included local deities, which were in many cases readily accepted into the pantheon. This could explain some of the localized folkloric traditions which still exist, such as Herne the Hunter in Berkshire. This same process allowed the inclusion of the Christian God into the belief system, as clearly happened with King Rædwald, 'he seemed at the same time to serve Christ and the gods whom he served before; and in the same temple he had an altar for the Christian Sacrifice, and another small one at which to offer victims to devils'.[29]

While this was completely unacceptable in a monotheistic religion based on supremacy of the few and control of power, it was perfectly acceptable and common in a pluralistic and open belief system.

The majority of religious activity would have occurred outside, with a particular focus on springs, groves and standing stones, though there were more formal sites used as well. Groves played a particularly central role in religious beliefs of Germanic peoples. Tacitus reveals that the Germanic tribes used groves as places of divination, sacrifice, 'a grove hallowed by the auguries of their ancestors and by immemorial awe'.[30] The sanctity and importance of certain groves was shared across the northern European landscape, the druids had a sacred grove at Anglesey in Wales, and the Norse had a similar sacred grove at Uppsala, Sweden. This commonality continued through Angle and Saxon times and were seen as 'places of ancestral knowledge or places for divination'.[31] Many of these groves were named after the god worshipped at the location and can still be found on modern maps of England including Thundersley, Thurleigh, Thursley, Eastleigh, Ingestre, Tuesley, Tuesnoad, Wensley, and many others. There are yet more sites named for these deities and attached to ridges, hilltops, tumuli, lakes and moors. There are many that no longer exist on maps, but which are attested to in historical documents.

Along with the natural features and places of worship, the Angles also had more developed sites of worship including a Wih, Træf, and an Eahl. These three types grow in sophistication and development. The Wih was an image standing in the open with no shelter. This could have been a carved image, a pole, an ancient tree or perhaps a standing stone.[32] There are still place names which tell us where we might find the Wih including, Wye, Weedon, Willey, Weeley Wing, Whyly, and many more.

A more developed Wih may be termed a Træf. The Træf was a Wih with some shelter afforded to the location, perhaps a small building or a tent over the sacred spot. These locations are likely still named with the Wih structures, so they may be difficult to identify in the modern landscape. The most developed site of worship was the Eahl. The Eahl was a fully enclosed wooden temple. As is the case with the Wihs, the locations of these Eahls can still be detected in some modern place names including, Alkham, and Elham. Many of these Eahls were the focus of Pope Gregory's direction to Abbot Mellitus during the period of conversion and the church's missionary work in Britain:

> The temples of the idols in that nation ought not to be destroyed; but let the idols that are in them be destroyed; let water be consecrated and sprinkled in the said temples, let altars be erected, and relics placed there. For if those temples are well built, it is requisite that they be converted from the worship of devils to the service of the true God.[33]

Much of the Angle religious practices are lost, but some of them continue to exist in folklore, folk traditions, and hidden in modern festivals. This was a belief system that can be characterized as having,

> a conception of the divine based on plurality (polytheism) or the immanence of divinity in the natural world; what does seem clear is that the religious system was based in the community; it was not controlled by any central authority; it was directly connected to the land and the natural cycles of the world [and] an ethic that values personal responsibility over rule-based prescriptions.[34]

Furthermore, the belief system focused attention on ancestral worship; it was open, and finally it was flexible. This was the spiritual world in which Penda lived, and a spiritual world for which he would become one of the last holdouts against the conversion to religions which were utterly foreign to the Angles. Penda was dedicated to his ancestral ways, but he was no religious zealot. Bede tells us that when Penda was a powerful king, he allowed for a pluralistic society and the continued preaching of the Roman religion in the lands he controlled, 'Nor did King Penda forbid the preaching of the word even among his people'.[35] This openness was not only a feature of the Angle religious practices but also a credit to the man himself.

The Angle belief system, kingship, and kinship were all intrinsically linked in this period providing social and communal stability across communities in the wake of the Roman Empire constricting. It is generally accepted that chiefs and kings played an important role in the maintenance of the belief system and that system also played a reciprocal role in the maintenance of the king. The king was the bringer of wealth, prosperity and luck to the people. If a king was unable to maintain those things, it would be seen that his *Wyrd* was waning and, 'when the kingdom's luck disappeared the king would be deposed or killed'.[36] This process acted as a check and balance against a king's authority and may have helped contain excesses of power, 'one feature of this system is that any abuse of royal power would be extremely difficult'.[37]

The Angle system of kingship should not be treated as signs of early democracy, but it does certainly align with Tacitus' remarks on first-century Germanic practices of kingship: 'They choose their kings by birth, their generals for merit. These kings have not unlimited or arbitrary power, and the generals do more by example than by authority'.[38] In the 600 years between Tacitus and Penda, it would appear little had changed by way of kingship as far as broad strokes go. Truly the turning point for the control of kingship authority came with the rise of Christianity where 'the monopolization of the power of religion by a centralized, hierarchic institution dependent on and allied with the king increased his influence over society'.³⁹ It stands that kings had more to gain from the influence and use of Christianity than other groups within Angle and Saxon society. With Penda not being near the top of the kingship hierarchy, it seems fitting that the draw to convert wasn't present for him and could have been one of the more tangible reasons he never converted, particularly if he always saw himself as a warrior first and foremost.

Kinship was a central component to the functioning of society in the seventh century, providing an identity, operating as a foundation for alliances and conflicts, and providing some level of community welfare. Between Penda's birth in AD 606 and the arrival of his ancestor Eomer, roughly 150 years had elapsed. In that time, tribal affiliation still existed amongst the people; they still knew they were Angles as opposed to Saxons or Britons, but the link was tenuous and one built on stories and folk memory. It is almost certain that none of the Iclingas since Eomer had ever returned to their ancestral home land of Angln. From the initial arrival of the Angles from the continent to Britain, kinship began to replace tribal affiliations. This process has modern examples as well, for example in the Anglo-sphere, Canada, New Zealand, and Australia. In these countries, many families can trace their ancestors' migration from Britain at some point in the last 150 years. While they all may have a folk claim to ancestral home, many people have no physical contact, or even kinship connections to these ancestral places. In the modern world we have communication systems and air travel which eliminate many of the barriers to maintaining these links, and yet they still slip away. For the Angles in the sixth and seventh century, connection involved arduous journeys which simply were not viable. With a view on the modern world, it is easy to see how quickly the connection to a tribe on the continent would decompose in short order.

Kinship in this period is remarkably similar to the modern day, where bilateral kinship was the standard, meaning that an individual traced their kinsmen through both their mother and father's family.⁴⁰ More specifically, the Angle kinship system is a 'non-unilineal kinship, in which every individual has, in general, the option of tracing affiliation to a set of persons through both his parents'.⁴¹ The benefit of this system is that Penda would have been able to rely on support from both sides of his family. The flexible bilateral kinship system also ensured Penda had a broad geographic network which he could turn to for support as needed, particularly while far from his home. These connections would become particularly useful as he began campaigning and building a reputation as a warlord.

Within this kinship system, Penda owed loyalty to his kin and his community. This loyalty did come with a cost, 'to belong to a kindred meant accepting an obligation to kill, or to be killed by, strangers, friends, or in-laws if their kin happened to be in feud with yours'.[42] The kinship also provided Penda with a measure of loyalty to him as a member of the group, 'they owed him the duty of avenging his death, either by prosecuting a feud, or by exacting wergild payments'.[43] The wergild was an ancient customary law that attributed a compensation value for the injury or death of a person, which must be paid to the kin of the victim by the perpetrator. These bilateral networks allowed for young men of the nobility to participate in fosterage with other families. Penda may have participated in one of these opportunities fostering deep connections between families and allowing him to develop as a future leader and warrior. Fosterage should be viewed as an apprenticeship under a different leader and warriors, allowing the young Penda to gain experience and training on the battlefield, and as a leader.

The etymology of Penda's name is often cited as a suitable clue to a possible Brittonic connection. The name does not appear to be Angle, and certainly fits the mould of a Brittonic name. The lands that Penda's father and grandfather lived and fought in overlapped the final redoubts of Brittonic kingdoms. In this border, area control likely oscillated between Angle and Briton dominance. It would have been in the best interest of any leader to seek stability through alliances and oaths if possible.

One of the leading methods to seal alliances was through marriage. Many women in this period became the linkages between kingdoms and the weavers of peace between nations. Examining the historical record for conflict between Pybba and the Britons or Penda and the Britons turns up no confirmed cases of conflict. This is an interesting finding as Bede and others would tell us that the Angles and Britons were firm enemies, so why weren't the Iclingas and the Britons fighting in the late sixth century and early seventh century? This could simply be a case of the records of conflict not being kept, but looking at Penda's thirty-year reign as a king shows the same tendency of peace with the Britons.

The lack of conflict, along with the etymology of Penda's name, provides circumstantial evidence about the connection between the Iclingas and Britons, perhaps as far back as Creoda, but certainly with Pybba. It seems reasonable to suggest that Pybba's wife, Penda's mother, was a Briton. This marriage seems likely to be the work of Creoda and presumably occurred before Pybba lost power to Ceorl. Creoda's goal would have been to link the Iclingas with a Brittonic family and prevent further conflict to the west of the Iclingas. Strategically this was an outstanding move as it allowed the Iclingas to focus their attention on the largest threat in Britain, the continued rising power north of the Humber.

Penda's future collaboration with Brittonic kingdoms could be based on kinship linkages through his mother's lineage. In the seventh century the Brittonic kingdoms were no more homogenized then the fledgling Angle and Saxon kingdoms, and so connection to one of them did not mean peace and connection with all of them. For the Iclingas, the kingdom with the closest proximity was Powys, though contact with Gwynedd may have occurred as well as the political boundaries shifted and fluctuated with the fortunes of leaders. The kinship linkages to Powys or Gwynedd also allows for the opportunity of fosterage for Penda in these kingdoms. This experience would include significant time adapting to a different method of warfare, different weapons, and expanding his knowledge of a second language. The Welsh annals record a nickname for Penda, 'Penda ap Pyd', or Penda Son of Danger.[44] The nickname is a positive one and shows a certain affinity between the Britons and Penda. This seems a more appropriate nickname for a warrior, given by colleagues, as it isn't particularly noble sounding and meant for a king. The nickname implies that Penda, Son of Danger developed his martial prowess in the company of Britons as a young man. While these skills would go on to serve Penda in the future, his exposure to a different culture and religion at a young age allowed him to construct a pluralistic kingdom capable of drawing together many disparate groups into a single confederated entity.

Traditional tribal connections remained though were surely distant, while kinship connections grew in importance and began to develop into a new layer of tribal construction. This process is mirrored by the decentralization of authority and localization of political and economic systems occurring across Britain in the wake of the Roman evacuation of the island. Within a single generation it is possible that kinship connections had been elevated above tribal affiliations and formed the primary authority and cultural identity of individuals. Over time kinship groups, particularly in the modern midlands, coalesced into the sæta groups. Although the sæta may not have resulted in kingships, they were likely the first multi-kinship identifiers to be generated in Britain following the arrival of Germanic migrants. Sæta is best defined as an inhabitant or resident in its singular form, but in the plural application it is generally accepted as a folk name or tribal name.[45] There are around twenty-six indefinable sæta groups on the historic record, but likely there were many more. Of the groups which can be confirmed, the majority occurred in the midlands, the future areas we would consider as the Mercian heartlands. These sæta groups would grow to include the Pecsæta, Scrobsæta, Magonsæta, Dornsæta, Arosæta, Wreocensæta and Tomsæta. The Tomsæta centred round Tamworth and the assumed centre of mass for Mercian royal authority. Some of these sæta would be forged together into a larger Mercian identity, while others such as the Magonsæta would achieve a level of independence under their own king.

The sæta of the future Mercian territories were not fully formed stable kingdoms; they were the buffer states and the 'no man's land' between mighty nations. The future Mercian lands were the seventh century version of modern

Belgium, Ukraine, Poland or Korea. All of these buffer nations are the products of powerful neighbours establishing and quasi-supporting their existence as long as they provided an advantageous cushion between the home territory and the predation of nation wolves prowling the land. However, when the balance of power and equilibrium of nations is unsettled, the buffer state becomes an easy target for aggression and subjugation. This is the world that Penda and all Mercians found themselves in: in the middle of the glen with the wolves on all sides.

There should be no doubt that at some level, Penda would see himself as an Angle, but more importantly he would see himself deeply connected to the Iclingas and likely to a broader proto-tribe or sæta. All of the cultural factors and kinship realities were pivotal to Penda in his young life, and would in time be indispensable as he rose to power. With Ceorl in power and older Iclingas brothers jockeying for greater control, it seems evident that Penda was a long way from any position which would be titled king. In his youth, Penda was developing the skills of his trade, war and leadership, but not with a focus on kingship.

Chapter Four
Mercia's Rise

It is unclear where or when the term Mercia began to be used as a reference for a kingdom. The historic record lacks information on the origin of the country and what scattered details can be detected were invariably written by others about Mercia, and not by Mercians. This creates gaps in the story of Mercia, but also clouds our understanding as the records are usually written from the perspective of a competitor or enemy. Some kingdoms and their identities are easy to understand; this is particularly visible in the south-east, where the migration began to take root. Here we see East Anglia, South Saxons, East Saxons and West Saxons. Naming conventions of Britain's seventh-century polities seem to follow a few general approaches of either a single word descended from the Britons, or a compound word of Angle or Saxon origin: Deira, Elmet, Lindsey, Kent, Bernicia, of Brittonic descent versus the East Saxons, West Saxons, East Angles, and South Saxons. However, there are polities that don't follow these trends: the Hwicce, Gewisse and Mercia. These three names seem to run against the general naming conventions. The Hwicce and the Gewisse may descend from the same source, perhaps after the name of an individual, or may be related to Brittonic naming conventions; but what of Mercia? Mercia truly is devoid of a patterned birth and explanation, to shake the naming trends which seemingly account for all of the other major polities of the era is surprising.

There are modern parallels to the naming conventions and process of polities in Britain through the migration period. Initially, places are referenced to something, and the earliest arrivals named themselves and their places in relation to their ancestral homes. In this, we arrive at East Anglia, South Saxons, and Middle Angles. In the modern world you have New York, New Brunswick, Nova Scotia, New South Wales and New Zealand. The second wave of colonizing no longer relies on the ancestral home and is based out of the initial colonies. It begins to use names already found on the land. Through this process we get Deira, Bernicia, and Lindsey. The United States of America provides a clear modern example where we see English and Latin-based names for states on the Eastern Seaboard, and these give way to indigenous-based names such as Iowa, Ohio, Tennessee, Mississippi, Kentucky, Michigan, Missouri, and Illinois. Of course there are certainly outliers to this in Anglo-Saxon Britain. Kent is a significant stand out; and in the modern USA, Massachusetts and Connecticut are exceptions to the rule.

This naming process seems to replicate in Canada as well with English and Latin-based nomenclature thoroughly referencing an ancestral homeland, eventually giving way to names derived from the history of the land and the indigenous peoples. All of this is important because Mercia is unusual. One would expect people or places to take a name from the land, similar to the sæta names on its border lands. While Mercia does show a disregard for an ancient Angle homeland it fails to show the usual connection to a traditional land name.

In general, the name Mercia is accepted as deriving from a border land, generally identified as the border between Britons and Germanic migrants. That understanding presents a falsehood that there was only one border between the Germanic Angles: Saxons on one side and Britons on the opposite side, when in fact there were many. In the east, Lindsey, Elmet, and Heathfield all appear to continue as Brittonic kingdoms south of the River Humber. To the south there was a significant border between the Gewisse and the Brittonic kingdom of Dumonia, the future counties of Cornwall, Somerset and Dorset. North of the Humber the borders between Brittonic, Scoti and Picts were more complex than any other area. While Deira and Bernicia were Angle kingdoms they shared borders with non-Angle kingdoms including Rheged, Strathclyde, Gododdin, and Catterick.

The term Mercia comes from old English word 'Mearc', which is a boundary, and gives way to the medieval term 'march' or 'mark'. This interpretation is likely correct, but still leaves many questions. There are 'march' locations still present on the modern map of Europe including the nation of Denmark, and regional names such as Telemark and Finmark in Norway; France also has the province of Marche which was historically the March Limousine. Casting back farther in time there are ample examples of regional marches established under Charlemagne and the Carolingian kings. These regional buffer areas, of which there were eleven in total, were used to encircle the Frankish empire and provide a series of bulwark states between the Frankish kingdom and other powerful nations. These zones of soft dominance were used effectively to first pacify future competitors, assimilate cultures, and inevitably draw the zone into the greater political establishment. It is worth noting that none of these marches predate Mercia, and none of them rose to the prominence of Mercia, nor did any of the Frankish examples survive as a polity. History does show one example of a people named for a march which does predate Mercia, and that is a Germanic continental people called the Marcomanni, whose name likely means 'Border People'.

All of these examples bar that of the Marcomanni share a number of characteristics not seen in Mercia. First off they all have a reference to the march, some compound or additional term which provides a reference and separates the march from the other march areas. Second, apart from the Marcomanni all of them occur after Mercia is established. An examination shows the Carolingians to be the major catalyst behind the use of the Marche and the designation of areas, but this kingdom was still 200 years adrift from the founding of the Mercian Kingdom. To complicate the consideration of the etymology and political origin of 'Mercia' is the 1,400 years of history since the establishment of the kingdom. Following 1066, the Normans made extensive use of the marches in their control of a conquered Britain; perhaps this was a political tool learned from Frankish history. This fact may have clouded the interpretation of 'Mercia'. It is the lack of a geographical reference with Mercia that makes it so difficult to outright accept the name. By the naming standards of the time, it is hard to envision a king or a group of people accepting their role in the land as being defined by their position between other nations. This implies a lack of national self-determination and is wholly reliant on the reference to other peoples.

Accepting the etymology of Mercia as arriving from the term march or boundary would suggest that these peoples formed a significant geo-political tool for a particular region not seen since the continental Roman Empire, nor used until the rise of the Carolingian Empire some 200 years later. If this is the case, one would expect to see greater use of the term maerc during this period, but that doesn't appear to be the case. Where is the Gewissemaerc, or the Humbermaerc or the Powysmaerc? The term Mercia, if related to maerc, is likely not an indigenous origin. It can safely be argued that the name occurred much later, and may be based on knowledge of the Carolingian Empire, where its use was frequent and developed as a wholistic political tool of control and dominance. Transmission of the term as a political tool likely came through the exchange of church officials from the continent. With close church ties between the English kingdoms and Frankia, knowledge of march zones and that naming convention could lead to the use in the English Kingdoms. It should not be forgotten that the term Northumbria did not occur until it was popularized by Bede, and perhaps the same can be said for Mercia.

If the etymology is related to march, then this region and people were most certainly named by other people. As the word is Germanic, it has to be another Anglo or Saxon kingdom that has provided the name. In the seventh century, Britain south of the River Humber was formed by scattered small sæta groups not yet coagulating into the larger nations of the heptarchy until you reach East Anglia, South Saxons, and Kent. The nearest kingdom to the south that may have had a watch on this region would be East Anglia, though it is still some distance away, particularly considering that the fenland around the Wash was much larger in this period. It is to the north of the River Humber that we likely need to look for the origin of the term Mercia, if indeed it relates to a march. A document written in the seventh or eighth century called the *Tribal Hidage* shows a general east to west axis largely along the Trent River, creating a borderland that divided north from south. The *Tribal Hidage* lists land size for kingdoms, and sub-kingdoms across Britain south of the River Humber. This fact is important in the interpretation of the name and the establishment of a date for the *Tribal Hidage* because the common understanding is that the referenced borderland is between Angle kingdoms in the east, and the Brittonic kingdoms in the west, specifically in the future nation of Wales. If the name truly derived from the ethno-religious border between the Angles and Brittonic peoples one would expect the term to be applied to an area in a north-south orientation, likely covering the *Tribal Hidage* areas of the Wrocsæta and Magonsæta.

North of the Humber River, there are none of the sæta polities, but there are a number of competing Brittonic, Pict, Scoti and Angle nations. By the seventh century, the dominant forces were Bernicia and Deira, with the likes of Rheged, Strathclyde, and Gododdin swinging the balance of northern supremacy between the two Angle nations. Northumbria as a political singularity was still hundreds of years in the future. The region along the Trent River makes sense from a strictly Deiran or later Northumbrian vantage point as a march, as the area borders smaller Angle seatas including the Pecseata, Tomsæta, Heathfield, along with Brittonic kingdoms of Lindsey and Elmet. If a Deiran king had overlordship north of the Humber, and had stretched south to at least Heathfield and Elmet, that version of Mercia would be a march, a border zone, and a buffer to the south. It must be assumed that the title of Mercia comes from a Deira or Bernicia source, a name given by others. However, there are other less explored options for the etymology of the name.

Perhaps the origin of the word Mercia is tied to the word for horse. Tamworth is traditionally held as the seat of Mercian power and one would expect to see a link of site names moving north from Oxford or south along the Trent, but neither of these occur. The land based multi-generational migration of the Iclingas, first south-west and then north relied on horse travel along ancient pathways and Roman roads. The horse was a highly symbolic animal in general for the Angles and it could be that the new kingdom being drawn together was named after the horse, or Maer. In this scenario, the Iclingas are showing reverence for an ancient symbol, but also their key to moving throughout the island. The tie to long-distance terrestrial travel would have shown the Iclingas the strategic importance of the Roman roads, and this could have led to the decision to settle at Tamworth along a major Roman road, and in direct proximity to other Roman roads. From this location the Iclingas could move against any of the major kingdoms and rapidly draw in smaller sæta groups. The access and control of the road system allowed the kingdom to maintain effective control across a large area, which is precisely what the Romans had in mind when they built it. Here we have an origin of the name based on land travel, but there is still a third possibility.

To the north-west of Mercia lies the River Mersey and the Wirral. A curious pattern on naming conventions occurs across Britain during this migration era. While place names are overwhelmingly replaced with Anglo and Saxon words, rivers are not. For one reason or another hydrological features maintain their Brittonic and in some cases even more ancient names. The River Mersey stands out as a definite anomaly, as the river's name is an Angle word, and not the original Celtic word. Why would this river take on a new name while others of equal or even greater influence on emerging kingdoms remain with their traditional names? More curious is that the generally accepted etymology for the river is the same as Mercia, it is named because it is a boundary, a march.

Prior to being named the River Mersey, this body of water was likely called the Meteia, a Brittonic tribe named after the waterway was the Metantti. Both the people and the water course are recorded by Roman sources, in particular Ptolemy who records them as the Seteia River and the Setantti people.[1] In the Brittonic languages the river's name meant 'Reaping one, she who cuts down'; the people in turn were 'Reapers, Cutters-down'.[2] The name's origin is perhaps related to the rapid rising and ebbing tide which could catch the unwary person.[3] The river is important here as it can't be ignored that the Angles and Saxons were renowned seafarers of the age. A case could be made that ships were landed in the River Meteia and a warband moved inland from there. Perhaps we are looking for the Meteiasæta as the origin of the Mercians. Another less romantic etymology for the River Mersey also exists through the word Mirce, meaning murky or dark. This would seem an appropriate description of the waters found at the River Mersey. The name of the river and people could have been misunderstood and simply translated to an appropriate word such as Mirce or Maecian. Maecian means to mix or stir, which could also fit as a description of the strong tidal forces found in the river's delta, and the very force that gave the river its original name, Meteia.

If a link exists between the Mercian people and the River Mersey it would appear a valid interpretation that the name of the people was born from the name of the river, and that it evolved over time and translation. While a border or a march could be insinuated here, the terms for murky, or to mix, seem like a much more accurate etymology for the river. The river does form a formidable boundary, but it is hard to see what the boundary separated. The region to the north of the river was not a place of power and was likely not of significant concern to those of the south.

Clearly the River Mersey and Mercia belong together and the etymology seems to make that link. The question then becomes: which reference was first and why? The argument that the people were so named because they bordered the Brittonic kingdoms makes sense, but then one may expect a riverine border between Mercia and Powys or Gwynedd to have the name 'Mersey' and not the northern border with little direct threat.

If the term Mercia was homegrown, it could represent an attempt to provide an acceptable name with broad appeal over a diverse confederation of traditionally independent sætas. This process would be familiar in a modern setting, such as the establishment of the 'United States of America', the 'Union of Soviet Socialist Republics', or the 'European Union'. In all of these cases you see the apolitical name, carrying no traditional tribal, ethnic, or state references, which is bland enough for all constituent parts of the confederation to accept. Only the most independent groups or late-comers to the polity could bristle against such mundane and sanitized naming conventions.

Of all these options, the general accepted link between Mercia and march still seems the most plausible without the introduction of new evidence to the contrary. However, it is important to remember that there is no definitive answer on the origin of the name. If we accept that the term 'Mercia' is based on the word 'march' then it was not an indigenously developed name. Instead it appears most logical that it was applied on the modern midlands by a power north of the Humber, before being taken on by the Iclingas in the future. By the seventh century the term Mercia provided its kings with a sanitized name to cover a vast territory with a diverse populace represented by multiple languages, religions, and group identities. As Penda entered adulthood, which is the first time he appears in historic records, it remains doubtful that he called himself a 'Mercian' and in all likelihood only saw himself in terms of his ancestral background, as a member of the Iclingas, and perhaps as an Angle. It's quite possible that he also felt a connection to the Britons and may have equally identified with them. Later authors have a tendency to over-state the ethnic rivalry between Britons and Angles. While there should be no doubt that they were involved in conflict frequently with one another, so too were the Angle kingdoms. This was an era when conflict was endemic and unless a king could achieve peace with his neighbours through oaths or marriages, the only other option was war. The idea that Britons and Angles were despised rivals comes first from Bede, but is followed by many other authors, and eventually drives the tales of King Arthur. It is difficult to find proof of the ethnic animosity, and in all likelihood most people saw all strangers in the same negative light, with no grander ideals based on the variance between Briton and Angle or Saxon.

In the year AD 626 Penda was twenty years old. He had spent his youth training, learning the skills of a warrior, and perhaps living with other noble families to round out his education and build connections with other groups. It's a fair assumption that as a twenty year old, Penda would be a seasoned combatant and based on his lineage could have had a small war band of his own. There are no recorded conflicts in the historic records for this period, but Penda would have been engaged in routine raids since his late teens. These raids were quick hit-and-run operations targeted at mobile wealth, perhaps some gold and silver, but much more likely cattle and livestock. The raiding was important to the warband and the warlord as it brought them wealth, kept them active, and allowed the continued development of martial skills. If a warlord wasn't able to keep his warband active and gaining wealth, it is reasonable to presume that the men would leave the group and go to serve another lord.

Each warband was held together by oaths and obligations. Warriors swore oaths which tied them to their lord, and required them to serve in his warband, and the warlord was obligated to keep them fed, and offer them opportunity to again wealth, status and prestige. Tacitus witnessed the outcome of a failure on the latter side:

> If their native state sinks into the sloth of prolonged peace and repose, many of its noble youths voluntarily seek those tribes which are waging some war, both because inaction is odious to their race, and because they win renown more readily in the midst of peril, and cannot maintain a numerous following except by violence and war.[4]

Penda began to establish himself as a warrior of some local renown, with a small warband conducting raids. He may well have inherited some of his father's seasoned warriors to help him in his early days on the land. As a warlord, Penda had to utilize each campaign season efficiently to provide for his warband, to keep his warriors happy and to attract more men to his warband. From a home in the vicinity of Pebworth, Penda could raid to the west against Powys, though it seems that there may have been marriage alliances in place so that wasn't a likely target. Going north was not viable either as that was Iclingas territory. To the east there may have been some isolated opportunities against small settlements. The south, however, stands out as a prime target for raiding. The Severn valley could be followed on either bank leading to worthwhile targets.

In AD 626 the future nation of Wales was made up of a number of kingdoms, generally of equal size, with the exception of those in the south-east. The north-west was Gwynedd, the north-east and east was Powys, and to the south-west Deheubarth. The south-east remained fractured into at least three small kingdoms, Gwent, Brycheiniog, and Morgannwg. Together these three kingdoms would have been of equal land mass to the other three Brittonic kingdoms of Wales, but in their splintered state they were susceptible to the predations of kingdoms and raiding warbands. On the west side of the Severn, the kingdom of Gwent provided a clear target for raiding. Gwent was relatively small by the standards of the other Brittonic kingdoms; it would have been susceptible to quick raids from warbands, particularly in the summer when the Severn would have been easier to cross. Access would have been easy enough for a small band on horseback. Penda would take them north-west to the crossing at Bridgnorth or a ford nearby and then south along the Roman road towards Gwent. This route passed through the future Mercian sub-kingdom of the Magonsæta, and these raids could have been part of the process of controlling this border land. As the raids continued, Penda was perhaps able to leave some of his warband in settlements within the future Magonsæta area to begin slowly controlling this region. This area had seen raids and conflict by the Iclingas in previous generations, most certainly by Penda's grandfather Creoda, who seems to have pushed Brittonic power east to Hereford.

South, along the eastern shore of the Severn River, would provide fertile grounds for warband raids, but also for the establishment of greater authority and power. This was the future territory of the Hwicce, stretching in the north from Pebworth, along the Severn River valley south to modern-day Bristol and east from modern Gloucester to the western edge of Oxford, creating a triangular territory of almost 4,500 square kilometres. This area was at a crossroads of multiple powers including the Saxon Gewisse moving from the south-east along the downs and the Thames River valley, the Brittonic Dumonians from the south-west in modern Somerset, Cornwall, and Devon; and the Iclingas Angles coming from the north. The land of the Hwicce no doubt had a population comprised of diverse tribal affiliations drawn from all of the nations around them and older Brittonic settlements. The lack of a strong central authority in this area made it a lawless country of expansion and raiding.

The Gewisse had been moving west along the downs, and out of their power centre along the upper Thames valley in the early part of the seventh century, culminating with the Battle of Beandun in AD 614. The Battle of Beandun is important as a line drawn from Oxford through Cirencester and onto Brean Down; the location of the battle provides a general northern border for the Gewisse, and a southern border for the Hwicce. Hwicce territory is triangular in shape which seems to be a natural fit to separate the Britons, Saxons and Angles. The variable nature of overlordship in this territory made it a treacherous place for all settlements, and it would be easy to see them as prey for the predators coming from the Gwisse, Iclingas, and Britons. Additionally, there may have been localized raiding parties operating on the land, making for a very dangerous place. For people living here, stability would only come with a dominant lord who was able to protect them against other lords and aggressors.

Between AD 626 and AD 628 Penda turned from raiding to establishing greater control and authority south of Pebworth and into the Hwicce lands. As his control to the south increased, he was able to draw in more warriors to his band and increase his power. By protecting parts of the Hwicce territory he was also able to draw warriors from these lands under his banner, perhaps leading to culturally mixed warband of Angles, Saxons and Britons. The origin of the term Hwicce is, like many other details of this area, a point of considerable debate. The most commonly accepted etymology is that it comes from a Brittonic term for 'most excellent' related to the modern Welsh word 'gwych'.[5] The Hwicce likely already existed as a political entity, but had their elite replaced by the Angles.[6] An alternative theory suggests that the Hwicce could have been 'a political entity created by the kings of Mercia, who installed a ruling dynasty over a mixed British and Anglo-Saxon.[7] This second theory is difficult based on the name of the people, which is clearly Brittonic in nature. It seems more likely that Hwicce achieved its stature as one amongst many Angle, Saxon, and Brittonic kingdoms through a more organic redevelopment of an existing polity, which grew in stature over a period of time.

Penda and the Iclingas before him were able to gain power and control in the Hwicce lands over time, through raids, battles, and eventually delivering protection to the local populace. Gradually, the local elite was replaced by members of the Iclingas and their warbands. The process of replacing leadership with a new one from a different culture and different land occurred with the Romans and would occur again in 1066 when the Normans arrived and replaced the English nobility with their own. Political decapitation also gave us the Angle nations of Bernicia and Deira, where the territories maintained their ancient names, but the elite changed.

What we can't know is whether Penda was placed in control of the Hwicce, or if he drew it together himself. In his future he shows little interest in conquering, though he is at war frequently. Over the next thirty years he will move armies to all corners of Britain, but never leave them in place; he always seems to return home. If this same tendency occurred when he was younger than it can be concluded that he was given a territory in the Hwicce. He was able to draw warriors to him through his fame and success in raids, eventually amassing a large enough band to execute campaigns farther afield and perhaps in an effort to protect his new Hwicce home.

In AD 626 the northern portion of what would one day become Mercia changed hands from the enigma we know as Ceorl to Penda's brother Eowa. Ceorl enters only a few sources and is not found in others. What limited details we have on him show that he forced Pybba out and ruled for the next twenty-nine years. During the three decades of his reign, Ceorl is not recorded throughout the available sources. Upon the death of Ceorl around AD 626, Eowa is able to launch a successful bid for the crown of the territory likely centred around Tamworth. Eowa's ability to take control of the kingship is remarkable as he was most certainly a distant contender following his father's dethroning nearly thirty years before. It is reasonable to say that Eowa had never known the Iclingas as kings, but he must have had a significant amount of backers amongst the elite and perhaps from a foreign kingdom, maybe from north of the Humber.

The *Anglo-Saxon Chronicles* and Bede tell us of the importance of AD 626 in other kingdoms. While the transition from Ceorl to Eowa cannot definitively be linked to the following events, they may have interacted or been a part of the same sweeping narrative. North of the Humber, King Edwin of Deira had achieved supremacy over Bernicia and now held a group of kingdoms together under a single crown. Edwin spent most of his youth in exile, being fostered by a number of kingdoms, including the court of Ceorl for a period of time, before finally arriving in King Rædwald's East Anglia. In AD 616 King Æthelfrith, Edwin's uncle, was actively hunting him down to stamp out any claim he may still have to the thrones of Deira or Bernicia which had been united into a single nation for the first time. Æthelfrith tracked Edwin down in East Anglia and attempted to bribe Rædwald to give up Edwin. When bribery failed Æthelfrith threatened Rædwald with war unless he handed Edwin over. Rædwald very nearly broke his oath of hospitality and protection, but his wife, the Queen of the East Anglians upbraided him and reminded him of his oaths. According to Bede, 'She dissuaded him from it, reminding him that it was altogether unworthy of so great a king to sell his good friend in such distress for gold, and to sacrifice his honour, which is more valuable than all other adornments'.[8]

Rædwald knew that Æthelfrith was now on his way south, the menace of war was no hollow threat. The king of the East Anglians opted to hastily march north against the aggressive Æthelfrith meeting him on the east side of the River Idle near Bawtry. Bede mentions that Rædwald 'raised a mighty army to subdue Æthelfrith; who, meeting him with much inferior forces, for Redwald had not given him time to gather and unite all his power'. This location is on a Roman road, allowing the East Anglian army to move quickly. The river here goes from a northerly direction, to a north-westerly direction, before an ancient crossing point just downstream from the bend. The strategic importance of the location is highlighted by the remains of an old Roman fort which protected the crossing at the River Idle. Rædwald arrived first and was able to pick the battlefield. He put his left wing along the River Idle, 200 metres south of the river crossing and the Roman road. To his right was the earthwork remains of the Roman fort, affording his right-wing protection. This provided a front of under 100 metres, the size of a football field. At the River Idle, King Rædwald of East Anglia positioned his force between the old fort and the river, forcing King Æthelfrith of Deira and Bernicia to cross the river and come shield to shield with the East Anglians. Rædwald's selection of the location allowed him to channel Æthelfrith's force into the centre of the East Anglian line, thus preventing the Northumbrians from turning their flanks.

Æthelfrith had no tactical advantage in this setting and was outnumbered, it was a trap that he was unable to extricate himself from. To turn away from the battle would have been an admission of defeat and the tacit yielding to the power of East Anglia, such a move would embolden rivals against his authority and lead to dynastic in-fighting, and revolt in Deira which would degrade his power at best, but most likely result in him losing the crown and his life. All Æthelfrith could do at this point was draw his force together and rely on their individual skill, this was the true test of the warbands oath to their king. If Æthelfrith took on a defensive posture his flanks would be wrapped by the East Anglians, so his only option was aggression and trying to punch a hole in the centre of Rædwald's line, giving the Deiran and Bernician warriors the ability to hack the line apart. Henry of Huntingdon states that Æthelfrith was,

> indignant that anyone should venture to resist him, rushed on the enemy boldly, but not in disorder with a select body of veteran soldiers, though the troops of Rædwald made a brilliant and formidable display, marching in three bodies, with fluttering standards and bristling with spears and helmets, while the numbers greatly exceeded their enemies.[9]

Æthelfrith may have used a 'Boar's Head' in this attack, forming his line into a wedge and smashing directly into the line of the East Anglians. This tactic would be sensible in an aggressive attack particularly if he was aiming at turning the disciplined shield-wall into a melee of individual combat, where his superior warriors could level the battlefield. At first Æthelfrith was able to gain some advantage in the early chaotic period of the battle, killing Rædwald's son and destroying part of the East Anglian force. Following the initial attack, Æthelfrith reforms and aims to attack the still-standing line of Rædwald. In the second attack, Rædwald stands firm against Æthelfrith, 'the Northumbrians made vain attempts to penetrate them, and Æthelfrith, charging among the enemy's squadrons, became separated from his own troops and was struck down on a heap of bodies he had slain.'[10]

Æthelfrith's aggression and lapse in strategic thought brought forward the destruction of his army, the collapse of his kingdom, and his own death along the river bank. Rædwald was now the key broker of power amongst the kingdoms of the Angles and Saxons, and his first move was to place Edwin on the thrones of Deira and Bernicia.

Over the next ten years, King Edwin would consolidate his authority north of the Humber. In time and with total control in the north, Edwin had an opportunity to begin moving south and exerting influence over other nations, in particular those of Elmet, Lindsey, and the lands adjacent to the south side of the River Humber. Edwin successfully used all of the tools available to him to build power, including fosterage with East Anglia, and marriage to Cwenburg of Kent, so that by AD 626 he was the single greatest power in Britain. Penda at this stage was campaigning with a warband, but not involved in the movements of kings. Edwin on the other hand was beginning to be a threat to southern kingdoms, particularly with his marriage to the Kentish dynasty. The Gewisse were most threatened by this move as it was yet another sign of the growing authority of Edwin, which Henry of Huntingdon records, 'had been raised to such a pitch of temporal power such as no English king had enjoyed before'.[11]

In the early months of AD 626 Cwichelm, one of the two kings of the Gewisse, hatched a plan to roll back the influence of King Edwin and the Deiran and Bernician kingdoms. Cwichelm dispatched an assassin named Eomer to the north to confront and kill Edwin. This task would have been made more difficult by the fact that kings in this period did not stay in one single centre. The lack of any public administration or government organ forced the king's court to travel between multiple royal sites on a never-ending tour to maintain control of the territory. This movement was a method of extracting taxes from nobility, it also provided opportunities for promotion and gift giving, and gave the king the opportunity to exercise control over legal matters as required. As Edwin's territory expanded, so too did his need to maintain royal centres across the subjugated area. All of this made Eomer's mission more complicated as he had to find the king without coming across as an obvious threat.

A court on the road would likely provide an opportunity for merchants, along with messengers from farther afield calling upon the king, and the assassin sought to blend into this mass of humanity. Eomer's hunt eventually brought him to the banks of the Derwent River. The Derwent runs in a southerly direction starting in the North Yorkshire moors and eventually draining into the River Ouse near the Humber estuary. Bede provides a few more details on the end of Eomer's hunt: 'He came to the king on the first day of the Easter festival, at the river Derwent, where there was then a royal township.'[12] The exact location of this royal estate on the Derwent is unknown, but along its water course is a town now called Malton. Malton descends from the Angle world 'mæthel',[13] a location where 'people met up at central places for feasts, rituals, and exchanges'.[14] If the local communities were already using this site as a location for legal proceedings and gatherings, then it would be an ideal location for the king's court to establish a regional centre.

About 20 April AD 626 Eomer was admitted into the king's hall under the guise of bringing a message from the Kings of the Gewisse, 'Whilst unfolding in cunning words his pretended embassy',[15] Eomer suddenly unsheathed a blade which had been coated in poison and lunged towards King Edwin.

> When Lilla, the king's most devoted servant, saw this, having no buckler at hand to protect the king from death, he at once interposed his own body to receive the blow; but the enemy struck home with such force, that he wounded the king through the body of the slaughtered thegn.[16]

Lilla died from his wounds; the king was gravely injured in the attack, and in the melee that ensued Eomer was able to kill one more thegn, called Frothhere. Eomer, the assassin sent by Cwichelm to curtail the power of Edwin, was 'immediately cut down by the swords of the king's attendants'.[17]

In the immediate aftermath of the attack the king was rushed away to York. This was likely due to its security, but also its proximity to care and the church. To add to the stress of the event, Edwin's wife went into labour in the hours following the attack, giving birth to a daughter. Lilla the brave thegn whose heroic actions saved the life of King Edwin was afforded a noble burial. His body was brought to the head waters of the Derwent high in the North Yorkshire moors, some thirty kilometres from the site of the assassination attempt. At this place Lilla was buried in a tumulus and marked by a stone cross now known as Lilla's Cross. A local legend records that Lilla had converted before Edwin and his selfless actions were one of the factors in Edwin's eventual conversion. If Lilla had converted, it is odd that he was not buried in a church yard, but the king's choice to bury him high up on the moors could be an example of the crossroads between Christianity and the Heathen faiths.

Naturally, Edwin needed to retaliate against the Gewisse for the assassination attempt. Unfortunately the record gets very sparse at this critical moment with both Bede and the *Anglo-Saxon Chronicles* being fairly non-descript. Bede tells us that Edwin raised an army and, 'marched against the nation of the West-Saxons; and engaging in war'.[18] What is clearly missing here is a location, a date, and even the combatants at the battle. If we take Bede at his word then it is clear that Cwichelm must have been amongst the dead in this campaign. Yet the *Anglo-Saxon Chronicles* tells us that Cwichelm was baptized and died in AD 636. The discrepancy is quite glaring and opens up another possibility. In the wake of the assassination attempt it would seem highly probable that Edwin would raise an army to seek revenge on the Gewisse. In order to attack them he would need to pass through the lands that would one day become Mercia. It would seem that this could only be possible with the support of Mercian nobles and warbands, to move across the land. It is worth considering that Bede may have got the details of this event wrong though. With Edwin tying in relationships and alliances with Kent, it was the Mercian lands that were most threatened. King Ceorl would be confronted with Northumbrian dominated lands to the north, east and south. The Mercian lands at this point were not united and even at their best were a loose confederacy. This fragmented land was unable to field an army large enough to confront Edwin's power. These lands were directly threatened by the Northern power, and assassination would seem an obvious approach from a lesser power who had real concerns about the authority of their neighbour. King Ceorl's reign comes to an end in AD 626 rather anonymously, as if he is forgotten on purpose. It would seem distinctly possible that it was not Cwichelm, but rather Ceorl that sent Eomer the assassin to Malton.

Alternatively, Ceorl had knowledge of the assassination and participated at some level in the conspiracy leading to his death at the hands of Edwin. With Ceorl out of the way, Edwin placed Penda's older brother Eowa on the Mercian throne. There would have been no love lost between Eowa of the Iclingas dynasty and the mysterious Ceorl. Nennius also provides a clue here by referring to the reign of Eowa, but also the future reign of Penda who he says 'reigned ten years; he first separated the kingdom of Mercia from that of the North-men'.[19] North-men in this context are the men north of the Humber, a very direct reference to Eowa's subservience to Edwin. There is one more clue from Henry of Huntingdon which suggests Eowa was subordinate to Edwin. Henry of Huntingdon has an entry of AD 628 that states, 'The Abbot of Pertaneu reported that he had seen an old man who was baptized by Paulinus with a crowd of people, in the presence of King Edwin, in the River Trent, near the town now called Fingecester (Southwell).'[20]

At first glance this quote seems innocuous, but it is remarkable as the location is well within the area assumed to be under Eowa's control, suggesting King Edwin had the freedom to pass through Eowa's land.

If indeed Cwichelm was the mastermind of the assassination attempt, then removing Ceorl and placing a friendly and subservient king on the Mercian throne provided Edwin with access to move against the Gewisse. Bede once again gives us some vague details on the outcome of Edwin's retribution telling us that he 'slew or received in surrender all those of whom he learned that they had conspired to murder him. So he returned victorious into his own country'.[21] Perhaps the mastermind Cwichelm was one of the lucky ones who surrendered to Edwin. At this point Edwin now had control north of the Humber, alliances with East Anglia, and Kent, and dominance over northern Mercia and the Gewisse.

Penda meanwhile was still in the lands of the Hwicce and Magonsæta, far to the south and west. Eowa's establishment as the Mercian king would have been celebrated by Penda, who shows a very distinct tendency towards protection of his family throughout his life. Although this is an era of mortal competition, even amongst members of the same ancestral household, Penda never showed this same propensity, he simply carried on with his life as a Thegn and warband leader. The *Anglo-Saxon Chronicles* do record a discrepancy though, in AD 626: 'This year Penda began to reign; and reigned thirty winters',[22] but this seems at odds with the narrative we find elsewhere. For example, Bede does not refer to Penda as a king during the Heathfield battle of AD 633, but as 'the vigorous Penda, of the royal race of Mercians'.[23] Nennius believed Penda reigned for ten years which would put his ascendency to the throne around AD 646.

Two interesting questions surface here: why do the *Anglo-Saxon Chronicles* record AD 626 as the start of Penda's reign?; and why do the chroniclers not speak of Eowa? The answer lies in the authorship of the chronicles. The *Anglo-Saxon Chronicles* are largely based on Gewisse and West-Saxon sources, so the earlier periods have limited references about northern concerns. Secondly, if Penda and his Hwiccans were the local threat to the Gewisse, then it would seem justifiable that they saw him as some type of king. In the next few years, conflict would erupt between Penda and the kings of the Gewisse which would certainly lend credence to this theory.

Chapter Five
To the South

Penda's authority and power had steadily grown as he took on the role of a warlord and the leader of a successful warband. He may have benefited from the installation of his brother Eowa as the Mercian king, raising his stature and authority in the Angle lands. Eowa was focused to the north and east, and exhibited little interest or control to the south; in this vacuum Penda was able to grow his authority and generally act independent of all external forces. Perhaps this independence of action with seemingly no deference paid to a higher authority is why early authors interpreted this moment as the beginning of Penda's reign as a king. However, it is equally possible that the Bede and the *Anglo-Saxon Chronicles* simply misinterpreted events which had occurred years before they were recorded. It seems unlikely, but it is entirely possible that Penda would crown himself as king at this point.

What is more likely is that in AD 626 Penda was a Thegn, with a direct line to a lineage of kings, giving him an opportunity to one day become a king and to establish lesser thegns below himself. At this time he had land and a warband, he was successful enough in raids and combat to keep his warriors at hand and to draw new warriors into his warband. Penda's connection with the Britons, likely through his mother but also through personal alliances, gave him and his land security to the west, and allowed him to attract not only Angle warriors, but also Britons looking for wealth and reputation. The Hwicce lands were at the crossroads with the Angles, Saxons, and Britons, and Penda's cultural flexibility and knowledge drew these disparate peoples together, providing Penda with the foundation of his power base.

Penda's continued rise in stature was partially due to the geo-politics which surrounded his fledgling kingdom of the Hwicce. On two fronts he had little concern of raids and conflict for he was protected to the west by his Brittonic connections and to the north by his brother. To the east were a variety of smaller Angle settlements and small sub-kingdoms, to the south-east were the Saxon Gewisse, and to the south-west the Dumonian Britons. These southern nations lacked alliances and connections through marriage or oaths to Penda and the Hwicce. By AD 628 Penda had gained enough power and notoriety to attract the attentions of the Saxon kings Cynegils and Cwichelm. What drew Cynegils and Cwichelm into contact with Penda isn't clear, but it could be that

Penda was raiding into Gewissan lands, forcing the southern kings into action. At the same time, Cynegils and Cwichelm believed that the Hwicce and Penda could be attacked and subdued easily, providing treasure and new lands to the Gewisse. The ill-thought-out operation to assassinate Edwin in AD 626 had placed them firmly under the control of Deira and Bernicia, certainly limiting their influence across southern Britain. With the Hwicce seemingly growing in stature, but lacking any clear patronage from a more powerful king, they may have been one of the few opportunities for the Gewissans to attack and hopefully begin regaining their own fortune.

Cwichelm and Cynegils seem to have shared the throne of the Gewisse, it is uncertain what that power sharing looked like. They may have acted together as co-rulers, or separated that land geographically, ruling each part independently. The connection between Cwichelm and Cynegils is still debated; Cwichelm may have been the son of Cynegils, or what seems more likely is that Cwichelm was Cynegil's younger brother. It was the younger brother's ill-conceived decision to set Eomer in motion. However, it was the older brother who shared in the punishment with Cynegils bowing to the authority of Edwin in order to protect his brother at the expense of his kingdom's subservience to King Edwin. Cynegils was now linked directly to Edwin, with Cwichelm's status gravely diminished. Although none of the historic sources name Cynegils as a conspirator and instead only mention Cwichelm as the instigator, if they were co-rulers, one would expect Edwin to treat them with equal contempt and condemnation. Until the point when they fell under the authority of Edwin, both Gewisse kings had been relatively successful overseeing the Gewissan expansion to the west and north along the Severn estuary where their kingdom abutted the Iclingas lands, that is until AD 626.

Throughout the early part of the seventh century, Gewisse had seen consistent success against the Britons of Dumonia, pushing them farther to the west. The *Anglo-Saxon Chronicles* entry for AD 614 says, 'in this year Cynegils and Cwichelm fought at Beandun, and slew two thousand and forty-six of the Welsh'.[1] If the losses for Dumonia are accurate, then the battle would be a serious set-back to any future Brittonic revival in the south-west. Replacing the lost arms alone would bankrupt most kings, let alone trying to replace the men that were killed. The 2,046 warriors would represent an entire generation of men for the Britons. The most convincing location of Beandun is Brean Down in Somerset.[2] Brean Down is a rocky promontory extending into the Bristol Channel between Burnham-on-Sea and Weston-Super-Mare. The peninsula that forms Brean Down is 1.8 kilometres long and 400 metres wide. From the isthmus Brean Down climbs to its peak, 100 metres over the Bristol Channel, providing long-distance views and a natural point of defence. The position is so advantageous that it has been in use since the late Bronze Age to protect people and project power. Over the ages, Brean Down was the site of an Iron Age hill fort, and a Romano-Celtic temple, a Victorian era fort, and a secret weapons facility in the Second World War.

Brean Down is only open to advancing troops from a narrow 200-metre wide isthmus to the east but even this is a difficult approach as the down rapidly gains height, forcing any attacking force to fight up a steep incline. All other cardinal directions are protected by both the sea and high cliffs, making the eastern approach the only option for an attacking army. The highest point of Brean Down is about three-quarters of the way down the peninsula, which would be the last defendable point of the redoubt. From its peak, Brean Down slopes towards the sea before terminating with cliffs in all directions.

In AD 614 the conflict between the Dumonians and the Gewisse may have culminated in the fight at Brean Down, but been proceeded by a number of battles in which the Britons were forced into successive retreats across the land under the weight of the Gewissan advance. Brean Down was a last bastion to turn the tide of the conflict against the Gewisse. The challenge with Brean Down is that it represents an all-or-nothing position. Once combat begins there is no line of retreat for the defenders and no option to reconstitute an army on another day. Defenders of Brean Down can tactically fall back along the length of the peninsula, but that is a finite luxury which end in cliffs and the sea.

The Britons, like all of Europe's northern peoples, could and did fight in shield-walls, using similar tactics to the Saxons, but they also used alternative tactics and strategies when applicable. Henry of Huntingdon gives us several references to the Britons' tactics for battles throughout the sixth and seventh century which utilize ambushes, nocturnal raids, reliance on ranged weapons, and multi-unit tactics. Henry of Huntingdon's entry for the year AD 508 speaks to the tactical acumen of the Britons in pitched battles:

> Their forces were arrayed in two wings of which Cerdic commanded the right and Kenric his son the left. Nazaleod (Briton) observing the right wing was the strongest charged it with his whole force for the purpose of routing at once the most formidable part of the enemies' army.[3]

Furthermore, Huntingdon's entry for AD 556 provides even greater reference to the Britons during large battles:

> Their battle array was formed by 9 battalions, a convenient number for military tactics, three being posted in the van, three in the centre and three in the rear, with chosen commanders to each, while the archers and slingers and cavalry were disposed after the roman order.[4]

The complexity here is clear to see, and the reference to Roman tactics is particularly interesting, if it is accurate. Both the Britons and the Saxons were exposed to Roman tactics as enemies, but also as members of the Roman military, in particular through the Foederati system. Although the memory of imperial control and contact was distant, the military lessons could easily have been absorbed by the Britons and Saxons to form a core part of their own military cultures. If the Roman tactics had survived to AD 556, then the knowledge and use of them may well have survived to the seventh century. The Roman legions used the shield-wall, but also had complex forms of it including the maniple system. This system was particularly effective in hilly or uneven battlegrounds, or when lighter skirmisher units needed to withdraw in front of the enemy. In an area like Brean Down, the maniple system would be effective over the undulating peninsula.

At Brean Down in AD 614 the Britons had an advantage in the selection of the battlefield; in general terms Brean Down provided a defendable position. Once Brean Down was selected, the particular location of the battle was to be decided by the Britons. They could defend the isthmus and arrange their force to protect their flanks by the natural limitations of the peninsula. This formation would provide the opportunity for tactical retreat or multiple defensive positions. Alternatively they could have arranged a defensive position at the peak of Brean Down, foregoing the defence of the isthmus all together. This second strategy denied the Britons the opportunity to retreat anywhere, but it would force the Saxons to advance a long way uphill against ranged weapons. If the casualty figures are accurate, then both the Briton and Saxon armies were significant in size. The Laws of King Ine written between AD 688 and AD 695 provide us with a near-contemporary view on army sizes with the following definitions 'By "thieves" we mean men up to the number seven; by "a band" from seven to thirty-five ; by "an army" above thirty-five'.[5] Over thirty-five men was an army, and the reported Brittonic casualties at Brean Down was 2,046 which was a huge show of force by both the Britons and the Saxon Gewisse.

An attacking force had to be much larger to confront an army with the advantage afforded by the lay of the land on Brean Down, perhaps 2,500 strong. The numbers of warriors at this battle was so significant that the outcome of the conflict would echo for generations. Arraigned in fighting order at Brean Down, there was no place to retreat for the Britons, and once their lines started to fail the battle turned into an outright slaughter, completely eradicating any resistance to Gewissan advancement in the near future. There was no quarter to be asked for nor given, and the Brittonic warriors were left with limited options, either stand and fall or be pushed off the cliffs into the sea. The destruction of such a large Brittonic force also left the Dumonian and Hwiccan lands more open for raiding and conquering by other nations, including sea raiders from the Welsh kingdoms. Penda would have been nine years old when the Battle of Brean Down occurred, and he most certainly would have been exposed to the tale of this fight, the potential frailty of the Britons to the south, and the value of the area as a target for raiding.

The year Brean Down was successfully attacked and the Dumonian army destroyed may have been the pinnacle for Cynegils and Cwichelm on the battlefield. They had established stability in Gewisse, and stretched their kingdom from the upper Thames river valley just south of Oxford all the way to the Bristol Channel. By AD 628 their Wyrd and poor choices left the Gewissan brothers not only subservient to King Edwin, but also facing a new threat emerging from the Hwicce lands along their north-west border lead by Penda. The Gewissan weakness following the assassination attempt was attracting the wolves.

Penda had achieved a level of regional dominance in the Hwicce lands, and with a larger warband, and more thegns to support, he was forced to look for bigger raiding targets, and perhaps a need for more land to provide to his thegns and warriors. The cycle of success on the battlefield drawing in new men would inevitably lead to larger targets, and a requirement of more land to settle these warriors on. Through the winter of AD 627, Penda had been planning for the campaigning season, gathering information from travellers and merchants, and eventually setting his sights southward on the old Roman city of Cirencester. At the local prearranged mæthel in the mid-winter, or perhaps in the spring at a celebration for Eostre, Penda would tell his thegns to raise their warbands and have them gather at an appropriate location before heading south.

The mustering of his forces may have also simply been prearranged, without the need of discussion at a mæthel, if there had been a regular mustering on a particular date every year. Mustering sites seem to have been preordained and well-known in this period, and may have been the original reason for the location of mæthel sites.[6] As the campaign season for war and raiding was fairly well-defined, it would seem appropriate that on a forecast date the warriors would come together and head out on to their duties. The sites chosen to muster an expeditionary force 'were located on significant long distance routes, accessible… and appropriate for the massed forward movement of the armies to engage the enemy'.[7] Although the mustering site for Penda's warband can't readily be pointed to, it may have been in Pebworth. It is interesting to note that Pebworth, a location named for Penda's father, is on a Roman road heading north to south with direct access to Cirencester. Pebworth's position would make it an ideal location to muster a force and move south along the Roman road.

There is no record of the size of Penda's army, only that 'a powerful army was assembled'.[8] No document exists that lays out Penda's reasoning for attacking

Cirencester, but it seems likely that he felt it was under-protected, and had some manner of wealth making it a worthy target. Cirencester was a quick strike for Penda and was easily accessed on the Roman roads. It could also be that Penda had already conducted raids in this area and knew what to expect. Assuming Penda had previously attacked around Cirencester, it would explain why Cwichelm and Cynegils were prepared to meet him there. Having faced previous raids from the Hwicce in the vicinity of Cirencester, the kings of Gewisse may have expected a similar experience as winter gave way to the spring in AD 628.

Cwichelm and Cynegils may have occupied different halls, providing administration and control over a divided country, or they may have lead from the same location. For the Saxons and Angles, the idea of two brothers sharing control was not unknown and can be seen in two of their origin stories. Saxo Grammaticus was a historian and theologian who wrote the first history of Denmark in the early years of the thirteenth century. In his first of nine books Grammaticus tells us a story of a King Humble. Humble had two sons, one named Angul and one named Dan. When Humble died, Angul and Dan, 'by the wish and favour of their country they gained the lordship of the realm and, owing to their bravery, got the supreme power by the consenting voices of their countrymen'.[9] The story of the sons of Humble is important as Grammaticus goes on to state,

> Angul, so runs the tradition of beginnings of the Anglian race, caused his name to be applied to the district he ruled. This was an easy kind of memorial wherewith to immortalize his fame'; and 'From Dan, however, so saith antiquity, the pedigrees of our kings [Denmark] have flowed in glorious series.[10]

The *Anglo-Saxon Chronicles*, Henry of Huntingdon, and Bede all record another story of brothers as equal leaders with the arrival of the first Saxon and Angle raids in AD 449, which we are told were led by the brothers Hengist and Horsa. Both of these stories, centred round brothers, are questioned by modern historians, but they should not be ignored as they appear to show a cultural acceptance and precedence for brothers co-ruling, which is important in the case of Cwichelm and Cynegils, and perhaps with Eowa and Penda.

Cwichelm and Cynegils had a large kingdom to administer, and like all kings of the era relied on a number of royal halls throughout their kingdom to provide effective control. Without an effective administration or government apparatus, control of the kingdom relied firmly on the continually movement of the king's court between these royal estates. In the 1940s, a series of aerial photographs showed crop markings which suggested a number of Saxon halls mingled in with older Iron Age features, possibly tumuli, in a small village on the River Thames a few miles south of Abingdon called Sutton Courtenay. The site was excavated in 2009 and was dated to the mid-sixth century. The main hall at Sutton Courtenay, 'measured 30.9m x 10.8 m, making it the largest Anglo-Saxon timber building found to date in Britain'.[11] The great hall was constructed using massive posts to form the walls and support the roof. External to these were another set of raked posts placed to counter the weight of the roof. Sutton Courtenay stands out amongst known royal sites across Britain due to its size, which was even larger than those built by the most powerful king at the time, King Edwin at Yeavering. The halls at Sutton Courtenay and Yeavering seem almost connected in their size and design:

> The close similarities of the great halls at Yeavering, Sutton Courtenay and Lyminge, may thus reflect a shared 'court culture' and a desire on the part of the leaders of the Gewisse to emulate successful innovations originating in other kingdoms.[12]

This connection of architecture and court culture between an Angle kingdom far to the north and a Saxon kingdom in the south can be attributed to the subjugation of Gewisse to King Edwin. Although this link is mere conjecture it is still an interesting linkage worth considering. The construction and design of the sites is so similar that it could be the same master craftsman who built them.

Assuming Penda's attack on Cirencester occurred early in the campaigning season, Cwichelm and Cynegils may have still been at Sutton Courtenay, preparing to travel around their territory through the spring summer and fall. The large size of the site would have allowed them to maintain a warband close at hand and able to react quickly to incursions and raids. Any delay in response was caused only by the distance to which notifications had to travel. Cirencester is equidistant from both Sutton Courtenay, and Pebworth, but would have been an easier travel for Penda's warband as they had direct access to the Roman roads, whereas the Gewisse kings would need to make use of ancient pathways to move their force.

The Gewisse warband would have needed to either move south to the ridgeway, then west before approaching Cirencester from the south-west, or to have moved west utilizing ancient footpaths. The ridgeway is an ancient pathway which follows the chalk downs in an east-west orientation, linking ancient Iron Age forts and religious sites along its 147 kilometre length. The ridgeway provided the backbone to the Gewisse lands and must have been a regular route for the kings and their warbands. If Cwichelm and Cynegils were expecting an attack at or near Cirencester they would have only been a few steps behind Penda with mobilization of their warbands. Alongside the deployment of the king's warband, one can assume that the Cirencester locals would have started mobilizing local defensive forces. These secondary forces 'drew upon a wider population beyond the warrior elite',[13] but could augment a hastily drawn together warband for defensive purposes. As Cwichelm and Cynegils travelled eastward with a warband, the local community at Cirencester called up local men armed with spears and few shields to prepare the cities defences. Penda's force would have been moving in a more methodical nature along the Roman road, in an effort to conserve energy for the fight ahead. This gave Cwichelm and Cynegils the breathing space to arrive at Cirencester after a hard ride and begin organizing and augmenting the local defenders.

Cirencester itself had been a Roman city, with extensive fortifications including defensive earthworks, stone walls, gates, and the River Churn on its east side. All of these components would have allowed the Gewisse to shelter and force Penda into a prolonged siege, but this wasn't the approach taken by Cwichelm and Cynegils. Penda and his force arrived to the north-east of Cirencester and would have set up a camp along the higher ground. About eight kilometres north-east of Cirencester is Foss Cross, the final high point along the road to Cirencester. This location would be defendable and provide a good place for an army on the move to rest. The proximity to Cirencester of Penda's camp would have been known by Cwichelm and Cynegils, and allowed them to make an assessment of Penda's strength leading up to the battle. At this point Penda as the aggressor still had the initiative, and would be able to choose when to attack Cirencester, but some of the tactical advantage would be swinging towards Cwichelm and Cynegils if they were able to maintain effective reconnaissance of the Hwicce force and properly assess its strength.

By morning, the Gewisse believed they were equal or greater in strength than Penda's force and opted to take to the field rather than wait for a siege to start. The exact location of the battle is unknown, but it would seem reasonable to believe it occurred to the north-east along the road, but still in sight of Cirencester's Roman walls. Cwichelm and Cynegils could have drawn their force up around the Tarbarrow tumulus, which is only about 500 metres from the safety of the Roman walls. This position would allow them some extra height to see the advancing Hwicce, afford them a safe line of retreat, protect Cirencester, and eliminate the advantage of fighting downhill for Penda. It is likely that Cwichelm and Cynegils had superior numbers on the battlefield with local defenders and their warbands, and now had some advantage of selecting the field.

Penda's advantage was tied to the fact that his army was made up of first-class warriors, as opposed to the Gewissans which was an augmented force of warriors and local defenders. Once the Hwicce warbands arrived on the battlefield they formed into a shield-wall in opposition to that of the Gewisse. Each man overlapped his shield with that of the man next to him. Swords were drawn and spears were levelled over the top edge of the shields. With enough men at hand a second rank was stacked behind the front line to provide immediate relief should a warrior fall, and to add weight to the entire line. Members of the second rank with spears could lunge over top of the first rank and inflict wounds on the enemy while they waited for their turn in front rank. Once Penda had decided on a line of advance, he took a position in the centre of his shield-wall, he would lead from the front, and buoy any wavering members of his warband with his presence. The circumstances of the attack forced Penda to push his shield-wall forward to a point just outside the maximum range of ranged weapons. Both sides were now in a phase of stalemate trying to fully assess the other side and gain whatever tactical advantage was available. Penda would be looking for the weak points in the line, judiciously studying each man in front of him. At the same time he would be trying to raise the confidence of his force, and decrease the willingness of his Gewissan opponents to stand and fight.

With the shield-walls positioned across from one another, the men on both sides sized up their opponents, seeking whatever advantage they could find, and holding back the rising tide of fear that was brought on by the anticipation of the slaughter which would occur when the two shield-walls met in earnest. Young warriors seeking to build a reputation would emerge from the shield-walls, call out their opponents and launch spears across the dead ground into the shield-wall on the other side. This duel continued back and forth, but still the shield-walls held their ground. It's possible that individual warriors accepted offers for single combat and met in the space between the walls. The two armies were firmly in a stalemate. As time marched on and left arms tired under the weight of the shields, the front rank was relieved by the second rank for a time at the front, until they also needed a rest.

The initiative to advance to contact was with Penda, but he couldn't find a weak point and was unwilling to commit his force to an outcome he couldn't predict. Cwichelm and Cynegils on the other hand didn't have to advance; they needed to hold the ground they stood on, and protect their route of retreat. Henry of Huntingdon says that both sides of the conflict 'vowed not to turn their back on their enemies, each firmly maintained its ground until they were happily separated by the setting of the sun'.[14] The armies withdrew from the field, the Gewisse retired to the city walls, and Penda led his men into the shelter of the nearby woods. Penda had set out on this raid in the hope of a quick strike and then return home; he wasn't expecting a siege to develop, and he was ill-prepared for it. The warbands were carrying limited supplies and could not sit at the gates of Cirencester and starve the city out. Aside from constructing ladders and scaling the walls, there seemed no way to get into the city either. The night was passed for most of the Hwicce men around campfires eating the limited supplies they brought, washed down with a few casks of ale.

As the sun rose on day two of the battle, Penda and the Gewissan kings 'were sensible that, if they renewed the conflict, the destruction of both armies must ensue, they listened to moderate counsels and concluded a treaty of peace'.[15] The *Anglo-Saxon Chronicles* also mention that this battle concluded with a treaty, lending support to the narrative Henry of Huntingdon provides. The upsetting part is that neither source explains what the treaty was. For the Angles, Saxons and Britons of the era, treaties were sealed with oaths which subjugated one party to another; the exchange of hostages; baptism and godfatherhood; or the interlacing of kinship groups through marriage. The stalemate on the battlefield would, at initial blush, seem to be a victory for the Gewisse, they had prevented the aggressive Hwicce from gaining anything. However, under deeper scrutiny it seems Penda achieved a victory. The Gewisse, their kingdom, and their kings had been held in place by a clever warlord, but he was not yet a king. This was clearly a blow to the prestige of Cwichelm and Cynegils, they had been bested by a man who wasn't a king and shouldn't have been equal to them. Unlike the Gewissan kings, Penda didn't have a kingdom to draw his power and authority from. While the kings of the Gewisse had been able to protect Cirencester and their warriors, it had come at a cost to their reputation, even before negotiations got under way.

Cirencester was Penda's first major confrontation and he showed the markers of effective leadership and all the characteristics of a successful tactician. In this period of time, 'warfare was characterized by the avoidance of battle wherever possible; concentration on small-scale clashes; the value of supplies and ravaging; recognition of the worth of surprise and cunning; an appreciation of prudent generalship.'[16]

The Battle of Cirencester highlights Penda's practical skills as a leader and a commander of men. Seeing his enemy give up the security of the city walls to meet him on a battlefield could have spurned him to rash action, similar to Æthelfrith's irrational charge at Bawtry in AD 616. Had Penda charged headlong into Cwichelm and Cynegils' lines, the story of Penda may well have ended before it started. In the setting of this battle, the Gewisse had selected a good position to defend from and had allowed themselves room to retreat to the safety of the city walls. Had they given ground in the open, they would still stand a high chance of seeing out a siege. Penda had made the correct decision not to throw away his force against a battle with questionable outcomes.

Penda appears to have the dominant position in the ensuing negotiations. He was able to lay claim to any lands north of Cirencester and along the Severn estuary, opening the door for the Hwicce to be centralized under Penda, and protected from future incursions of the Gewisse. Cwichelm and Cynegils must have achieved security along their northern border as part of the treaty otherwise it's hard to see why they would accept the loss of future territorial expansion to the north. Neither party would have been willing to submit to the other through oaths, leaving marriage as the only viable option for completing the treaty. The historical records tell us that Penda agreed to marry his sister to Cynegils' son Cenwalh. This marriage tells us something of the bargaining positions of both parties; Cynegils was providing a future claimant to his throne, but Penda wasn't providing access to any throne. Penda was getting the better result by building a future claim to the Gewisse throne for his future nephews. The marriage also effectively recognized Penda as an equal to the kings of the Gewisse, and it is here that he may finally have been recognized as a king for the first time.

But did the result of the stalemate on the battlefield warrant such a lopsided treaty, and could there be more to this story? We know at some point that Penda married Cynewise, but we don't know much about her. It's possible that this marriage was a product of the treaty negotiations. Based on naming alliteration connections, it is feasible that Cynewise is of Gewissan stock, and could be as close as the daughter of Cynegils. Cynewise's betrothal to Penda would have balanced the outcome of the negotiations for Cwichelm and Cynegils, providing them a direct attachment to Penda's hall. This arrangement provided the kings of Gewisse with some level of benefit; one can imagine Cynegils bristling at the thought of bringing his enemy's sister into the house of his son, and retaliating by upping the demand to have his daughter in the house of Penda. While Penda still comes out of this agreement in the better shape, Cynegils will have felt he had established a deeper hook into the great hall of Penda.

It is unlikely that Penda's sister nor Cynewise were at Cirencester, so agreement on dates to complete the marriages formed part of the negotiations. The treaty conclusion benefited Penda with increased prestige, and a kingdom to rule, but it neglected to provide booty to his thegns and warband. To keep his men placated, Penda could have used the opportunity to settle them in halls across the Hwicce lands, from Pebworth south along the Severn valley and as far east as Wychwood in Oxfordshire. Penda was now a lord capable of giving land to trusted warriors and thegns. These men wanted the land, and Penda needed them on it in order to control the territory. Penda already had peace with the Britons to the west, his brother Eowa to the north and now the conclusion of the

Gewissan treaty also gave Penda security to the south, making him vulnerable only from the east and along the Severn watercourse. In effect, he had secured his homeland from the deprivations of raids and conflict, and could focus his warbands on being expeditionary in nature. The security Penda established provided him with an opportunity to dedicate more time to internal matters and deepening his control of his own territory.

The campaigning season generally closed in late October, and the conclusion of the treaty and marriages logically occurred before this, perhaps in the midsummer, overlapping other traditional festivities and allowing both sides to settle into new routines. For Penda's sister and Cynewise, this must have been an uncomfortable and difficult period of time, leaving their families and joining a new kinship group. Cynewise and Penda's sister were the weavers of peace between the Gewisse and the Hwicce, they became part of their new kindreds, but maintained a connection to their ancestral kin and homes. It was these links that helped maintain the peace between nations. Such arrangements also increased royal households' skill-sets and knowledge of the world around them.

Unfortunately we know very little about these women, but we can infer certain aspects of their lives based on those of future women, as very little would change throughout the Middle Ages. Cynewise and Penda's sister would become the centre of their new families, raising children, managing the household, hosting visitors, maintaining domestic life, and potentially maintaining government and control while their husbands were away. For the Angles and Saxons in the pre-Christian period, the veneration of motherhood was a critical feature as is seen in the celebration of goddesses before the migration, and certainly after it with the continued worship of Eostre. Bede tells us that in mid-winter,

> They began the year on the 8th kalends of January [25 December], when we celebrate the birth of the Lord. That very night, which we hold so sacred, they used to call by the heathen word Modranecht, that is, 'mother's night', because of the ceremonies they enacted all that night.[17]

The veneration of female attributes and deities doesn't eliminate the fact that this was a male-dominated society, but nor should we think that Cynewise and Penda's sister didn't play a crucial role in the events of their age, nor were they ignored within the dominate culture. Over her life span, Cynewise would become the measure for all queens of the age, and be the firm roots for the future Mercian supremacy, which would go on to dominate the power structure in Britain until the rise of Wessex in the ninth century. Her children would affect the future and leave a lasting impression on the secular and religious worlds, become kings of Mercia and canonized saints. In the future, the steadfastness, trustworthiness and abilities of Cynewise provided Penda with the backstop he needed in order to venture throughout Britain during the campaigning season while she maintained the duties of leadership at home. Kingdoms were forged by battlefield success, but quenched through marriage. The skill of the king and the need for ancestral connection made both avenues critical to supremacy and claims of kingship. Success was not just on the battlefield, but at home through the support of powerful families and relationships.

The year AD 628 was the public beginning of Penda. Until this point he was leading localized raids as a leader of a warband. The stalemate at Cirencester was an overwhelming success for Penda, though at the time it may not have seemed that way. In strategic terms he had engineered de-facto acknowledgement of his leadership as a king, and his homelands as some form of kingdom. The outcome of the battle does seem to support the idea that this was a raid, a military venture seeking mobile wealth with a planned withdrawal. Had the AD 628 southern campaign been driven by territorial acquisition, it seems likely that Penda would have been forced to commit to a combat action in order to generate a convincing victory and thus lay claim to the city of Cirencester. The action against Cwichelm and Cynegils by Penda at Cirencester ended the northern expansion by the Saxons until Alfred the Great took the Wessex throne in the ninth century. While the nation of Mercia was still distant, the formation of strong southern and western borders set in motion the growth of the Mercian nation which would be a dominant force throughout Britain until the ninth century.

The Iclingas now counted two kings with two kingdoms as their own: Eowa to the north and Penda to the south. While Eowa was subservient to the King of Deira and Bernicia, Penda had gained a substantial autonomy and control in the lands of the Hwicce without subjugation to more powerful kings. He was firmly operating on his own accord. The Hwicce were growing in stature, and with the defeat of the Gewisse, now had territorial integrity in all directions save for the east. Penda's ability to secure the territory and protect the people from future incursions tied the people directly to him, and furthered his authority. Although the authority Penda now had was not vested in the people in a directly democratic approach common in the modern world, he was reliant on the support of people to maintain his power. Penda needed to be successful in order to attract thegns and warriors into his service. His role was to bring success to these men, who in turn would stay and protect the land and the people who worked the land. If he was unsuccessful, he would be put aside through one method or another. The people relied on Penda for protection, and in turn Penda relied on the people for power and authority.

Chapter Six
Cadwallon

Cirencester had been a triumph for Penda and the Hwicce. They could now count themselves as equals with Eowa's Iclingas kingdom to the north and the Gewisse to the south. Following the success at Cirencester in AD 628, the records go quiet on Penda until AD 630. After wintering in his hall with his new wife, it's more than likely that Penda and Cynewise were expecting their first child. The exact order of children is difficult to establish, but it was either his son Peada, or one of Penda's daughters, Cyneburh or Cyneswith. Peada would go on to be a King of Mercia, and both Cyneburh and Cyneswith would be canonized as saints. All of Penda's children would convert to Christianity in his lifetime, but he seems to have harboured no ill-will, nor forced them in any particular direction. Their decisions on religion were left entirely to them to determine the path forward. As home life changed for Penda, he still had the responsibility to maintain his warband through the acquisition of wealth, and this meant raiding. His actions at Cirencester opened up the opportunity to raid Dumonia to the south-west, the future locations of Somerset, Devon, and Cornwall. Dumonia remained an independent Brittonic kingdom at this point, but was now under increased pressure from the Gewisse and the Hwicce. Each foray south brought new information, which could support the next raid, and future campaigns.

Things in the south had achieved some stability and routine by AD 629, but this was not the case across Britain. Actions in the north began to send ripples across the island and led to significant changes elsewhere, including Penda's future. The weavers of Wyrd were at work, linking individuals, events, and decisions with one another across the great tapestry of time and space. Although the distant events would seem inconsequential to Penda at the time, they would grow in importance to him and to the future of Britain. The *Annales Cambriae* are a series of chronicles written in Latin and compiled in Dyfed, Wales around the tenth century, and record that in AD 629 there was a 'besieging of King Cadwallon in the island of Glannauc'.[1] This event isn't recorded in the *Anglo-Saxon Chronicles*, though the repercussions of it were caught by Bede. The dearth of resources recording this event would suggest that this moment was seen as non-consequential, but in reality this was a critical moment in the future of Penda and the greater power dynamic across Britain.

In the ensuing years following the assassination attempt by Eomer in AD 626 at Malton, King Edwin had converted to Christianity along with his court and many people within his nation. His conversion occurred on Easter of AD 627 in York, where he set about building a church, and followed shortly by the construction of a second one at a royal township called Campodonum, not to be confused with the Campodunum of Boudicca's era. Bede tells us that following his conversion, King Edwin was 'zealous for the true worship'.[2] King Edwin's conversion was important as it changed some aspects of conflict in Britain. Where the traditional purpose of conflict was territorial and wealth driven, a new layer of evangelist religious conflict surfaced. The power and influence of King Edwin led other kings and kingdoms to follow him into conversion. The general historic view of this period has been framed with overtly Christian sentiment, where the superiority of Christianity as the one true faith was preordained to succeed. Through this lens, kings such as Edwin look like they are advancing the common good, but this is far from the truth. The traditional religions of the Angles and Saxons were devolved and lacked control and authority, they were a folk religious system owned by individuals. Christianity, on the other hand, held some practical elements that support the growth of kingly authority including the centralization of power, the establishment of hierarchal power, and the ability to record through written word. Edwin's conversion was about authority and control, something he was ready to expand by AD 629, by renewing conflict with the Britons, in particular with the Kingdom of Gwynedd.

Gwynedd was the northern Brittonic kingdom of the future nation of Wales. Bede tells us that 'Edwin reigned most gloriously seventeen years over the nations of the English and the Britons, six whereof, as has been said, he also was a soldier in the kingdom of Christ. Cadwallon, king of the Britons, rebelled against him.'[3]

In order for Cadwallon to rebel against Edwin, he must have already been subservient to him. In AD 607, Edwin's predecessor and persecutor, King Æthelfrith had lead a campaign into Gwynedd inflicting a crushing defeat on the Britons,

> Æthelfrith, the formidable king of the English, of whom we have spoken, having assembled a vast army, made an immense slaughter of the perfidious nation at the city of the legions which is called by the English people Lege-cester but by the Britons, more correctly, Kaer-legion.[4]

The Battle of Chester, as it would become known, stands out amongst the endemic warfare of the age based on the reported size of the engagement which is comparable to what was reported at Brean Down. The *Anglo-Saxon Chronicles* provide further detail on the Battle of Chester,

> Æthelfrith led his army to Chester; where he slew an innumerable host of the Welsh; and so was fulfilled the prophecy of Augustine, wherein he saith 'If the Welsh will not have peace with us, they shall perish at the hands of the Saxons.' There were also slain two hundred priests, who came thither to pray for the army of the Welsh.[5]

The defeat at Chester was catastrophic to the Brittonic kingdoms of Gwynedd and Powys, and ensured they would not be capable of threatening Angle dominance for nearly twenty years. By AD 629, Gwynedd had regained sufficient power that Cadwallon led his rebellion against Edwin. This could have started as raids on settlements under the protection of Edwin, but it quickly turned into an aggressive counter-insurgency campaign by Edwin.

In AD 629, Edwin must have marched an army through the territory of Eowa to reach Gwynedd, and in all likelihood Eowa and his warriors would have been drawn into the western invasion. This army would have used the Roman road system through Chester, then west, shadowing the coastline to the Menai Strait. We have no record of significant battles in the AD 629 invasion, though it is likely that there were skirmishes and ambushes occurring. In fairly rapid order, Cadwallon withdrew to Anglesey, a location that could be more easily defended by forcing his pursuer to conduct an amphibious attack. This didn't deter Edwin, who continued his pursuit onto Anglesey, with Cadwallon eventually achieving a defensive position at Glennauc, or Puffin Island. Glennauc is a small rocky island on the north-west shore of Anglesey, separated by 800 metres of ocean. Glennauc is only 1 kilometre in length and 300 metres at its widest point. Its size alone meant that it was not going to provide Cadwallon and whatever force remained with him a real chance of survival. As a final act in his rebellion, Cadwallon and his force fled to Ireland, denying Edwin the opportunity to destroy his enemy.

Although we lack details, and even a timeline for the events, Bede tells us that Edwin 'subjected to the English the Mevanian islands'.[6] The Mevanian Islands are Angelsey and the Isle of Man. One theory states that Edwin was relying on a fleet of vessels and mariners from Rheged, which owed him some render.[7] In this theory Edwin, along with Deiran, Bernician and Rheged warriors, invades the Isle of Man and then launches an amphibious invasion of Anglesey, avoiding the necessity of marching through Mercian and Gwynedd territory. But the question that surfaces is: if an amphibious assault wasn't a barrier, then why would Cadwallon flee to Glennauc, and why wouldn't Edwin follow him there and destroy him at that location? The only reason would be a lack of vessels at hand, suggesting that the initial expedition against Cadwallon was based on a land invasion and not by sea.

The twelfth-century monk Geoffrey of Monmouth picks up the story of Cadwallon from this point. Geoffrey is a controversial source, and the veracity of his *Historia Regum Brittaniae* has been a regular topic of debate since it was completed sometime around AD 1136. The *Historia* is most renowned for popularizing the Arthurian legends, but amongst modern historians has largely been viewed with scepticism, verging on outright disregard. Geoffrey's sources have never been fully determined, though he tells us in his own words that he drew the information from an ancient book 'written in the British Tongue'.[8] Between 2014 and 2017, Bournemouth University conducted in-depth research into Geoffrey of Monmouth's writings and found 'sufficient evidence to suggest this was no work of make-believe'.[9] This study went even further to establish that Geoffrey of Monmouth's work was, 'likely compiled from a variety of sources most likely originating from the south of England'.[10] While some of the details found within the *Historia* must be discarded, particularly those most distant in time, the general narrative cannot easily be disregarded, particularly in a time period of few other references.

Geoffrey of Monmouth opens the story of the exile of Cadwallon by telling us that he fled first to Ireland. This was a common enough event in this period, as the future King Oswald was also forced into exile in Ireland.[11] Edwin was now free to subjugate Gwynedd, and strip it of wealth,

> burning the cities before him, grievously afflicted the citizens and country people. During this exercise of his cruelty, Cadwallon never ceased endeavouring to return back to his country in a fleet without success; because to whatever port he steered, Edwin met him with his forces and hindered his landing.[12]

It would seem that Cadwallon's journey to Ireland was to raise more warriors to retake Gwynedd, but his failed return would suggest that he wasn't able to raise enough men. From this point Cadwallon heads to Armorica, modern-day Brittany in France. Armorica had been settled by refugees from the Roman provinces of Britain, and the connections between the Britons on either side of the Channel most surely endured throughout this period of time.

Geoffrey of Monmouth takes a bit of artistic license at this point in the story, telling us that in Armorica, Cadwallon learns that King Edwin has a Spanish advisor named Pellitus who is skilled in telling the future, and it was he who was able to foresee each of Cadwallon's attempted landings at Gwynedd after he had fled to Ireland. It could be that the characterization of Pellitus was based on the priest Paulinus. Paulinus was from Rome, and had come to Britain as part of the Augustine mission to convert the Angles and the Saxons. Paulinus ended up in the court of Edwin, and eventually converted and served King Edwin. Cadwallon hatches a plan to send his cousin Brien north to Deira to assassinate Pellitus, thus preventing Edwin from utilizing any further knowledge or support from his advisor. Brien hastily returns to Britain and heads to the north, in much the same vein as Eomer had years earlier on his assassination operation. Brien is seeking to find Edwin's court in Deiran lands and heads to York. This tells us that Edwin did not winter in Gwynedd following the events at Angelsey, but instead returned to his kingdom before the winter set in and the campaigning season ended. Brien could have sailed up the east coast of Britain and straight into York, though this would seem unlikely as it would imply he knew the exact location of Edwin and Pellitus, and leave him only one exit route.

A more likely and safer route would be to travel north through the Irish Sea coming ashore at the wild lands north of the Mersey estuary, perhaps at the Ribble and Alt estuaries. This area still had strong, and nominally independent, Brittonic communities, many of whom would support Brien's mission. These wild lands were close enough to Deira that Brien was able to gather news on the location of Edwin's court, which he learned was in York. On horseback and with the benefit of Roman roads, Brien would be in York in no more than four days. Once in York, Brien found Pellitus outside the church and slayed him amongst a crowd in the street. We know that Paulinus died in AD 644, and if he was the same person as Pellitus then clearly the assassination was not successful, in spite of what Geoffrey of Monmouth tells us. Brien then 'retired from that place and went to Exeter, where he called together the Britons, and told them what he had done. Afterwards, having dispatched away messengers to Cadwallon, he fortified that city'.[13]

Exeter provided an excellent fallback position for Brien based on its location and its attributes. The city of Exeter began its existence as a Roman legionary fortress immediately after the first-century invasion. The site was not a standalone outpost, but part of a larger Roman defensive network. This network drove regional stability through the pacification of the Britons and led to an enormous influx of people to the area, perhaps increasing the local population by 10,000.[14] Within a single generation, the Roman legionnaires were required farther to the north, and the city changed from a base of occupation, to a centre of local commerce, driving further growth and population booms. Archaeological finds at Exeter have unearthed thousands of animal bones and dozens of stockades suggesting that Exeter was a critical market hub for the sale of rural driven goods such as livestock.[15] As a key economic and trade hub, Exeter suffered heavily in the wake of the Roman Empire's contraction in the fourth century. As communities start to withdraw from the larger economy and became isolated and self-sufficient, the need for regional market networks collapsed, and with it the use of Exeter. The archaeological record saw substantial animal butchering until the fourth century, and then a void until the eleventh century, clearly showing the large scale abandonment of the site.[16]

Exeter, however, was not a simple market town. Its origins as an outpost of the Roman Empire gave it particularly useful attributes. By the third century, Exeter was entirely enclosed by a stone wall ten metres high, and three metres wide, enclosing ninety-two acres of land.[17] The city wall was serviced by a gate house allowing for access to be denied by would-be defenders. Additionally, the entire wall was circled by earthworks of varying sizes. To the west of the city, the River Exe added another defensive measure, but also a route to the sea. Exeter, like all Roman cities, was attached to the Roman network of roads allowing for rapid movement across the landscape, which support logistics, troop movements, and communications. For Brien and Cadwallon, Exeter had other benefits. Its position was nearly as distant as possible from King Edwin, with multiple kingdoms between Deira and themselves. Exeter was also in a hinterland, wedged between three warring factions, meaning its effective control by any group was questionable.

Geoffrey of Monmouth tells us 'Penda, King of Mercians, with a very great army of Saxons, came to Exeter and besieged Brien.'[18] Historians generally discount this action, primarily because there are no corroborating sources, but it would seem to fit with the action that Penda conducted at Cirencester; the critical question is, what was his motivation? If we disregard the story of Brien and the assassination, then Penda could be conducting a raid on the city in search of mobile wealth, in particular livestock. If we allow for the story of Brien, or some version of it, than perhaps Penda was out for a bounty, or to curry favour with Edwin, or even to support his brother Eowa. Whatever the motivation, Penda and his warbands are moving south against Exeter.

The area along the Severn estuary, through Cirencester and south to Exeter, was of dubious control and no doubt suffered incursions from the Hwicce, Gewisse and Dumonians at regular intervals. After Cirencester curtailed Gewissan expansion, the road to the south would have been open for Penda. Travel to Exeter was simple enough with multiple routes available to Penda, either by the Roman road which parallels the Severn estuary, or through Cirencester. Penda had to traverse 200 kilometres, which would take him about ten days. This expedition was substantially more complex than the raid on Cirencester, so some logistics support would have been required. Carts pulling food, tents, weapons, would surely have made up part of the procession, allowing an average of twenty-four kilometres per day to be covered.[19] The final approach to Exeter would come from the east. There is no high ground from this direction, providing Penda with limited field advantages in the immediate approaches to Exeter. About five kilometres to the west, where the southerly route meets the westerly Roman road to Exeter, is a small hill called 'Gypsy Hill'. This would have been the best location for Penda to encamp his army prior to moving against Exeter.

With good weather, the time to attack the city would be in the early morning using the glare of the rising sun to the disadvantage of the defenders. As Penda approached Exeter he was no doubt expecting a force to meet him outside the walls, but the opposition refused the invitation, choosing instead to stay securely behind the city's walls. Penda now had a siege to handle. As a warlord, men swore oaths to Penda to serve him, but that oath came with a price, and that price was reputation and wealth. Penda needed to deliver wealth to his men or face losing them. He had no option but to try to conduct a siege against Exeter, something he, like all Angle, Saxon, and Briton commanders, was entirely unprepared for. Penda brought his camp closer to the city wall to support the siege. The city would most likely receive relief from the west, and as he constructed his strategy he would be sending riders out in all directions to assess how to seal off the city. His camp was now in a vulnerable spot, but he must have analyzed the risk of attack from the Gewisse in the east as inconsequential, keeping his focus to the west.

Cadwallon by this point was beginning his trip to Exeter, coming from Ireland, or from Armorica. To disguise his movements and support the mobility of his army his best route was to approach from the south of Exeter, using the Exe River to bring his army directly to the city. As he entered the Exe estuary, he may have been met by a local person who was able to provide him news of the Angle army camped at the eastern gate. It would do Cadwallon no good to be trapped inside the walls, so it is reasonable to think that he disembarked his force and moved them due north to the Roman road. Once there, he was able to march them directly into the rear of Penda's encampment. Penda would have had some early warning of the approaching force by stationing a picket two kilometres to the west at a junction. The picket rider rode hard to warn Penda of the approaching force, and in the limited time afforded by the warning, Penda would be drawing together his force into a defensive shield-wall. This was no easy feat, as he still had to concern himself with the defenders of Exeter. Penda had to focus some contingent of his force on Exeter's gate and the bulk of his force on the approaching army.

Cadwallon also separated his force, 'he divided his force into four parts, and then made no delay to advance and join battle with the enemy'.[20] Cadwallon had a made a shrewd tactical movement and, with the city's walls, could now fully surround Penda. Penda was forced to draw his army in closer and form a defensive box, he was trapped. There would be no success in a break out and no hope of survival once Cadwallon committed his forces forward. But Cadwallon was hesitant to close the gap and offer combat. While he was certain he would succeed, it would cost him some portion of his army. Cadwallon was an experienced commander, and he could see that the warlord he had trapped was a hardened warrior, and while he was certain he could defeat these Angles, it would come at a cost. Cadwallon was motivated by revenge against Edwin, and would prefer to keep his army intact, to be used in the reconquest of his home and the defeat of Edwin. Cadwallon called Penda forward to speak, and offered him the opportunity to survive the day, and achieve wealth for his army if he would help defeat King Edwin. From Geoffrey of Monmouth we are told that Penda, 'finding no other way for his own safety, he surrendered himself to Cadwallon, and gave hostages, with a promise that he would assist him against the Saxons'.[21] This was a fair offer, and one which Penda was in no position to turn down. Cadwallon had the oath of Penda, but he must have still held some reservations about him, after all they were from different people, with different religions. They did, however, share two characteristics: the first was a distaste for the overlordship of Edwin, and the second was language. Penda's family and his territory was made up of Britons and Angles, making bilingualism a necessity for him.

The night after Cadwallon's attack must have been a difficult one for Penda. Wyrd can seem cruel at times, yet this turn of events would be a major catalyst for his future success. Though he would have not understood the importance of these events in the moment, he most certainly would have seen the hands of the Norns at work, weaving the great tapestry of wyrd and binding events and people together. Until he met Cadwallon, Penda had focused his attentions to the south; but from AD 630 he would turn north, like the midwinter's sun. For Cadwallon, Exeter provided him access to Penda's warriors, but also the support of the people of Exeter whom he relieved, and likely warriors from Dumonia who would have heard of his actions outside of the city walls. The events at Exeter had caused Cadwallon's army to swell in size, giving him a true opportunity for success against Edwin. Cadwallon's challenge now was to keep this diverse group together long enough to succeed against King Edwin. Achieving regular success and gaining wealth to distribute amongst the warbands would go a long way to maintaining control over this army.

Additional sources including Bede, the *Anglo-Saxon Chronicles*, and Henry of Huntingdon verify that Penda and Cadwallon were working together against Edwin; but all of these sources lack any reference to how Penda and Cadwallon came together, so we can't easily dispel the story painted by Geoffrey of Monmouth. There are intriguing similarities between life and activities of Penda and Cadwallon and the Arthurian legends that were born out by Geoffrey's writing. A study of the similarities between the fiction and reality shows that Uther Pendragon had a real-world model,

> This is Penda of Mercia, who fought against the expanding power of the English kingdom of Northumbira. Penda's main ally in his struggle was a very powerful British ruler, Cadwallon, King of Gwynedd. Indeed like the fictional Aurelius, Cadwallon was originally the senior partner in the alliance. It was only the British king's death in battle that made Penda the leader of the coalition.[22]

Beyond the general similarities shared between Uther Pendragon and Penda, there is a significant overlap in the sequence of events found in the Arthurian legends and the life of Penda which implies that the saga of Penda formed the backbone of the Arthurian legend, 'the point-by-point analogues between the careers of Cadwallon/Penda and Aurelius/Uther are too numerous to be coincidence'.[23]

The timeline for this series of events started with Edwin's suppression of Cadwallon through the campaigning season of AD 629. The activities surrounding Brien, if they occurred, would be through the winter of AD 629 or in to the early months of the following year. For Penda, his participation began in the spring with the opening of the campaign season and his march against Exeter. If Penda marched early, the entire episode may have come to a conclusion by mid-May. This left Cadwallon with a full six months to lead a resurgent fight against Edwin. With no base of power to defend and with a hastily organized army, which likely wouldn't survive intact over a fruitless campaigning season, he had to move quickly. Penda would have been counselling for rapid advancement against Edwin in order to keep his own warband together and suitably supplied with wealth and reputation. The inclusion of Penda was a boost for Cadwallon, as he would be able to march his forces through Hwicce unmolested, thus providing the most rapid advance, and maintaining the element of surprise as they pushed north through Powys and into Gwynedd.

Penda departed first, perhaps leaving a small contingent to act as guides for the larger Brittonic contingent of Cadwallon's army. Penda would first head to his own home to resupply, perhaps gather more warriors and then rendezvous with Cadwallon's force at Onnenau Meigion or Six-Ashes; all told it was a thirteen day journey from Exeter. There is a legend that a battle occurred at Six-Ashes between Penda and Cadwallon but that story 'may be a mistaken reference to a combined hosting of the Britons and the Mercians at that place in

630 A.D'.[24] The exact location of this meeting and preparation for conflict may have been on Tuck Hill at the current site of the Holy Innocents Church.[25] It is quite possible that this meeting location was an ancient grove with religious significance to both the Britons and the Angles. The location is remote and finding it would have been a challenge if it wasn't already a well-known feature by both parties. Penda arrived with fresh supplies, a few extra warriors, followed by the arrival of the larger Brittonic force under the leadership of Cadwallon. This combined army included warriors from many nations and may have been the first of its kind; warriors from Ireland, Armorica, Dumonia, Gwynedd, and Hwicce were now present. As the army encamped at Six-Ashes, word would be spreading to other Brittonic nations drawing more warriors in from Powys and perhaps Angle lands upon hearing that Penda was marching.

By mid-June AD 630 Gwynedd's reclamation force was at its strongest and ready to enter the Brittonic lands to the west. The first major step was to cross the Severn. The army could have moved north to Bridgnorth which may have had some Roman infrastructure and a bridge still in place, but this route would surely be watched by any Northumbrian army still lurking in the country. Instead, the army could have crossed at Quatford, along some ancient foot tracks, which would help conceal them as they advanced against Edwin. This crossing allowed them to shadow the Roman road moving east to west, without losing the element of surprise. The Roman road eventually swings from west to south-west before re-establishing a more westerly direction at Craven Arms. Some ten kilometres north of Craven Arms is a town called Clun, which has traditionally been linked to a Welsh poem praising Cadwallon. The poem says 'Cadwallon's assembly to the hill of Caradog's fort'.[26] Caradog's fort has never been fully identified but Clun is on the shortlist. This could have been the location of the first skirmish between Cadwallon and Edwin.

From Caradog's fort, the army left the footpaths and began using the Roman road to speed up their march. Once on the roads, the army would expect to clear twenty kilometres per day, allowing enough time to move the baggage train, set up and dismantle the camp. This was an army attempting to move fast, so there may have been limited tactical considerations in selecting the location for each night's camp, perhaps using rivers and small hills as defensive locations. The march would have taken around five days, and the use of the Roman roads was critical as it allowed Cadwallon to move rapidly without exhausting the force by travelling on rough trails. Throughout the march, Cadwallon was picking up intelligence from the locals which allowed him to slowly zero in on the Bernician and Deiran force at an Iron Age fort situated on Cefn Digoll.

Cefn Digoll, or Long Mountain, is a promontory which overlooks the Roman road linking modern-day Newtown and Shrewsbury. On top of Cefn

Digoll are the remains of an Iron Age ring fort, today called Beacon Ring. The fort is oval in shape and includes significant earthwork defences constructed in series, including a ditch and bank. This position provided commanding views of the local area and an excellent defensive position for an expeditionary army. The town of Newtown in AD 630 was a crossroads, perhaps with a small Powys hamlet but nothing more. Cadwallon's army would have pushed a few miles north-east along the road and then set up camp. This would have been a tense night knowing they were within a day's march of an enemy who had a defensive advantage using the earth works at Cefn Digoll. During the night Cadwallon and Penda may have sent light troops out to protect the camp from a surprise attack, but also to reconnoitre the enemy's position at Cefn Digoll. For the Angles, this could have included sending out specialist warriors such as the Herewulf, the Wolf Warriors. The Herewulf entered battle with no armour, clothed in the skins of a wolf. This warrior tradition is recorded by Plutarch in the Roman period and, and was still active through the later Viking period.[27] These warriors were noted for operating alone and silently, making them ideal for watching the enemy at night.

Cadwallon would supply guides to help get the warriors close enough to the Cefn Digoll, before dismounting and moving forward silently on foot. The Briton guide would need to take care of the horses, while the Herewulf began prowling the shadows, looking for weakness amongst the defenders, much as the wolf seeks to pick off the weak from a herd. Sound, along with sight, provided them details about the defenders, how many were present, and where they were from. In a dark still night, the voices of men gathered around a fire would carry deep into the darkness. The Bernician and Deiran men posted at Cefn Digoll must have known by this point that there was an army lurking in the countryside, but perhaps they were comforted by the superiority of their position, surrounded by the ancient defensive earthworks. The small reconnaissance team returned before sun-up to provide Cadwallon and Penda with as much detail as they could. The warlords now had some serious issues to address; they likely had the superior force, but assaulting an army in a defensive position like Cefn Digoll would come at a cost, and could derail further action. Cunning was needed in this case.

There are folk tales of a fight between Cadwallon and Northumbrian forces at a place called Forden which is halfway between Newtown and Cefn Digoll. This location has been theorized to be the location of King Oswald's defeat in AD 642, which we will return to later. While this argument could be accurate, it could also be that the source material has been confused over time, and that while there was a fight here involving Penda and men from north of the River Humber, the wrong battle was overlaid. This battle is along the road headed for Cefn Digoll, which could be a part of the AD 630 campaign. For example, the armies may have made initial contact at Forden, with the Northumbrians then conducting a tactical retreat to the safety of Beacon Ring, the Iron Age fort at Cefn Digoll. Alternatively, knowing the strength of the Northumbrians, perhaps Cadwallon and Penda lured them out of their defensive position into an ambush at Forden. These types of techniques are identified in the *Anglo-Saxon Chronicles* as previously mentioned. A successful ambush at Forden would deplete the defenders of warriors, and could be followed up with the full scale assault on Cefn Digoll. Either way, the army from north of the Humber found itself in a defence position behind the earthworks of Cefn Digoll. Cadwallon on the other hand found himself confronted with a difficult attack against an army who had the advantage of selecting the battlefield atop Cefn Digoll.

The assault at Cefn Digoll would likely come from the south-west through the modern-day village of Kingswood. From this route the attackers would be able to gain elevation quickly, and then have a generally level final approach to Beacon Ring over the final two kilometres. This route was likely the ancient footpath running along the spine of Cefn Digoll, providing the attackers with some ease of movement. At some point, the two forces put their shield-walls into the field and battle ensued. It is unclear if Edwin was present at Cefn Digoll, but it is clear that the battle was a resounding success for Cadwallon and Penda. While the battle didn't finish off Edwin's army, the conflict was anything but bloodless. A series of Welsh poems known as the *Welsh Triads* recorded in the thirteenth century says of the battle, 'Cadwallon when he went to the Action of Digoll, and the forces of Cymry with him; and Edwin on the other side, and the forces of Lloegr with him. And then the Severn was defiled from its source to its mouth'.[28]

If Edwin was present, the resulting retreat from Gwynedd would have been the low point of his reign, ending his successful expansion into Gwynedd and Powys. Such a defeat could embolden other subjugated peoples to rise up and confront the Deiran and Bernician hegemony.

A ninth-century Welsh poem called 'Canu Llywarch Hen Saga' includes a reference to Cefn Digoll. In the poem, Beacon Ring on Cefn Digoll is identified as Cadwallon's Camp. The poem states that Cadwallon stayed here for seven months carrying out seven skirmishes per day against Edwin's forces.[29] This poem is fairly distant from the events, but it may be capturing elements of the historical fact. After removing Edwin's main force from the location, the Cadwallon and Penda army may have been forced to rest and recuperate at the location for a period of time. By the time they had succeeded at Cefn Digoll, the army had been in combat or on the move for nearly two months; by July AD 630, all parties were in need of a break. This location can effectively use the Roman road system to move smaller components of the army through the countryside to continue conducting resistance activities against Edwin's forces. By the end of the campaign season, Edwin would need to withdraw from Gwynedd and Powys, leaving Cadwallon free to return to his home.

King Edwin's withdrawal seems to have been to the north, but not without further skirmishes. The Welsh poem in praise of Cadwallon records, 'Riddance of the affliction of Llong, place of swords'.[30] Llong is fifteen kilometres to the west of Chester, providing the line of retreat for Edwin, and also showing that this was a fighting retreat. The fight at Cefn Digoll did not result in the total destruction of Edwin's force, but was enough of a loss that the northern army was forced to withdraw from the western kingdoms.

Gwynedd and Powys were once again under their own control, and Edwin's invading army was so severely mauled that it would take several years for him to present a threat to any of the nations south of the Humber. Cadwallon and Penda were able to call more men to their respective banners based on their battlefield success. For Cadwallon, men from across the Brittonic Kingdoms were drawn to the first Briton to lead a successful campaign against the dominant Angle and Saxon nations. The Britons as a larger group had suffered twenty-seven years of failure born on the backs of the crushing defeats at Brean Down and Chester. Cadwallon was a fresh hope for Gwynedd, and it is reasonable to presume that his story was spreading through the Brittonic kingdoms where he represented a future for the Brittonic people.

It is easy to envision Penda at the centre of his shield-wall, hacking and slashing his way through Edwin's forces, as Cadwallon's mixed army forced the invader backwards. Penda was a man of his age and fitted the mould of the heroic Germanic warrior king. He was successful on the battlefield through his tactics, but more importantly through the edge of his own sword. He had proven time and again that he was capable of taking on any foe, but would not enter a battle without deep reflection. Penda was certainly a man of great reputation by the conclusion of the actions in Powys and Gwynedd, surely deserving the nickname he had earned from the Britons, Penda ap Pyd, or 'Penda Son of Danger'.

Although Edwin hadn't been eclipsed as the ultimate power broker, his rule and dominance was teetering on the edge. As fall arrived and winter closed in, and armies across Britain began returning to their homes, the power dynamic in Britain had shifted significantly to the west. In early October AD 630, Penda and his army would depart Cadwallon's company to return to their own lands. Penda had been forced to participate in this campaign, but he dedicated himself to its successful outcome, and in the process had earned Cadwallon's trust and perhaps genuine friendship. The two kings may have exchanged young men in fosterage, and arranged a meeting date early in the next spring. Unlike so many other partnerships and alliances, this one doesn't seem to include any of the usual actions to bind the nations together such as marriages or baptisms. The explanation must be that Penda had sworn an oath, and nothing more was required to keep them bound together. This would show a high degree of trust between the two men, in particular on the part of Cadwallon. There is, however, a hint of a more common arrangement written by Geoffrey of Monmouth which says of Cadwallon's son Cadwallader, 'His mother was Penda's sister, by the same father but a different mother, descended from the noble race of the Gewissians. For Cadwallon, after his reconciliation with her brother, made her the partner of his bed, and had Cadwallader by her'.[31]

An alliance sealed by marriage would be the more cultural acceptable method of ensuring the alliance between Cadwallon and Penda, and would help explain how the two men were capable of operating together for an extended period of time. The connection between Penda and the throne of Gwynedd also helps explain the long-held peace Penda enjoys with the Brittonic kingdoms.

Chapter Seven
Hatfield Chase

Bede paints the picture of both Cadwallon and Penda as ravenous warlords, focused only on the destruction of all that was right in the world. In Bede's view these men would destroy the world that the angelic kings of Northumbria were struggling to construct. His characterization of these kings and warlords is one of aggressive predators, capable of nothing but devastation. Neither Cadwallon nor Penda were gentlemen, but they also were no different from any other successful warlord of the age. The historic records tell a story of successful warriors, but ones that were not aggressive to the point of recklessness. Following the success of AD 630, the chronology seems to suggest a period of general peace across Britain, perhaps a time to replace warriors and rebuild warbands in preparation for the next wars.

The *Anglo-Saxon Chronicles*, Bede, Henry of Huntingdon, along with the Welsh and Irish Chronicles all have a gap in time from AD 630 to AD 633. The *Anglo-Saxon Chronicles* contain one single entry covering these missing years in which we are told that Oswald was baptized. There is no mention of Penda or Cadwallon following the success of AD 630, which could show that neither of them fit Bede's characterization. Instead, Penda and Cadwallon returned to the regularity of normal life, which likely included continued raids closer to home and the strengthening of their own armies. This was a calculated rest period to regenerate their forces, before another campaign. It took maturity as a strategist to hold back and not gamble on pressing on to Deira. The seat of Cadwallon's power in Anglesey is some 200 kilometres from Penda's Hwicce lands, and separated by territories of other people. In order to maintain their ongoing relationship, significant effort on both of their parts was needed.

Penda was certainly the junior partner following the events at Exeter, but the success at Cefn Digoll may have altered the relationship between Cadwallon and Penda into a more collegial partnership, and one that would survive the quieter period where they focused their attentions closer to their own homes. This quiet period is also a sign that Edwin's army had been substantially degraded by the conflict with Cadwallon and Penda; had this not been the case, a rapid invasion in AD 631 and follow on in AD 632 would have been expected. Edwin must have spent the ensuing years shoring up his own authority in Deira and Bernicia, in order to maintain his throne. Although Edwin had united the two Angle kingdoms north of the Humber, he still had Brittonic and Scoti competitors along his borders vying for power. He was also faced with internal threats, in particular following the disastrous campaign in Powys and Gwynedd. Angle and Saxon kings in this era were not sacrosanct; their positions only lasted as long as their success on the battlefield held out. Deira and Bernicia seemed particularly susceptible to the intrigues of dynastic infighting with numerous Æthelings holding legitimate claims to the thrones of either kingdom. These claimants were sheltered and supported by Angle, Saxon and Briton kings all hoping that they could gain greater influence if they backed the right candidate. For Edwin, this meant multiple candidates plotting to take one or both of his thrones.

King Edwin's authority extended south of the Humber, in particular the lands of Eowa Iclingas, the Brittonic kingdoms of Elmet, and perhaps Lindsey, in the region of modern-day Lincolnshire. Penda's involvement in the Cefn Digoll campaign and support of Cadwallon would not have gone unnoticed by Edwin, and likely made for some unpleasant conversations with Eowa. While Eowa and Penda seem to have been largely amicable, they were now firmly on opposing sides, inevitably marching towards a conflict that would place the Iclingas in direct confrontation with one another. Eowa reigned because of support from Edwin, his rise to power showed a calculated nature, with little concern for family relationships or national independence. Penda, on the other hand, would show a continued concern for his family, and conflict with his brother was likely something that affected him greatly. While outright hostilities between the brothers hadn't occurred, one would expect that they were both doing their best to bolster their numbers, and trying to pull in warriors from the same locations, likely leading to more split loyalties and divided families. In Eowa's favour was the backing of the most powerful king in Britain, and a relatively stable kingdom. Penda, however, was proving to be a masterful leader of men, and a successful warlord. For many warriors and nobles there were difficult decisions to make. Across the lands that would become Mercia, men were choosing one side or another, hoping they had chosen the right king to follow: Eowa and Edwin, or Penda and Cadwallon.

Following the successful campaign against Edwin, Cadwallon had returned to Gwynedd and retook his throne. During his exile, the throne may have remained vacant, with people relying on the support of local nobles to provide protection and leadership. Alternatively, Edwin may have selected his own king for the role, as was common in this period. Unfortunately there are no clues at the moment to tell us what happened. Cadwallon's success at Cefn Digoll certainly increased his profile and made him the most powerful Brittonic king. He would now have more ability to draw warriors to him from farther afield, motivated by the opportunity of battlefield success. His contacts with Ireland,

Dumonia, and Armorica gave him a deep pool of warrior talent to draw from. Cadwallon was also shoring up support closer to home, by sending emissaries to the other Brittonic kingdoms, seeking support and warriors from Powys, Deheubarth, Morgannwg, Gwent and Brycheiniog. It's conceivable that he was also building links along the north-eastern shore through Rheged, Strathclyde and smaller Brittonic settlements. All the while he was maintaining contact with his Heathen partner Penda ap Pyd.

Since entering the written record in AD 628 Penda had successfully confronted the Gewisse and achieved a positive result without having to fight, he had lost against Cadwallon without a fight, and he had participated in delivering Edwin's first heavy defeat. These three events are interesting, as rarely in this era did leaders fail and survive. His men must have appreciated his sensibilities; not wasting their lives with impunity, he was willing to seek alliances and treaties as viable conclusions to conflict. This was based either on Machiavellian considerations, or on a general concern for the lives of those around him. Bede tells us that Penda was 'a most warlike man',[1] and while he never walked away from a fight, it seems to belittle both his compassion and his strategic disciplined calculations during conflicts.

By AD 631 Penda had earned a reputation as a distinguished leader and warrior. John of Worcester, a twelfth-century monk and chronicler, describes Penda in an entry for AD 633 as 'a prince of distinguished bravery'.[2] Henry of Huntingdon uses the sobriquet 'Penda the Strong' throughout his work. This is interesting as he doesn't supply any other nicknames for the key characters. Bede tells us Penda is 'warlike', and the Britons' nickname 'Penda son of Danger' speaks to his bravery. Many of these characterizations are attached to activities and events that occurred early in his rise, and generally before AD 633. The early dates attached to these attributes show these are characteristics Penda had from a young age and developed since childhood, rather than favourable attributes applied by chroniclers after he rose to prominence. These are all the traits expected of a warlord and king within the Heathen belief system, and easily found in heroic tales of Beowulf, Woden, Thunor, or Hengist and Horsa.

Following the failed assassination attempt and subsequent success against Cwichelm and Cynegils, Edwin converted to Christianity in AD 627. For Edwin, conversion brought him closer to the continental rulers and allowed him to centralize power and authority within his court. The man that converted Edwin was a Roman missionary named Paulinus. Paulinus had been sent by Pope Gregory to support the conversion of the Angles and Saxons in AD 601. He spent the first twenty-five years of his mission in Kent, before accompanying Edwin's Kentish bride Æthelburg to Bernicia and Deira. Once in Bernicia and

Deira, Paulinus oversaw the construction of several churches including those at York and Campodonum. Bede tells us that at Yeavering Paulinus,

> stayed there with them thirty-six days, fully occupied in catechizing and baptizing; during which days, from morning till night, he did nothing else but instruct the people resorting from all villages and places, in Christ's saving Word; and when they were instructed, he washed them with the water of absolution in the river Glen.[3]

Paulinus brought something other than a new faith to Edwin; he also brought trappings of Imperial Rome. The Angles were well aware of Rome as their ancestors had fought for and against the Romans. The last real contact between these peoples was likely fighting for Rome as part of auxiliary units or Foederati. The stories of this empire would still be available to people in the seventh century. What's more, the remains of Rome's occupation of Britain were still visible in the ruins of cities, forts, bridges and the remaining Roman road system. Paulinus was able to tell Edwin of the glories of the Roman Empire, and explain to him both the vastness of it, and its methods of governance and control. Much of this must have appealed to Edwin as he did take on roman characteristics:

> His dignity was so great throughout his dominions, that not only were his banners borne before him in battle, but even in time of peace, when he rode about his cities, townships, or provinces, with his thegns, the standard bearer was always wont to go before him. When he walked anywhere along the streets, that sort of banner which the Romans call Tufa, and the English, Thuuf, was in like manner borne before him.[4]

Edwin had a number of royal townships throughout Deira and Bernicia, but the most important were York, Yeavering, Campodonum and Bebbanburg. Bebbanburg was the great defensive site of the Bernician kings. The fortress at Bebbanburg is a rocky outcrop on the North Sea, situated perfectly as a defensive position. Even without the addition of palisades, walls, gates and guard towers, the position is formidable. York in the seventh century was known as Eoforwic, and was a key place of trade. The suffix 'wic' is common throughout Britain, and is generally tied to market places and sites related to particular craftsmen. More specifically there is a strong connection between 'wic' sites and maritime or estuarine based market places.[5] These were locations where wealth could be attained through means other than raiding and warfare. In Kent, trade with the continent effectively ended the era of the warlord as the kings of Kent could trade for wealth and no longer needed to attack their neighbours. North of the Humber, York was the key market city for the Deiran kings, elevating the importance of the city. As the Christian conversion began, York's stature continued to climb as it was the site of Deira's first church. Campodonum's importance was also based around the construction of one of the earliest churches north of the Humber.

Yeavering's initial importance was perhaps to balance the closed nature of Bebbanburg by creating an open royal settlement. Yeavering had no palisades, but did have large stockades to draw livestock in for trade and taxation. Until the discovery of the royal hall at Sutton Courtenay, Yeavering had the claim to the largest Angle or Saxon hall in Britain. What makes Yeavering particularly interesting is the inclusion of a semi-circular grandstand. This wooden construction is the only one known in Britain and has similarities to Roman amphitheatres and coliseums. Archaeologist Brian Hope-Taylor conducted extensive research at Yeavering and remarked on the grandstand that it reflected 'the highly sophisticated aspirations of those who caused it to be built'.[6] The underlying Roman inspiration, and the ambition behind the grandstand at Yeavering, are yet more connections to Edwin and Paulinus.

It can be reasonably concluded that at some point in AD 632, Penda and Cadwallon met with one another. This meeting would see the development of strategy for the campaigning season the following year. Perhaps as a matter of simplicity the pair met with their nobles and a select warband at Cefn Digoll or Six-Ashes. Both locations offered them safety from prying eyes, and ease of travel. By the flight of the raven, Cefn Digoll was about ninety-five kilometres from both Penda's and Cadwallon's kingdoms, in the friendly kingdom of Powys. Powys certainly owed its freedom to these two men and would welcome them both.

Cadwallon would be the instigator here, seeking to bring Penda willingly into the invasion of Deira, and perhaps farther. Penda may still have a sworn oath to support Cadwallon, or he may have been freed from that based on the defeat of Edwin. Using hindsight and based on the future events, it seems that the oath was cleared, and Penda's assistance was being asked for rather than demanded. Penda was a willing participant; he had warriors to keep and ever-expanding warbands that could not be maintained through localized raiding. Penda had effectively sealed Hwicce from border security concerns through marriage, treaty, and war. While there were options to the east, Penda likely didn't have an army large enough for such an expedition on his own. Weighing up all of this issues, he would willingly go with Cadwallon, north of the Humber into the heart of Edwin's lands in search of wealth and reputation. The men must have agreed on a location and time to bring the army together and begin the march. The spring Equinox would have provided an ideal date, as it would have been known to both men, and easily interpreted; Eostre's celebration for Penda, and Pascha for Cadwallon.

Cadwallon had a significant army at his disposal by this point, but the inclusion of the Hwicce, under the leadership of Penda ap Pyd, was a force multiplier. Penda was likely to draw other Angles, Saxons and Britons to his banner based on his reputation as a fierce warrior, but also a calculating and thoughtful leader of men. Penda's Heathen beliefs likely buoyed Cadwallon's trust in him, as Penda wasn't pushed or controlled by any external forces, there was no influence from other kings, or priests in his decisions. Penda would rely on his own skills and intelligence, along with Wyrd to carry him through combat. Nor had Cadwallon seen in Penda any drive to conquer lands, that motivation was not present, making him an ideal partner. On the field, Penda was a warrior in search of reputation, wealth, and a noble death, but not land or power. Cadwallon on the other hand was seemingly motivated by revenge and power alone.

The two men continued to balance one another out very well, and if they themselves recognized that, then it could be assumed that they had developed a friendship, not just a military alliance. This pairing should shake all modern notions of ethnic tensions present in the seventh century. Here we have a Christian Briton and an Angle Heathen capable of forming an incredibly strong alliance, and fielding an army of a size and strength which would alter the fabric of power in Britain. These men were not held apart by language, past, religion, or culture. Either this relationship is novel, or it could be a sign that the acrimony between Briton and Angle was a product of later writers, and not a reflection of reality in the seventh century. It is perhaps a balance between both of those interpretations, further pushed by the increasing power of the Roman church, who viewed Penda and Cadwallon with equal disdain: Penda as the Heathen and Cadwallon as the Heretic.

Something unexpected occurred in the lead up to the AD 633 campaign; Cadwallon had two sensible options to advance along en route to attack Deira. The first was to march east to Chester then north-east through Manchester, Leeds and onto York. The second route was to go north to Preston then east to York. This second route would provide less warning to Edwin but would have been a longer march. Both of these lines of advance allowed the invading armies to skirt lands that were fully within Edwin's sphere of influence and controlled by powerful kings, in particular Eowa, who was firmly under the direction of King Edwin. The Hwicce would have been safe to march north and link up with Cadwallon near Chester before moving on, also avoiding contact with Eowa and his South-Humbrians. For one reason or another, these routes were not selected, and the army of Edwin was met much farther south and to the east along Ermine Street. Ermine Street is the main north-south artery moving from London, through York and on to Hadrian's Wall. The meeting place of armies was near the site of the Battle of the River Idle in AD 616, which had brought Edwin to power.

The only justification for the armies meeting here must have been related to freshly gathered intelligence by Penda and Cadwallon about the movements of Edwin. Over the past year all sides had been building the strength of their armies and preparing for battle. Edwin needed to show that he was still the most powerful king in Britain, but to do this he needed to defeat Cadwallon and Penda. Edwin called his warbands to York, where they were told that they would march south, draw in more forces and then launch an attack. As Penda was still the smaller threat by size, Edwin would target him first, before turning his attention on Cadwallon. King Edwin was planning to move his force south through Eowa's territory and defeat Penda, before turning north-west against Powys and Gwynedd. However, this was a strategic plan built on the backs of many assumptions. For starters, Edwin was working on the flawed theory that Cadwallon and Penda's alliance was one of convenience and had not survived the past two years. Second, Edwin was assuming he was the only aggressive actor at play, not expecting that Cadwallon and Penda were also in an offensive posture. Finally, Edwin assumed that this plan was secure and wouldn't be leaked to the opposition.

Cadwallon and Penda must have found out about the plan early enough to alter their strategy for the campaign. If the combined force was in Chester when they found out, they could move through Eowa's territory to the south-east without much concern and with two primary options using the Roman roads before turning north-east near either near Tamworth or Derby and then towards Doncaster. Penda and Cadwallon may have selected a more difficult route through the Peak District moving due east. At least half of this approach would have been on footpaths before picking up a minor Roman road at Buxton. This was a move of 140 kilometres; it would have been a forced march under difficult circumstances and terrain, but in the best case would put the army in a strong position to confront Edwin within seven days. The challenge here is that the army would be exhausted and forced to confront a relatively rested enemy.

The third strategic option, and seemingly likely move, would be to place the army in a position that it could intercept Edwin on the march, without wearing down the force through a difficult march. This was to move the army along the Roman road linking Chester, Northwich, Stoke-on-Trent, and Derby. Moving the army here placed themselves along Edwin's likely route of advance to the south and allowed Cadwallon and Penda to intercept him along the Roman road. There are a curious series of place names and folk stories between Nottingham and Doncaster which seem to suggest Edwin was present in and around Sherwood Forest. As individual stories and locations these are easily ignored, but in conjunction with one another they do suggest something occurred here, which supports the theory of Cadwallon and Penda advancing from Derby on a north-east trajectory.

Penda and Cadwallon must have been successful in their redeployment, arriving in time to hear news that Edwin was moving through Sherwood Forest, off the main roads. Amidst the traditional boundaries for Sherwood Forest is a location called Edwinstowe. This has been interpreted as either 'Edwin's meeting place' or 'Edwin's resting place'. A local tale states that Edwin's body was hidden here after his death at the Battle of Hatfield Chase. But this would mean he was carried south, past the line of victors, which seems doubtful. What seems more probable is that Edwin drew his forces together at this location perhaps to consolidate more warbands, or to give the army a rest; what he didn't know at this point was that Penda and Cadwallon had found him, and were now on the hunt.

Operating inside Sherwood Forest would be within the comfort zone of traditional Brittonic fighting techniques, giving Cadwallon more confidence as they advanced north. At Edwinstowe, an early morning attack by Cadwallon into the camp would have a devastating impact. This type of ambush had been successful in the past and would suit this situation perfectly, as Edwin's camp had limited protection and was relying on being unseen as its protection. Silently Cadwallon positioned his force at the edge of the wood, sitting in the shadows and waiting to attack Edwin's sleeping force. Ideally such an ambush would happen in the early morning light, before the sun had fully risen, giving the attackers some light to see and ensuring the defenders were deeply asleep. Penda's force generally fought differently, in a shield-wall, and may have been held back from the ambush, perhaps setting a shield-wall to Cadwallon's rear as a defensive support should Cadwallon need to withdraw. Once the ambush was launched, Penda could quickly draw his force up into the shield-wall and begin advancing methodically in the wake of Cadwallon's onslaught. The shield-wall was a secondary wave of death for any of Edwin's men who tried to flee to the south. If an ambush of this nature occurred, the Britons would tear through Edwin's camp as his thegns struggled to gain control and establish defensive shield-walls. Some of the warband would have been able to make a stand against the Britons, but they would have melted away at the sight of Penda and his shield-wall methodically advancing forwards. In this proposed scenario Edwin now had to get his army off the killing field and formed up in some order in the woods to take away the advantage that Penda would have with his shield-wall. Cadwallon on the other hand would need to temper down the blood lust of his men and begin to form them up following the initial ambush, lest they perish in small parties against the reforming Northumbrians. Edwin was short on options in the morning light but needed to find a defensive position to regain control of his force. Local legend suggests that Cuckney may have provided a location for Edwin to organize his army.

Cuckney is a small hamlet seven kilometres north-west of Edwinstowe and within the boundary of the seventh-century Sherwood Forest. In 1951, the church at Cuckney was undergoing substantial refurbishment, including underpinning work which required excavations to take place directly below the church itself. During this dig, a mass grave was unearthed containing 200 men, many of whom seemed to have died by violent means. Lidar surveys and archaeological digs have identified earthworks at the location, which may have provided a defensive position. It is possible that the earthworks were natural, and enhanced at some point. A local story holds that it was at this position where Edwin died, and the Battle of Hatfield Chase occurred. As a site for the primary battle, Cuckney seems unlikely, but it could be a viable location for Edwin to retreat to. It is close enough to Edwinstowe, and positioned at a bend in the river, with some natural features that could make it a hastily defendable position. With enough time afforded to him, Edwin may have been able to enhance the earthworks, and eventually bury wounded men who died at the site. Unless Penda and Cadwallon attacked this location and were then forced to set camp here, they would have no reason to bury Edwin's fallen men, so the interment would most certainly be a task for King Edwin's army. The ambush at Edwinstowe and the stay at Cuckney is conjecture, built on the available place name evidence and local folklore of the area. However, this series of events does go some way to explaining these items in the context of the fight between Penda and Edwin.

Edwin now found himself in the same position he had been in at Cefn Digoll; he had been out-thought and out-fought by Cadwallon and Penda. The respite at Cuckney had allowed him to regain command of his army, but his losses and the time of year were forcing him into a rapid retreat. From Cuckney, Edwin pushed his force north along footpaths, arriving after a few days at Bawtry. Edwin had been here before, at the side of Rædwald when he had defeated Æthelfrith and claimed the thrones of Deira and Berncia. Penda and Cadwallon were rapidly closing the gap to Edwin. Once Penda and Cadwallon had picked up the Roman road at Bawtry they would be able to quickly attack York. Edwin knew this, and he knew his only option was to find a location that provided him some field advantage and force Penda and Cadwallon into a pitched battle. Edwin pushed north from Bawtry for another seven kilometers, before finally stopping his army, and turning to face his pursuers. On 12 October, the armies finally made contact at what has become known as the Battle of Hatfield Chase. 'This dramatic event took place, it seems, south-east of Doncaster on the old road to Lincoln, where it fringed the marshland of Haethfelth, later Hatfield Chase.'[7] The location will not have been off the road, as either side of it are on unstable moorland and, as it was late in the campaign year, it is fair to assume that the moorland was already starting to swell with the winter rains. A likely site for the battle could be just before the road crosses the River Torne. Edwin, like many other kings, would meet his end on the banks of a river. As he drew his force together to defend the river crossing he was confronted by the combined armies of Penda and Cadwallon. Penda 'the Strong', Penda 'Son of Danger', would be chomping at the bit to engage Edwin in the shield-wall. Penda's reputation was built on moments like these, positioning himself in the centre of his shield-wall, with his warbands right at the centre of the advancing line and the flanks held by the more mobile Britons. Edwin had no option but to defend to the very last man, forcing him to condense his warbands and restrict the frontage of his position. Penda likely turned to the boar's head formation in order to smash the very centre of Edwin's force, and kill Edwin as rapidly as possible. The boar's head began moving forward, with Penda close to the very point of it.

Edwin's men stood still, gripping their shields tightly, tensing their bodies against the future. Penda scanned their shields and faces honing in on a final location to direct his attack against them. As the Hwicce approached, they hit their shields with weapons and let out terrible yells. They approached in a methodical and slow manner in order to keep the shape of the shield-wall, and ensure their footing held. Penda's boar's head struck into the defenders' wall, the weight of it forcing the centre of King Edwin's line to begin sagging and bowing out of shape. The fight would have been desperate work for Edwin, there was no exit from this place. The moment the structure of Edwin's line started to unravel, Penda and his force would pour into the void and begin the real damage, hacking and cutting down men with impunity. Edwin was likely near the centre of his forces and would have stood out prominently amongst the Deiran and Bernician army by way of his helmet and armour. Penda and his men were looking for the king, once he was dead the remaining defenders would lose the will to keep fighting. Henry of Huntingdon gives us the end point of the battle, 'King Edwin was killed by Penda the Strong.'[8]

Bede records that Edwin's 'army was either slain or dispersed. In the same war also, Osfrid, one of his sons, a warlike youth, fell before him'.[9] Henry of Huntingdon goes on to provide more details of the battles aftermath:

Reports say that in the battle just mentioned the plain of Hethfeld reeked throughout with red streams of noble blood; it was indeed, the scene of a sudden and deplorable slaughter of the bravest warriors. For Cadwallon, who was a most powerful king, was at the head of an immense army; and Penda the Strong was truly the strongest.[10]

There is another interesting outcome in the immediate aftermath of the battle and that is recorded by Bede, where Eadfrid, a son of Edwin, 'compelled by necessity, went over to King Penda, and was by him afterwards slain in the reign of Oswald, contrary to his oath'.[11] This appears to show an exchange of hostages, but seems out of place in this scenario as no peace was achieved at the battle. Hostage exchanges were a common occurrence and used as an insurance policy between kings, but in this case it makes little sense with King Edwin already dead and Eadfrid holding no power with Bernicia or Deira. It could be that this hostage was not taken on the battlefield at all, but instead agreed upon by Cadwallon and Edwin's successor at a later date. It may also be that Penda took Eadfrid in as an exiled Ætheling as other nobles grabbed at the seats of power in Deira and Bernicia. Bede's accusation that Penda broke his oath is a serious accusation in this age. However, it is recorded by Bede as a secondary concern, and so little detail is provided meaning further exploration of the incident isn't possible.

Unlike Edwin, Eowa goes on to rule for another ten years, so it seems that he either survived the fight at Hatfield Chase, or more likely that he wasn't there. If he wasn't there he may have headed home just prior to the battle, in the same way that Edwin was headed back to Deira, as a normal part of the campaigning season. The battle happened in October, and this would be the normal moment for armies to break up and return to their winter quarters. Though, it would mean that Edwin had made a fatal calculation in allowing Eowa to depart just prior to the battle. Edwin may have believed his troubles were largely over when he left Sherwood Forest, and cut Eowa loose at the time to head home. Or it could be a case that Eowa abandoned Edwin earlier, or was simply not a part of Edwin's campaign against Cadwallon and Penda.

In the wake of the battle, Cadwallon and Penda drew the army together at a camp. Small parties were sent out to acquire food and drink if possible, bodies were buried, and any booty from the fight was collected and given to Penda and Cadwallon. As the night set in, the fires were lit and men tried to rest, while the gentle sounds of lyres played softly to the telling of stories and riddles. In this setting Penda and Cadwallon divided the spoils of war, including the personal belongings of Edwin.

The Staffordshire hoard has components to an exquisite Angle helmet, quite unlike others that have been found. In particular, this helmet held a crest of red hair running front to back, 'the inspiration for its form can be traced ultimately back to the crests of Roman Imperial helmets' (Fern et al, 2019). This helmet shares many similarities to the Sutton Hoo helmet, 'apart from the iconic helmet from Sutton Hoo mound one, none of the other helmets has decoration of die-impressed panels or bands of figural and zoomorphic ornament'.[12] The design, elements and construction of the Staffordshire hoard helmet suggest it was made in an East Anglian workshop, perhaps the same one that made King Rædwald's famous helmet.

Aside from Paulinus' Roman influence, Edwin's close links with East Anglia could explain the design of the helmet, and its place of manufacture. At the Battle of the River Idle in AD 616, Edwin would have seen King Rædwald in his gleaming helmet and must have been inspired by the spectacle of it. On circumstantial evidence only, it would seem possible that the Roman styling of the helmet could be traced to Edwin, and the influence of Paulinus. This helmet had been inspired by Rome, crafted in East Anglia, ruled in Northumbria, lost in Hatfield, and interred in Staffordshire. Such a powerful object would not have ended up with a thegn or warrior; this was a prize for a king, and it would seem appropriate that if Penda put Edwin to the sword that the prize, or parts of it, went directly to him.

Some of Edwin's men made it off the battlefield at Hatfield Chase, and they would be riding hard to York, Campodonum, Yeavering, and Bebbanburg, bearing news of the defeat. These messages would be passed through neighbouring territories and the Æthelings, backed by foster kings, would begin raising warbands and placing their claims on the thrones of Deira and Bernicia. King Edwin's head was taken from the battlefield by his men and brought to York and, 'afterwards taken into the church of the blessed Peter the Apostle, which he had begun'.[13] To accomplish this macabre retrieval, a small group of men must have returned to the scene of the battlefield as soon as it was safe to do so. By this point the king and the dead warriors had been stripped of their weapons and valuables. Once the men found King Edwin, they rode into York, which was already seeing to its own defences as Cadwallon and Penda were still on the land, and not a great distance from the town.

Cadwallon and Penda's first target following Hatfield chase was Edwin's royal township of Campodonum, the site of Paulinus' second church. The exact location of Campodonum has long been debated, partially through translation confusion and the spectre of a misprint in its spelling, confusing the places of Campodunum and Campodonum. Campodonum has been placed at Doncaster, Slack, and a number of other locations over the years. The lack of apparent defences at Campodonum, and the language Bede used to describe the church there as 'Fecit Basilicam – He made, not built a basilica',[14] implies that the church was a repurposed building. The reuse of Roman temples was common in the former Roman Empire, 'Constantine gave several basilica to be converted into Christian churches, and Edwin probably did the same'.[15] In the seventh century the common term for Christian church was 'temple' not the Greek, 'Kuriake or vernacular form cyrice'.[16] Templeborough stands out as the only former Roman location with 'temple' in its name in the vicinity of Hatfield. It seems highly probable that it was the temple at this Roman site that became Edwin's Campodonum. This put the royal township within a single day's hard ride to the south-west of the battlefield, and along the route Cadwallon and Penda would take to return to their own kingdoms and winter quarters. What was found at the site is hard to say, but it was sacked and then burned as Bede recounted, 'in Campodonum, where there was then a royal township, he built a church which the pagans, by whom King Edwin was slain, afterwards burnt, together with all the place'.[17] So complete was the destruction of Campodonum that it was never rebuilt and largely forgotten in time.

As Campodonum burned, Æthelings assumed the thrones of Deira and Bernicia. The new king of Deira was Edwin's cousin Osric and in Bernicia, 'Eanfrith the son of Æthelfrith, obtained the kingdom'.[18] Both of these men had lived in exile during the reign of Edwin, 'For all the time that Edwin reigned, the sons of the aforesaid Æthelfrith, who had reigned before him, with many of the younger nobility, lived in banishment among the Scots or Picts.'[19] This pattern of exile amongst Britons is common in the period, and furthers the argument that the endemic fighting between Britons, Angles, and Saxons was not driven by ethnic conflict but by territorial competition between all parties. As the Northumbrian kingdoms teetered on the edge of chaos, Edwin's Kentish wife, children and Paulinus fled,

> there seemed to be no prospect of safety except in flight, Paulinus, taking with him Queen Ethelberg, whom he had before brought thither, returned into Kent by sea, and was very honourably received by the Archbishop Honorius and King Eadbald.[20]

Paulinus also grabbed some of Edwin's wealth and brought it with him to Kent including 'a large gold cross, and a golden chalice'.[21] As these items were altar goods, they would likely be housed in either the York or Campodonum church. Campodonum's fate, and the fact that Paulinus left by the sea, would imply that these goods were in York and that this was where Edwin's family departed from.

As the campaign against Edwin wound down, the combined force parted company, with the Britons heading west into Gwynedd and the Hwicce under Penda turning south. Penda had freed Eowa from Edwin's control, and it is conceivable that he marched his force south from Campodonum directly to the crossroads between Tamworth and Lichfield, only four kilometres from the resting place of the Staffordshire hoard. An army marching this closely to Tamworth would not have gone unnoticed and it seems logical that Penda and Eowa would have met nearby. At this meeting Penda shared his success with Eowa and informed him of the death of Edwin. That Eowa was no longer under the control of Edwin must have been met with both joy and anxiety; he was no longer subservient to any king, but he now had to worry about the rising stature of Penda, and the threat he presented. Eowa would come to believe his kingdom and his position were threatened not only by his brother, but once again from the nations north of the Humber, who under new kings may seek to attack south of the River Humber. Upon the death of any king, all alliances ended and the competition for power began anew.

Penda was greeted in his own hall by Cynewise and his children. The hall would ring with celebration upon the return of the warbands. Penda now had to redistribute land and rank to replace the men who died on campaign, and award the warriors who crushed Edwin's army. In the hall men were given weapons, and wealth was distributed. Lyres would be passed around the hall as people told stories and made boasts for the next year. This was a time of celebration, but also a time to remember the warriors who had left middle-earth.

Chapter Eight
North of the Humber

Cadwallon spent the winter in the same way he had spent all winters since defeating Edwin at Cefn Digoll; re-establishing his control over Gwynedd, drawing in new warriors to his warbands, and sending emissaries to more distant Brittonic kingdoms seeking support for more action in the north. The message this year was different however. Edwin and the united provinces of Deira and Bernicia had been destroyed and the northern nations were now ripe for a campaign of conquest. Cadwallon would attack Deira and then push on to Bernicia in the next campaign. With the death of Edwin, the Britons in the north, including the kingdoms of Rheged, Strathclyde, Gododdin along with Elmet south of the Humber, may be willing to join the men from Gwynedd, and further the destruction of Deira and Bernicia. Cadwallon had proved that he was capable of confronting the most powerful kingdoms, but to do it again he needed to strengthen his army.

Penda had also been recruiting men to his warbands, and the action at Hatfield Chase, along with the march through Eowa's land, had increased his own profile making him a more attractive leader for men seeking riches and prestige. Men without an oath sworn to another thegn, or men whose kings and thegns were failing to deliver opportunities for the acquisition of wealth, reputation and land would be eager to join an active and successful king such as Penda. In early generations of Germanic leaders, Tacitus observed that they, 'cannot maintain a numerous following except by violence and war'.[1] Although Tacitus made this observation centuries before, the culture surrounding the Angles in the seventh century was still very closely linked to the continental people of Tacitus' 'Germania'. Nationality, tribal affiliation, and even religion were all fluid concepts, with kinship being the most important connection. As long as a man was not breaking an oath or a bond of kinship, movement between kingdoms and people would not have been a concern. The flexibility of movement for members of the warrior classes is reflected in Beowulf, where we see a warband of the Geats coming to Heorot to support the Danes in spite of being from different tribes. The Angles and Saxons had no compunction in joining other nations for military action as single warriors or members of a warband, and can be seen in their participation with the Roman Empire as

Foederati, and the story of Hengist and Horsa fighting for the Romano-Celtic King Vortigern.

As Cadwallon prepared for his expedition to the north, he must have asked Penda to join him on campaign after the success they had both experienced over the past few years. The available historic evidence doesn't mention Penda in any of the following actions which occur north of the Humber, and so it must be implied that he wasn't there. This tells us that he was no longer beholden to Cadwallon by an oath, and was now able to make decisions on the involvement of his warbands against Deira and Bernicia. It would, however, be reasonable for him to allow a small warband made up of younger warriors seeking combat experience to support Cadwallon. The benefit to Penda is that warriors were kept busy, but also gained experience in war, and learned from Cadwallon and his Brittonic army. This warband's inclusion in the fight may have led to tales of Penda being in the north, when in actual fact he wasn't there.

Through the campaign of AD 634 we see only the name of Cadwallon, and no mention of Penda by Bede or in the *Anglo-Saxon Chronicles*. However, Geoffrey of Monmouth and Matthew of Paris both record Penda's participation in their later chronicles. Matthew of Paris was a monk writing in the sixteenth century stating, 'Penda was also sent this year the king of the Mercians, by Cadwallon king of the Britons, with a very large number of armed men in the region of the Northumbrians'.[2] The discord between records cannot rapidly be reconciled, and leaves the possibility on the table that Penda participated in the AD 634 campaign against Deira, though this seems unlikely, not least because of the outcome of the campaign. The silence of the records which were written closest to the time of the events must take supremacy on the debate, in which case it appears that Penda played no personal role in the third campaign by Cadwallon against Deira.

Penda's decision not to be involved in the northern expedition did not deter Cadwallon's preparation nor his decision to carry on with the attack north of the Humber. No doubt Cadwallon greatly desired to have Penda with him, but he must have remained confident that he had a force large enough at hand even without the Hwicce. The swelling of the Gwynedd army likely came from emboldened Brittonic kingdoms in the west, and perhaps from across the Irish Sea. The initial target for Cadwallon was York, this was the closest major centre within Deira, and would provide some riches due to its importance as a marketplace with links to the sea. Seizing the town would also ensure Cadwallon didn't have Deira warbands operating behind his advance. The likely location to gather the disparate warbands together prior to the advance could have been at Chester, or the Mersey estuary. From here, Cadwallon's force could skirt the lands of Eowa and make a direct assault on York. Utilizing the Roman road linking modern-day Manchester, Leeds, and then York meant the army could attack swiftly. This route may also catch the Deiran defenders off-guard as they may have been focused on the southern route through the last year's battleground, paralleling the shore of the Wash.

The attack on York occurred with no significant issue, and isn't directly recorded in the source material, but it is implied in the context of events following Cadwallon's seizure of the town. York may have been undefended or lightly defended, and fell quickly to the Brittonic army. The city was not exposed to a prolonged siege and the lack of information on a battle at York makes it safe to assume that the city was taken largely intact with limited or no damage to it. Acquiring an undamaged city with effective defences in place would be attractive to Cadwallon as a forward base to operate his campaign from. Osric, the new king of Deira, was alerted to York's fall, and was immediately compelled to act. York was the gateway to the north, by road and by sea, it protected the hinterland of Deira, and also acted as a key market centre for sea borne trade. Without York, Deira simply wouldn't be able to exist. Osric didn't have the benefit of time, and was now hastily seeing to the construction of an army capable of attacking Cadwallon and regaining control over York. The newly crowned king of Deira had to achieve success at York or he would be unable to slow the advance of Cadwallon across his nation. Osric had no options but to advance on York.

After gathering what forces he could, the freshly-minted King Osric of Deira marched on York, he believed that the men from Gwynedd were now sealed-up in the city, with no option but to weather a siege behind York's walls. Cadwallon, however, was not disposed to avoiding a fight nor waiting behind walls to be starved out, and upon seeing the advancing army, 'put Osric to death; for, being rashly besieged by him in the municipal town, he sallied out on a sudden with all his forces, took him by surprise, and destroyed him and all his army'.[3]

This was not the first time Cadwallon had been involved in a siege. He had learned many lessons about sieges at Exeter, and Edwin's confrontation with him at Glannauc. Cadwallon must have realized that if he allowed a siege to set in Osric would be afforded the opportunity to draw more help in and slowly tighten the noose. Cadwallon's advantage lay in his aggression and speed, something he would lose if he had allowed a siege to begin. The king of Gwynedd was really confronted by limited options as Osric appeared outside of York, the best opportunity for success was a rapid attack against the inexperienced and under-prepared Osric.

Exactly how this confrontation played out is impossible to know. Osric was probably approaching York from the east using the Roman roads to move his hastily formed army as quickly as possible to York. As he approached the city,

Osric needed to establish a camp before making the final push and establishing the siege. Bede says that the attack by Cadwallon took Osric by complete surprise, meaning that Osric wasn't formed up for combat. This wasn't an ambush, but rather the gates of York were opened and the whole of Cadwallon's force attacked. Osric must have been resting his men close enough to the city walls that they were unable to form a defensive position once the Britons began streaming out of the gates. Osric's lack of experience in major combat actions was glaringly exposed in comparison to the seasoned expertise of Cadwallon. In the ensuing slaughter, Osric and his army were utterly destroyed.

For the second time in two years, Deira was without a king. More concerning for them was the extreme degradation of the kingdom's ability to protect itself and its communities. Over the last two years, subsequent warbands had been put in the field and been eradicated by Penda and Cadwallon. The combat losses at both Hatfield Chase and again at York would leave Deira in a desperate position, and compel whatever local leadership was left to rely on second-tier defensive forces for protection. These forces would not stand up against an assault by the well-drilled Brittonic army, but may be able to see off smaller foraging parties. The defence of settlements and towns was no longer under the purview of a king and his army, but was to be looked after by the locals alone. Each town and hamlet in Deira was now an Angle outpost isolated from the rest of the nation and forced into a regime of complete self-sufficiency. The entire cultural system of leadership and protection was failing in Deira. Darker days could be on the horizon as well if people were called out of the farm fields in order to take up arms against Cadwallon; without people tending the crops and the mass theft of livestock by Cadwallon's forces, the region could face a serious threat of famine in short order.

Campaigns in the seventh century generally came to an end as autumn set in, and the spoils of war were transported to the victor's home kingdom, but according to Bede this didn't happen when Cadwallon invaded Deira. Following Osric's defeat, Cadwallon 'occupied the provinces of the Northumbrians for a whole year, not ruling them like a victorious king, but ravaging them like a furious tyrant'.[4] Cadwallon was engaged in a war of domination, not in the customary practice of raiding, though if we can trust Bede, he doesn't seem to have been interested in ruling Deira and Bernicia either. The idea of Cadwallon staying in Deira over the winter, forces the consideration of some interesting possibilities. For starters, perhaps Cadwallon wasn't a king after all, but instead a noble with no direct connection to a king similar to Penda's reality before Cirencester. If this is the case, then he had no need to leave Deira, and could easily overwinter north of the Humber. Or, perhaps Cadwallon left Gwynedd under the care of his eventual successor Cadafael Cadomedd ap Cynfeddw. Cadafael is interesting as he doesn't seem to descend from nobility, and therefore would not be seen as a rival for the throne by Cadwallon. Cadafael in this theory was the protector of Gwynedd, managing the affairs of the kingdom in Cadwallon's absence.

A third possibility is that Cadwallon was not from Gwynedd at all, but was instead a Briton from north of the Humber:

> nothing in the Vita Columbae, Historia Ecclesiastica, or the Irish chronicles would encourage us to locate Cadwallon in Gwynedd. The identification of Catguollaun as rex regionis Guenedotae in the Historia Brittonum is an authorial gloss on material otherwise drawn from Northumbrian sources and is a product of the synchronizing tendencies of a writer working two centuries after the events he is describing.[5]

As is the case with so much from this period, it is difficult to untangle the truth, and we are forced to make educated estimates of what was occurring without further evidence being found through historical records or archaeology. However, with no evidence to the contrary, the safest assumption is that Cadwallon was a king of Gwynedd, and he had left control of that crown with a trusted individual while he overwintered in Deira.

Bede and future authors would have us believe that the actions of Cadwallon were driven by ethnicity, or even religion, but if that was the case why hadn't he attacked Eowa or even Penda who shared borders with Gwynedd and Powys? If Cadwallon was on a mission to eradicate the Angles and Saxons from Britain then attacking far to the north seems odd as it kept pockets of Angles behind his line of advance. It seems more likely that this was a war of revenge directed at Deira and Bernicia, motivated by the actions and conduct of Edwin, and perhaps Æthelfrith before him. Cadwallon was avenging the domination of Edwin over Gwynedd, and then looking to destroy any further risk of a repeat of the northern Angle nations rising again.

With Osric dead and Deira largely devoid of any remaining defensive capacity, Cadwallon went on to drain Deira of its mobile wealth. His warbands had free reign over the entire Deiran kingdom, moving anywhere with impunity and pillaging as they went. The period of Cadwallon's occupation is cloudy, including the location of Cadwallon's winter camp in Deira, though there are many theories, including a return to York. Cadwallon's entire campaign was directed at the total destruction of Deira, and to push his power farther north; retreating to York for the winter would release the pressure he was placing on Deira, and Bernicia. The king of Gwynedd wanted to continually threaten Bernicia, which to this point had not been overly impacted by the destruction of Deira. Bernicia at this stage still had its warbands largely intact, its agriculture and economy still functioning. As autumn turned to winter, the largest barrier to the north would be crossing the River Tyne, and it is this natural barrier that dictated where Cadwallon would winter.

The River Tyne and its general vicinity is renowned for the Roman infrastructure which defends, crosses and prevents access to the north and the south. All of these qualities made it an attractive centre for Cadwallon to establish his winter quarters. The River Tyne and its associated settlements and roads would provide an effective communication, transportation and defensive position for the Brittonic army as it waited for the arrival of spring. Scholars have theorized that Cadwallon set his camp at the disused Roman fort at Corbridge on the north bank of the River Tyne. This seems a reasonable location which was serviced by Roman infrastructure and could support Cadwallon's logistic and communication needs.

Corbridge had originally been established by the Roman Legions to control a crucial strategic ford over the River Tyne. The ford at this location had been used for generations before the Roman invasion. Originally the Britons of the area had named the ford, Corioritum, which meant 'army ford' or 'hosting ford'.[6] The naming of the location speaks to the importance of this location, and the value it held to generations of military men: 'In the case of Corbridge "host-place ford" seems a very suitable name for the strategic crossing of the River Tyne.'[7] This was a strategic location that allowed trade and armies to move north and south. During the period of Roman conquest in Britain, the first action the legions took at Corioritum was to control the north side of the ford, preventing the free use of the crossing by the tribes from the north. To accomplish this a Roman fort was built at the location. As in many other cases, the fort drew in civilians, and slowly grew into a small town complete with a market, Roman temple, and fountain. By AD 160, the Romans had upgraded the river crossing from a natural ford to an eleven arch, 140 metre stone bridge. This bridge was enormous, considering 'Roman bridges were noted for their durability and performance, than for their length of span, which rarely exceeded 70 to 80 feet.'[8] The span at Corbridge was nearly eight times the length of the average Roman bridge and was likely the largest in Britain. The construction and maintenance of this river crossing was an enormous investment by the Roman government. Generations of legionnaires would march across this bridge on their way to and from the garrisons on Hadrian's Wall.

The River Tyne is no small waterway, and it has routinely destroyed bridges all along the water course, right up to the present day. In 1771 a particularly devastating flood destroyed all the bridges over the River Tyne bar one. This flood in 1771 was nothing particularly special, on average the river suffers from a serious flooding event every 90 years.[9] Under normal conditions the River

Tyne has a flow rate of 44 cubic metres per second, but under flood conditions the average flow is 974 cubic metres per second, or more than twenty times the normal rate.[10] The modern need to keep bridges in place over such a powerful river requires routine maintenance and repair. During and after the Roman period the need for regular repair existed as well. 'In the last quarter of the fourth century resources were thus still being expended on keeping the main routes open, and presumably the river bridge was still being maintained.'[11]

On the north side of the River Tyne the Romans built the Stangate Road. This road provided the primary east to west route to service Hadrian's Wall. Floods in the last part of the fourth century damaged the north bank of the river significantly enough to force the Roman administration to alter sections of the Stanegate Road. This re-routing required a new bridge to be built to the west at a place called Cor Burn. This smaller bridge is important as pottery found at the site dates the construction of the Cor Burn bridge to around AD 370 A.D.[12] What is telling is that the local bridges were still under the care of the Romans almost into the fifth century. Based on the last known Roman connection with the bridge in AD 370, and the drastic Roman contraction in the following fifty years, it would seem that the bridge no longer received maintenance and repair service around the mid-fifth century. By the time Cadwallon was operating along the River Tyne the bridge at Corbridge had potentially been without service for upwards of 260 years. With the River Tyne's estimated ninety year flood return, along with the impacts of the Dark Age cold period, it's fair to say that the un-serviced bridge was faced with at least three significant flood events between the last known flood on the river around AD 370 and AD 634.

The Corbridge bridge was a marvel of engineering, but didn't include the use of concrete in its construction, instead relying on gravity and iron pin connections to hold the bridge together. These iron connectors are a 'flat rectangular bar with curved-in waist, now commonly referred to as a "dovetail" clamp'.[13] The connection was made by stone masons cutting clamp grooves into the two stones, and the clamp placed into the recess, connecting the stones together. Each of these clamps was a potential point of failure, particularly with corrosion and weathering. Based on the construction methods, requirement for regular servicing, and the power of the River Tyne's regular major floods, it seems highly likely that the bridge was not serviceable by the time Cadwallon was in the area.

A serviceable bridge here would have been a critical point for Bernicia's defence, potentially garrisoned by a warband at the Roman fort, but that is not mentioned in any of the historic record. With no functional bridge, there would be no reason for Cadwallon to winter at Corbridge, which at this point is an abandoned ruin, and probably not a comfortable location to keep an army. While Cadwallon could have forded the river and wintered at Corbridge this would put him in a strategically weak position with no route of retreat in the case of a Bernician attack. The safer winter location was on the south side of the Tyne, where the likelihood of a Deiran attack was negligible due to their crushing defeat at York.

If Cadwallon wasn't at Corbridge for the winter, where was he? The most likely candidate is the town of Hexham, which is only five kilometres to the west of Corbridge. The etymology of Hexham provides the primary clue, the Old English name was Haegstaldtham meaning 'Young Warriors Village'. In both the *Historia Britonnum* and the *Annales Cambriae*, the location of Cadwallon's last fight is called 'Cantscaul' which is 'Old Welsh for "enclosure of a young warrior"'.[14] It seems likely there was a settlement sufficient enough to support Cadwallon and his army through the winter. He would have felt safe from the primary military threat of Bernicia from the north in this location, as the winter rains would cause the river to rise and make a forded crossing difficult and more dangerous than usual. On the south side of the River Tyne, Cadwallon was able to maintain a route of retreat, and continue sending out foraging parties to keep the camp supplied through the winter. This location would also allow Cadwallon to restart his northern campaign as soon as the rivers could be forded, keeping the pressure on Bernicia.

Once Cadwallon was settled in Hexham, King Eanfrith ventured down from Bernicia with only twelve soldiers to speak with Cadwallon at his winter camp. Since Cadwallon had cornered Penda at Exeter, he hadn't ended a conflict through negotiations and it is rather surprising that King Eanfrith thought he may be able to bargain his way out of conflict with Cadwallon. The Bernician warbands had faced Cadwallon and Penda at Hatfield Chase, they had watched his army decimate Deira over the last year, and knew what he was capable of. Eanfrith and those around him clearly believed they couldn't defeat Cadwallon once the next campaign began, and accepted that their only hope was to negotiate with him in one way or another. King Eanfrith's trip to see Cadwallon could be the first time they met, and Bernicia was looking for peace with the powerful king of Gwynedd. An alternative theory is that Eanfrith had already sworn an oath to Cadwallon, and was entering his court for further discussions. Following the death of Edwin, Eanfrith was able to take over the kingship of Bernicia so rapidly that some have speculated he was already in an alliance with Cadwallon. If Eanfrith and Cadwallon were in some alliance or relationship, it greatly benefited Cadwallon as he was able to fully dismantle Deira without fear of an attack out of the north.

Unfortunately for King Eanfrith and his twelve men, Cadwallon was in no mood for conversation and he killed them all on the spot, leaving both Angle nations north of the Humber without leaders. The *Annales Tigernach* (AT), a chronicle from Ireland, includes one more detail on Eanfrith's death: 'What is perhaps interesting to note is AT's assertion that Eanfrith was beheaded'.[15] Following the defeat of Edwin at Hatfield the chroniclers mention that his head was retrieved from the battlefield and returned to York. Based on Eanfrith's treatment, it could very well be the case that Cadwallon had Edwin decapitated as well. Eanfrith's naivety had cost him his life, and would now put Bernicia in turmoil, similar to Deira. Deira and Bernicia were now on their knees, and desperate for a protector from the predations of Cadwallon. The year and reigns of Osric and Eanfrith were so disastrous to both nations north of the Humber that Bede wrote,

> that year is looked upon as ill-omened, and hateful to all good men; as well on account of the apostacy of the English kings, who had renounced the mysteries of the faith, as of the outrageous tyranny of the British king. Hence it has been generally agreed, in reckoning the dates of the kings, to abolish the memory of those faithless monarchs, and to assign that year to the reign of the following king.[16]

At the time of Eanfrith's death, the Ætheling Oswald was still in exile with the Picts, north of the Firth of Forth. Oswald was the brother of Eanfrith and the next Ætheling to rise to the challenge of the Bernician throne. During his time in exile Oswald had been raised as a Christian, and unlike Osric and Eanfrith he was a true believer. Eanfrith had been exposed to the same exile and as Oswald, including exposure to Celtic Christianity, but was much older than Oswald, and may have had a deeper connection to his Heathen culture. When their father Æthelfrith died in AD 616 at the River Idle, Oswald was only 12, but Eanfrith was 26. Upon taking the Bernican throne, Eanfrith renounced Christianity and returned to the Heathen faith, this was more than likely done to gain support from some sector of the Bernician nobility, once again showing the flexibility of conversion as a tool to achieve or maintain power.

Oswald was different than Eanfrith, and had spent much of his youth in exile, certainly with the Picts, but potentially spent time in Ireland as well, learning both religion and the Celtic style of combat. The Irish saga *Togail Bruidne Da Derga* mentions Oswald clearly:

> On the northern side of the house I beheld nine men. Nine very yellow manes were on them. Nine linen frocks somewhat short were round them: nine purple plaids over them without brooches therein. Nine broad spears, nine red curved shields above them. 'We know them,' quoth he. 'Oswald and his two foster-brothers, Osbrit Longhand and his two foster-brothers,

Lindas and his two foster-brothers. Three crown-princes of England who are with the king. That set will share victorious prowess.'[17]

From an early age he had been exposed to Christianity, in fact the majority of his life had been surrounded by Celtic Christian societies. In particular, Oswald had spent most of his exile in Dal Riata, home of the Christian monastery at Iona. Oswald's exposure from a young age supported his religious growth and led him to develop into a true believer.

Oswald would have heard of the march of Cadwallon, the deaths of Edwin, Osric, and his brother Eanfrith. With support and perhaps a push from the King Domnall Brecc, who had protected him, Oswald went south to claim the throne. Domnall Brecc was keen to see Oswald succeed as it would lead to a relationship on which the kingdom of Dal Riata could rely, and perhaps even direct the Bernician king. Bernicia was still largely unmolested by Cadwallon, and under its own protection. In order to establish his claim to the throne and gather forces Oswald must have visited Yeavering and then Bebbanburg as these were the key centres of power. He had to prove to the thegns that he was worth backing, and would be successful against Cadwallon. The inclusion of Pictish warriors in his retinue would help make his argument. Oswald would have been a strange sight for the nobility of Bernicia: while he clearly had a claim to the throne, he spoke and acted like the Picts having lived with them for nearly twenty years, in fact the majority of his life.

As soon as Oswald had gained control of the throne, he began quickly drawing together available warbands, and augmenting the Bernician force with the support of Dal Riatan, and perhaps Irish warriors who had come south with him. Oswald was at least partially successful in these endeavours to draw an army together as he was able to organize a force to march south against Cadwallon, 'after the death of his brother Eanfrith, advanced with an army, small, indeed, in number'.[18] If Bede is correct that Oswald was carrying a smaller force against Cadwallon, he would need to rely on cunning in order to win.

From Bebbanburg, Oswald was able to utilize the southbound Roman Road, before turning west along the Roman 'military way' road which shadows the south side of Hadrian's Wall. After a four day march the Bernician army arrived at a point two kilometres north of Port Gate. This point was an ideal setting for a final camp before the tactical maneouvring began. From his camp at Port Gate the next and final camp was only seven kilometres to the west at Heavenfield, which closed the gap to Hexham and would keep the army fresh and capable of marching again at night to launch a dawn raid against Cadwallon's position.

At Heavenfield we are told that 'Oswald, being about to engage in this battle, erected the symbol of the Holy Cross, and knelt down and prayed to God.'[19]

There is a small church near to this location which has claimed to be the spot where Oswald camped and raised the cross. With the risk of Cadwallon launching an attack on them, maintaining close contact with the remnants of Hadrian's Wall and any other defensive works was prudent. The Roman defensive turret now called Turret 25B is only 100 metres from the site of the church. In the 1950s, Turret 25B was excavated and a rectangular hole was identified in the centre of the Turret. Since that excavation, the hole has been interpreted as the potential location for the placement of Oswald's Cross.[20,21]

After a brief rest at Heavenfield, Oswald may have led his army on a night march in order to position his force for the final dawn attack on Cadwallon at Hexham. Oswald stirred his army and moved them along the road which shadows Hadrian's Wall farther to the west, crossing North Tyne at Chester's bridge or using the nearby ford. Chester's bridge and the bridge at Corbridge 'were built at the same time, perhaps by the same team of masons or under the direction of the same architect'.[22] Chester's bridge crosses the smaller North Tyne River so it may have survived into this period. However, it also may have been destroyed by flood waters, as had its larger sister at Corbridge, forcing Oswald to use a ford. Once across the North Tyne River Oswald moved his force south to the Ring fort at High Warden, before finally fording the South Tyne River a few kilometres west of Hexham.

Crossing the ford would have been a difficult process in the dark, but was necessary to place Oswald and his army within striking range of Cadwallon as the sun rose. Once across the South Tyne, Oswald was now within reach of Cadwallon, less than three kilometres separated them. As the morning's first light began to show, Oswald was 'advancing towards the enemy with the first dawn of day'.[23] Cadwallon was not ringed by a wall, and had assumed that the river would protect him from Bernician aggression. It seems likely that he was totally unprepared for the attack, and even though Oswald's force was smaller, they had the element of surprise, leading to the slaughter of much of Cadwallon's army. This dawn raid on a resting army was a classic technique of the Celtic tribes, and something Oswald had been exposed to during his exile. Cadwallon had failed to understand his enemy, and was expecting to confront Angle warbands who would fight almost exclusively in shield-walls, he was completely unprepared for the Celtic tactics employed by King Oswald.

As Oswald's force of Bernician and Pictish warriors streamed into Hexham and began the slaughter, Cadwallon and a cadre of warriors were able to organize a hasty defence and began retreating. First they were pushed eastward under the weight of Oswald's attack, before turning south following the Devil's Water, 'the impious commander of the Britons, in spite of his vast forces, which he boasted nothing could withstand, was slain at a place called in the English tongue Denisesburna, that is, the brook of Denis.'[24] Cadwallon may have made a final stand at a ford somewhere along the Denisesburna, but he was caught and finally defeated by Oswald's forces. Cadwallon's defeat is important as it is the last time the Brittonic nations are ever able to launch and sustain a serious campaign against the dominant Angle or Saxon kingdoms. It also marks the last time that the western Britons would have a direct land border with the Britons of the north.

The political landscape had altered significantly once again, and Oswald was now in a position to assume the dual thrones of Deira and Bernicia as Edwin had in AD 616, following the battle of the River Idle. The impacts of this event reached Penda as well. He had been able to refocus his energy internally over the past two years with the success of Cadwallon pushing the largest danger on the island to a point of failure. However, with the change in power dynamics, Penda would once again be forced to consider the threat presented by a resurgent Bernicia and Deira.

King Edwin had used the church to further the control of his territories, and while Oswald would also benefit from this reality, he was motivated by a true faith in the religion, and in particular its evangelical nature. One of Oswald's first actions following his defeat of Cadwallon, and assumption of both the Deira and Bernicia thrones, was the establishment of the Christian church.

> Oswald, as soon as he ascended the throne, being desirous that all the nation under his rule should be endued with the grace of the Christian faith, whereof he had found happy experience in vanquishing the barbarians, sent to the elders of the Scots, among whom himself and his followers, when in banishment had received the sacrament of Baptism, desiring that they would send him a bishop, by whose instruction and ministry the English nation, which he governed, might learn the privileges and receive the Sacraments of the faith of our Lord.[25]

Oswald was clearly prepared to follow the example set by King Edwin in establishing a broad reach and power throughout Britain. In AD 635, shortly after establishing his reign, he became the godfather for Cynegils of the Gewisse. This relationship implies that the Gewisse were subservient to Oswald's authority, and drives the question 'who made the request?' For the Gewisse, they still had Penda on their northern border, who had proved to be capable of defeating them. From the stand point of Cynegils, establishing a treaty with Oswald was a wise move to compete against Penda, and protect himself from future conflict with the Hwicce. Oswald and Cynegils sealed a multifaceted alliance according to Bede:

Oswald, the most holy and victorious king of the Northumbrians, being present, received him as he came forth from baptism, and by an honourable alliance most acceptable to God, first adopted as his son, thus born again and dedicated to God, the man [Cynegils] whose daughter he was about to receive in marriage.[26]

Cynegils' conversion may have been driven by the value of the relationship with Oswald, at the same time conversion stood Cynegils and the Gewisse in opposition to Penda. The relationship between the Gewisse, Deira and Bernicia nations was certainly starting to look like a resurrection of Edwin's world, and would have been a concern to Penda, who also had connections through marriage to the Gewisse.

Throughout this period Eowa would have been in an extremely precarious position with rivals and potential enemies along all of his borders. While Penda had always maintained a peaceful relationship with his brother, his rising power must have threatened Eowa. Oswald represented an even greater threat to Eowa, as he was no longer in a subservient relationship with Deira since the death of Edwin. During Cadwallon's campaign there seemed to be no threat coming out of the north, but with Oswald able to unite the northern nations and his new influence over the Gewisse, there was an ever growing pressure from the north. Eowa doesn't feature very much in the historic record, which is surprising considering how close his kingdom was to a number of significant events. He seems to have done just enough to avoid major conflict, and was perhaps willing to enter into alliances as the junior partner simply as a measure of self-preservation, this was certainly what had happened with Edwin's patronage.

Eowa could have turned to Penda to further their mutual defence, but perhaps this alarmed him as Penda had been a decisive part of Edwin's defeat at Cefn Digol, and his death at Hatfield Chase. Standing together with Penda was sure to bring the wrath of Oswald south of the Humber, which Eowa was determined to avoid. Eowa saw an internal threat from his powerful brother Penda, who could seek to unite their thrones under a single Iclingas king. The external threat he would have been most alarmed by was the spectre of Oswald marching south in order to attack Penda, marching through his South-Humbrian lands, and his nation being devastated along the way. It seems that in the end he chose to offer his allegiance to Oswald. Based on Oswald's conduct with other kings, it would seem a fair expectation that part of the alliance would be the baptism of Eowa, which in turn would further isolate Heathen men like Penda.

The chronicles all go quiet between AD 635 and AD 642, these seven years are virtually missing from the historic record. The *Anglo-Saxon Chronicles* does have a number of entries, but they relate to baptisms of the Gewisse, and the death of the king of Kent. The *Annales Cambriae* has an even longer gap covering AD 633 to AD 644, though they do seem to be off by two years when compared to other sources. Even Bede is curiously quiet in this period of time, with many of his entries covering longer spans of years. Oswald spends these intervening years shoring up his power in the north, and slowly drawing more nations under his influence: 'He brought under his dominion all the nations who inhabited Britain, viz. the Britons, the English, the Picts, and the Scots'.[27]

Penda had not been engaged with a serious conflict since AD 633 and the following actions in the aftermath of the Battle of Hatfield Chase. Future events would lead us to believe that he wasn't idle in the ensuring years, but was likely conducting raids and extending his influence eastward, through the minor kingdoms which were left in the wake of the initial Angle expansion. The *Tribal Hidage* records a variety of small kingdoms and people that may have slowly been turning to Penda including the Færfingas, Hendrica, Unecung-ga, West Willa, East Willa, and others. Looking towards the future, it is most certain that Penda was still successfully recruiting warriors throughout this period of time, and that must imply that his warbands were still very active conducting raids and small scale conflict. Although these operations were minor in nature, Penda was clearly doing enough to keep his warriors supplied with wealth and reputation.

Chapter Nine

Eastward

By AD 641 Penda had achieved security for the Hwicce, through war, marriage and alliance. Security at home was a luxury that many other nations didn't have, and it provided Penda with the opportunity to raid great distances from his own home without much concern. In broad strokes he had stability to the north, partnership to the west, and dominance to the south. Penda's ongoing success, and the loyalty of his thegns, eliminated the risk of internal strife in the Hwicce territory as well. The stability Penda had built for his people was priceless, and felt by the lowest ceorl up to Queen Cynewise.

Aside from territorial security, Penda had another advantage over his rivals: Queen Cynewise, who was able to run the kingdom during his long absences. We know precious little about Cynewise, and only see her name written once, when Bede tells us that hostages from a king were under her care. We can imply that she was trusted and powerful by that one line alone. Cynewise also stands out in the works of Bede as: 'She is almost alone in this period, as a Mercian noblewoman who is mentioned neither as a saint nor a connection with a foul murder.'[1] This infers her importance, even to a man whose work is so deeply tainted against Heathens as Bede was. We know that Penda saw his children converted, but it seems that Cynewise remained a Heathen alongside Penda.

As spring arrived in AD 641, Penda would be turning once again to Cynewise to support his expedition and maintain the kingdom in his absence. Penda's duties as a warlord required him to keep his warbands active, and if there was no major conflict at hand, then raiding was the order of the day. The only avenue left open for him to raid was to the east, across the centre of England and as far as the North Sea. With Penda's reputation and power, he needed to come up against a suitably wealthy and powerful nation; it simply wouldn't be enough to pick off a small sub-kingdom as the wealth wouldn't be there.

In his earlier years, he had launched two larger scale raids; the first at Cirencester, and the second at Exeter. Both of these had been raids aimed at defeating a local garrison, gathering wealth and returning home rapidly. He had mixed results in his raids against these cities, and neither operation had resulted in the acquisition of any mobile wealth which was his ultimate goal. In the end, both raids had ended in positive outcomes for Penda, though at the time he wouldn't have been able to fully recognize the opportunities Wyrd had put on his doorstep. Having been forced to swear an oath to Cadwallon at Exeter, Penda had supported the campaigns in the west, and Edwin's eventual defeat at Hatfield Chase. These were both long-range campaigns led by Cadwallon. Penda had never led an army on expedition of the magnitude he was now preparing for, he was surely relying on the invaluable lessons and experience he had gained under Cadwallon's tutelage during the campaigns against Edwin.

Penda set his sights far to the east: an invasion of East Anglia. He would cross the lands of the Middle Angles, using the Icknield Way. Although we can't know all the reasons behind his decision to attack the East Angles, it is possible to explore some of the generalities he was interpreting. Following the defeat of Edwin, Penda was likely aware of the craftsmanship being produced in East Anglia. This was a clear demonstration of that nation's great wealth, driven by its continental connections and seaborne trade, which provided him with the motivation for invasion. As Penda looked at the tangled alliances throughout kingdoms, it became clear that East Anglia was largely on its own, and had no direct connection to the northern powers of Deira and Bernicia, in fact there may still have been animosity between them, providing Penda with opportunity. East Anglia had close relationships with the Saxon and Jutish nations of the East Saxons and Kent, but this entire region had based its security and stability on trade, conversion, and continental relationships rather than military, unlike the majority of kingdoms in Britain during the seventh century. For an aggressive warlord, the potential payoff coupled with the apparent military weakness of East Anglia was a target too tempting to leave on the table.

Attacking East Anglia was a serious undertaking, and included moving his mobilized Hwicce force some 160 kilometres eastward to the frontier with the East Angles, potentially through territory that was hostile, or at the very least unwelcoming. Penda must have felt his own territory was secure enough to remove his warbands so far from their homes, another sign of the security he had been able to establish for the Hwicce. What is particularly interesting in this is that it suggests his alliances and relationships with the Brittonic kingdoms on his western border had survived the death of Cadwallon. Penda had a relationship with the Britons predating Cadwallon, and his support in clearing the west of Edwin must have caused his stock to climb.

Penda's other key alliance was with the Gewisse, though somewhat more precarious as it had been formed on the back of a stalemate battle, and entered into begrudgingly by Cynegils and Cwichelm. The treaty with the Gewisse was a broad success for Penda in which he walked away with the lion's share of the spoils. The Gewisse were quiet enough in this period, and were of little concern to Penda, though their fresh alliance with King Oswald would need some level of active monitoring. Still, the Gewisse were not at a point to threaten the Hwicce, otherwise Penda would not have been able to march so far from his nation's heartland.

Eowa to the north, like the Gewisse, had drawn close to Oswald in a belief that Penda was the bigger threat to him than a resurgent Bernicia and Deira. This assumption was based on Eowa's own insecurity, as Penda had never shown any inclination for territorial gain against his brother. In fact Penda seems to have been firmly on the battlefield in most cases to raid and bring back wealth, not to increase the size of his own territory. Eowa, however, was likely competing with the reputation of Penda, and that reputation was attracting more warriors, allowing the Hwicce to grow in strength.

To the east of Penda was the land which would one day become the Middle Angles, but in the early part of the 640s it was a patchwork of smaller sub-kingdoms which were unable to compete with the machinations of the larger kingdoms. This group of smaller polities had been able to maintain their independence, most likely through the protection they provided as a buffer between the Saxon states in the south, and Angle nations. These small nations perhaps started as warbands, which were able to take over existing Brittonic tribal groups, removing the nobility and replacing it with their own. This is the same process that propelled the Iclingas nations now under Eowa and Penda; they were centred round a powerful family, which through its success attracted other members.

For these Middle Anglian nations, the rise of Penda was a source of discomfort as his increasing power and influence was upsetting the balance they relied on for their own existence. The introduction of a new authority and broker of wealth must have brought many of them to the conclusion that they could no longer maintain their own kingdoms through the good will of neighbours, but would now need to choose sides. These smaller nations were still tied to the traditional cultures of the Angles and Saxons, and had largely been ignored by the Christian missionaries, who focused their attention on Kent, Sussex, East Anglia and the Gewisse. The changing culture in these larger neighbouring nations may have provided an initial catalyst for the sub-kingdoms to side with Penda. It is also entirely possible that some of the nations closest to the Hwicce had already been absorbed into the larger nation through war, marriage, and oaths. The thegns and kings of the Middle Angles, who weren't keen on being subservient to the Iclingas, may have provided initial warnings to King Ecgric of East Anglia that Penda was on the move, giving the East Anglians five or six days to pull together their army and begin preparing their defences.

It would take Penda eight days to move his force to the East Anglian border, if he already had control of the right of way, but it would take much longer if he didn't have access or control through these lands. The route of advance was shadowing the initial route the Iclingas had taken on their march west, and in fact Penda and his army may well have ended up at Ickleton before crossing directly into East Anglia. At Ickleton stands an ancient bowl barrow just off the Icknield Way. This barrow and ditch has been weathered and ploughed for generations, but as Penda moved his army here the barrow would stand out in the landscape. The barrow provided a good spot for a sacrifice to appease any of the wights that stalked the land, and to show veneration for Icel, whom the town was named for. The sacrifice would be a simple affair, with Penda and others leaving food, ale, and medicinal plants at the barrow. With very few exceptions, it seems that the Angles did not employ a regular priestly class to see to the Heathen traditions, and that these duties fell to kings, thegns, and other leaders. Penda, as the king, led this service, which may also have been used to renew oaths between men as they marched towards battle.

The sacrifice may have been followed by other formal warriors' traditions on the eve of battle. The helmet found at Sutton Hoo, which has been linked with the Angle King Rædwald, included several depictions of warriors dancing. In these scenes, two men wear horned helmets with raven heads at the end of the horns. Each man carries a sword in an upright position, and two spears in the other hand, gripped in such a way to produce an 'X' shape, with the points aimed towards the ground. The men have their sword arms interlinked, apparently stepping toward one another. At the moment of contact the men have all of their weight on their front foot, while their rear foot is being dragged forward on the top of the toes. The imagery is developed to show the constant movement of the men and the image has been interpreted as a dance connected with warriors and Woden.

A similar image was found in Sweden, showing a single dancer, nearly identical to the Sutton Hoo men, along with a berserker. The biggest difference in this image is that the horned dancer from Sweden only has one eye, implying that this image is of Woden. Linking these images together, we may see the origin of the rite being between Woden and a berserker, but passed on to other warriors, who in turn conduct the rite in honour of Woden. The commonality of the dance imagery shows that it was widespread, and potentially a deep cultural practice amongst the Northern European tribes. Tacitus may have witnessed one of these dances hundreds of years before for he stated that 'youths who practise the sport bound in the dance amid swords and lances that threaten their lives'.[2] If the dance threatened the dancers' lives, it must have been conducted with speed and aggression, relying on the skills of those participating to keep themselves safe. Tacitus goes on to tell us that these dances were common at all events, and served both martial and spiritual purposes.

Back at Ickleton, these same types of dance were providing entertainment, along with mental, spiritual, and physical preparation for Penda's warriors as they readied themselves to attack East Anglia. The dances, accompanied by chanting, rhythmic striking of shields supported by the soft sounds of the lyre, would spread across the quiet landscape at night, perhaps picked up by East Anglian patrols out on the land. The haunting sounds would add a measure of fear and anxiety to the East Anglians, who knew that battle was imminent. The East Anglians could do nothing but wait for Penda and the Hwicce to emerge from the land and launch their attack.

A modern map of East Anglia appears to have a poor defensive position to the landward side. There are no hills, mountains, rivers or other natural barriers to slow an advancing army moving from the west. However, in the seventh century, East Anglia was endowed with formidable natural defences. The Fenlands to the north were significantly larger, filling in the low ground almost as far south as Cambridge. While parts of the Fens could be crossed, and pockets of solid ground existed, such as Ely, the majority was a lowland swamp. Some of it was permanently submerged, while other parts were susceptible to seasonal flooding, particularly in the winter. Throughout this era, the impact of the Dark Age Cold Period (DACP) generated wetter conditions, in particular through the middle part of the seventh century, with the 'most extreme phase of the DACP, an average was given as AD 625'.[3] This paints a picture of the Fenlands being at their wettest, and likely greatest range, during the first half of the seventh century. The available routes to and from East Anglia were constricted because of the fenlands to the north, and the East Saxons to the South. Coming from the west, this effectively left the Icknield Way as the only viable route in and out of the territory. The frontier of East Anglia was further protected by a significant earthwork ditch, providing a defensive position if an invading army was operating cross-country, forcing armies to stick to the roads. The ditch is now called the Devil's Dyke which,

> is a massive linear defensive earthwork 7.5 miles long running NW - SE, comprising a large bank, 12 - 18 feet high and up to 70 feet wide with a deep ditch on the SW side up to 17 feet deep and 65 feet wide.[4]

The Dyke ties together the southern point of the Fenlands at Reach to the town of Ditton Green. Its position would force an invading army to funnel onto the Icknield Way and deny the use of the open country to enemy forces. It seems possible that the Devil's Dyke was predated by other earthworks constructed by the Iceni tribe, but that these were significantly improved by the East Angles over time. The Devil's Dyke clearly tells us that East Anglia's strategy for self defence was one of a conventional front line, denying access to the nation. By providing a single point of advance, the East Anglian leaders would anchor their shield-wall to the Devil's Dyke and draw in the attacker to a point the East Anglian king controlled. This static defence system was rather novel in Britain at the time, with most nations relying on a defence in depth tactic, supported by isolated strong points. The Romans had used static defence in the north at Hadrian's Wall extremely effectively, but this required constant deployment of garrisons, and site maintenance. From an infrastructure standpoint, static border defences were expensive to build, operate and maintain. They required significant effort on behalf of the king in the resourcing, organizing and administering, something the Romans were very good at; but without a governmental administration, this would be difficult for the average Angle or Saxon kingdom.

The weakness of the East Anglian system was that it required early warning of an advancing army in order to garrison the Icknield Way, at the gap in the Devil's Dyke. Assuming that a small picket of riders was regularly maintained to provide early warning along the Icknield Way, the logical point would be at Worsted Lodge, where the Icknield Way intersects a Roman road, providing the East Angles the ability to identify threats from the north, south and west. Once an army was detected, the rider would have to set off at a breakneck pace to begin the alerting process. One would assume that before this final warning was required, the king and his thegns already had knowledge that an army was on the move through the messages from travellers and merchants. If this was the case, then the warning rider merely had to make it to the gap that had formed between the end of the Devil's Dyke and the southern shore of the Fenlands some thirteen kilometres away. The East Angles were relying on a complicated defence system requiring early intelligence, detection, alerting and rapid mobilization to an imminent threat, and finally the warriors available to fight at the gap. If any of these components failed, the East Angle kings would not be able to ensure the combat took place at the Devil's Dyke gap. This defensive system had to occur without the benefit of a bureaucratic administration, and was thus held together by the king and his thegns.

East Anglia had been ruled by the powerful King Rædwald until his death around AD 624. The defeat of Edwin's uncle Æthefrith at the River Idle in AD 616 effectively left Rædwald as the most powerful king in Britain. Rædwald's victory was the catalyst for generations of Deiran and Bernician power held first by Edwin and then Oswald. The destruction of Æthefrith also led to widespread peace and stability amongst the Angle and Saxon territories. No doubt conflict was still occurring, but in more isolated pockets, and not on the scale of a major battle. It is not a coincidence that there is an increase in nation-on-nation conflicts in the years after Rædwald's death as kings and warlords attempt to fill the power vacuum left in his wake.

King Rædwald's burial reflected the power he had achieved in life and is the most elaborate Angle grave ever found. It included grave goods from as far away as Byzantium; gold, silver, weapons, and an entire ship. This ship burial at Sutton Hoo is one of only three known ship burials in Britain, and shows the power and wealth of the East Anglian king, but also a connection with the ancestral home of the Angles in Scandinavia. The burial of a 90-foot ship, which would have been dragged up hill to its final location, required an immense amount of personnel, once again showing the importance of Rædwald and the power he had amassed during his reign.

Rædwald was, however, not infallible, and seems to have been rather indecisive and weak when put under direct pressure. Bede records the story of Rædwald nearly breaking his oath to Edwin when King Æthefrith,

> sent messengers to bribe that king with a great sum of money to murder him, but without effect. He sent a second and a third time, offering a greater bribe each time, and, moreover, threatening to make war on him if his offer should be despised. Rædwald, whether terrified by his threats, or won over by his gifts, complied with this request, and promised either to kill Edwin, or to deliver him up to the envoys.[5]

Edwin only escapes this fate because the Queen of East Anglia steps in on his behalf and upbraids Rædwald,

> for when he [Rædwald] had privately made known to the queen his intention of doing what I told you before, she dissuaded him from it, reminding him that it was altogether unworthy of so great a king to sell his good friend in such distress for gold, and to sacrifice his honour, which is more valuable than all other adornments, for the love of money.[6]

Unfortunately for the future kings of East Anglia, the tendency for indecisions, and moral challenges, would plague their dynasty, as would the aggression of Penda. Rædwald was succeeded by his son Eorpwald in AD 624; he was converted with the help of King Edwin, but he had a habit of oscillating between the Heathen and Christian faiths. His religious indecision eventually led to civil unrest and internal strife which culminated in his assassination, 'by one Ricbert, a Pagan'.[7] In the wake of the assassination, Ricbert may have held the throne for a few years, or Sigbert may have taken it as soon as he arrived from Gaul; unfortunately there is no record to confirm one way or the other. The fact that we don't know who held the throne following the death of Eorpwald speaks to the turmoil in East Anglia.

Eorpwald's brother Sigbert had fled to Gaul upon his brother taking the throne and, like Oswald, was a true believer in the Christian faith. Sigbert would have received word of his brother's demise, and from that point it was a race to secure the throne against other claimants. Upon his return to East Anglia and ascendency to the throne, Sigbert dedicated much time and effort to the conversion of the East Angles. Having reigned for a period of time, Sigbert, eventually,

> quitting the affairs of his kingdom, and committing them to his kinsman Ecgric, who before had a share in that kingdom, he entered a monastery, which he had built for himself, and having received the tonsure, applied himself rather to do battle for a heavenly throne.[8]

The swing between religions, and the irregularity of a king abdicating and selecting his successors, rather than the traditional succession processes, continued to act as agents of destabilization within East Anglia in the seventh century. Following the death of Rædwald in AD 624, East Anglia descended into almost twenty years of internal instability which ebbed and flowed as power changed hands, but was always lingering under the surface. Sigbert's abdication after what seems to be a period of success and stability for East Anglia was just another destabilizing factor for the kingdom. The internal discord may have been yet another attractor for Penda as he planned his annual campaigns.

The date and the location of Penda's first battle with East Anglia is unknown, but if the East Anglian defensive system was functional, then we should assume it occurred at the Devil's Dyke gap south-west of Newmarket. If the defensive system didn't work, or perhaps wasn't fully developed by this time, then the battle may have occurred anywhere along the Icknield Way between Newmarket and the Thetford forest to the north-east. The land here is flat, with limited defensive positions to be had, perhaps with the exception of a few scattered fords and woods. Based on what Bede tells us, it seems that the defensive system was functional, and that King Ecgric did have some early warning of the approaching force: 'The nation of the Mercians, under King Penda, made war on the East Angles; who finding themselves no match for their enemy, entreated Sigbert to go with them to battle, to encourage the soldiers.'[9]

Ecgric must have had access to some clear intelligence on the size and movement of Penda's army as it approached East Anglia in order to warrant removing Sigbert from the monastery. Sigbert responded to the request to lead the East Anglian army,

He was unwilling and refused, upon which they drew him against his will out of the monastery, and carried him to the army, hoping that the soldiers would be less afraid and less disposed to flee in the presence of one who had formerly been an active and distinguished commander.[10]

The monastery in question was likely at Bury St Edmunds, or as it would have been known to Sigbert, Beodericsworth. From this location, it would be a single day's march to the gap at the Devil's Dyke, where the army would wait for Penda to approach.

Sigbert's removal from the monastery shows a lack of trust in the abilities of Ecgric to lead the defence of the nation, providing further evidence of the internal strife in the nation. Pressing Sigbert back into service, and lacking trust in Ecgric, is a direct outcome of Ecgric not being chosen by the thegns, but instead being placed on the throne by Sigbert. The lack of trust between the thegns and their king must have impacted the morale of the warbands; none of this was a recipe for success, particularly against a renowned warlord like Penda. At the very top, the leadership of East Anglia seemed unsteady and divided, something Penda would be certain to take full advantage of.

With Sigbert pressed into service, the two armies finally came to a point of contact. As Penda approached the gap in the Devil's Dyke and the East Anglian shield-wall, he once again turned to the aggressive boar's head in order to punch a hole in the defender's line. This strategy would be particularly devastating against a defensive line which was already teetering on the edge of failure before they even arrived at the battlefield. Penda placed his own warband at the leading edge of the formation, and as he had done against Edwin, he was personally leading from the front. It was important that the first point of contact between Penda's boar's head and the enemy inflicted maximum damage, hopefully tearing a hole clean through their lines. The more confusion Penda could sow into the East Anglian lines the better. Before the shield-wall made contact, younger warriors, and the Herewulf warriors, skirmished out in front of the line, throwing spears and attempting to disrupt the defenders formed up in the shield-wall. The fearsome display by the Hwicce was in stark relief to that of the defenders. Sigbert had refused to carry a weapon into the battle, instead he 'would carry nothing in his hand but a wand'.[11] While his courage to go unarmed may have encouraged the most Christian of the East Angles, it would have been seen as a complete dereliction of his leadership duties by the hardened warriors. A king and leader's role was to fight and kill on the battlefield, not wave a stick around. Once again the destabilizing forces were at work within the East Anglian lines. As Penda led his men forward, the East Anglian forces were silent and wavering. While some men would be staunchly holding their ground, other men were unconsciously sliding backwards; this was not a line that would be able to take the weight of Penda's attack.

As the boar's head made contact with the East Anglian shield-wall, Penda and his chosen men at the tip of the attack hacked and slashed their way through Sigbert and Ecgric's line. The objective was to punch a hole in the centre of the line, allowing Penda and his best warriors access behind the East Anglian shield-wall, once this was achieved the slaughter would begin. The more confusion that Penda's attack could sow the better as it would give him and his most seasoned warriors the freedom to attack the defenders one on one.

The battle did not last long, and both Sigbert and Ecgric were killed. Based on the single line from Bede, it would appear that Sigbert and Ecgric did their duty leading from the front, Sigbert 'was killed with King Ecgric; and the pagans pressing on, all their army was either slaughtered or dispersed'.[12] The Angles, Saxons and Britons lived in a difficult world and were 'a quintessentially pragmatic people',[13] Sigbert's actions to ride into combat unarmed would have been seen as ridiculous by the Angle warriors. Sigbert was cut down with complete disdain. While the East Anglia defence system was advanced, its weaknesses now showed. Many men died on the field, but a large portion of the East Anglian army likely fled from the slaughter. Penda had no interest in their pursuit as this was not a battle for territorial dominance. With poor leadership and no defence in depth, the entire kingdom was left open to Penda to raid, but first he would collect weapons and wealth from the battlefield.

One of the most peculiar items from the Staffordshire hoard is the priest's head mount. This item is a small subconical mount with a column and apical disc, and

> bears a striking resemblance to the head-dress worn by the prophet Ezra in the well-known image in the *Codex Amiatinus*, one of three great Bibles written, with Bede's participation, at the monastery of Jarrow-Wearmouth, probably not long before 716.[14]

The headdress may have been a sign of higher authority within the church but was certainly not a common sight, 'there being no other evidence for similar headdresses in the Anglo-Saxon period, or indeed in the early church elsewhere'.[15] The spectacular cloisonne and gold work shares many similarities with items originating from East Anglia. The link to East Anglian craftsmen, and the clear special significance of the item, implies that it was not worn by an average member of the church. 'Bede states that the high-priest's headdress represented the "dignity of the priesthood" and might be seen as having connotations specifically of archiepiscopal authority'.[16] The single highest member of the church whose death can be directly linked to Penda is Sigbert of East Anglia.

It seems unlikely that the headdress was an Angle invention, and must have been based on a continental source, perhaps an illustration in a manuscript. Before devoting his life to the Church, King Sigbert,

> ascended the throne, being desirous to imitate the good institutions which he had seen in Gaul, he founded a school wherein boys should be taught letters, and was assisted therein by Bishop Felix, who came to him from Kent, and who furnished them with masters and teachers after the manner of the people of Kent.[17]

With his personal knowledge and connections to both Canterbury, and Gaul, it would seem plausible that Sigbert had seen similar items either in text or in person. While we are told Sigbert was armed only with a simple wand to lead the army against Penda, it would make sense he was also armed with the power of his religion,

> a head-dress symbolizing spiritual leadership, as Bede envisaged, would be a powerful and necessary symbol of ecclesiastical authority. Significantly, in the case of the Staffordshire example, this is enhanced by the assumption of the visual vocabulary and appearance of insignia associated with contemporary secular authority.[18]

Sigbert the former king, devoted to his religious faith, with his exposure to continental culture would seem a worthy owner of such a remarkable item, particularly as he leads the East Anglian army against King Penda.

The defeat of Ecgric and Sigbert's army left East Anglia open to raiding by Penda's forces. Penda marched his army further into East Anglia, and established a defensive position along his route of retreat. From this key point he was able to send raiding warbands out into the country to bring back whatever wealth could be gathered. The initial target for the raid could have been Exning. This town may have been the primary garrison for the Devil's Dyke Gap. Looking farther back, it is claimed that this was the capital of the Iceni, and the home of Boudicca during the Roman occupation. There are connections between Exning and the East Angle Wuffingas dynasty as one of King Anna's daughters is reported to have been born there in AD 631. Penda's raids could easily have reached the monastery at Beodericsworth, perhaps making off with some of the gold items housed at the monastery. While Penda had destroyed the East Anglian army, he didn't press the advantage as Cadwallon had following the defeat of

Edwin. There is no record of him reaching the royal township and Rendlesham or the powerful monastery at Cnobheresburg, leaving the impression that the raid was localized. This action against East Anglia was not about conquering land, but was a true raid conducted to carry wealth back to Hwicce. Following the raid, Penda turned the army around and returned to his home with weapons and wealth in plentiful supply, ready for distribution to his warriors and thegns.

The Catholic and Anglican churches assigns 29 October as St Sigbert's Day, which is likely the day that he was martyred at the Devil's Dyke. The date is interesting as it implies a few details we otherwise wouldn't know from this campaign; the first is how late in the campaign season this is as the vast majority of serious combat events happen before September ends. The late date may be a sign that Penda was restricted in his advance, and may have had to bring the minor nations of the East Angles under his control in order to continue the march to the east. Second, the late date would likely require Penda to turn back towards Hwicce in short order to ensure the fords didn't swell to high. Third, if Penda had to fight his way to the East Angles, he clearly had a large force capable of sustained action. Fourth, the length of time it took him to move across the land must have given Ecgric ample time to draw his forces together. Finally, Penda's limited action after the battle may have been driven by the lack of time before winter truly set in.

The ease with which Penda had destroyed the most prepared defence in Britain, and one of the most powerful Angle nations, would have alarmed all of the kings in Britain. Penda had crossed a vast distance and was still able to overwhelm a well prepared defence, meaning almost no nation was safe from him. Eowa would have been particularly distressed by the success of his brother, and wondered if one day the Hwicce army would march against him. North of the Humber, Oswald must have been considering what to do about Penda. Oswald had nominal control of the lands north of the Humber, an oath from Eowa south of the Humber, and an alliance with the Gewisse. The only areas that weren't under his influence were the Britons of the west, Kent, East Anglia, and Penda. Of all these nations only Penda remained a Heathen, and only he seemed to present a real threat to the security of other kingdoms. There were minor nations which were beyond Oswald's reach, but many of these were inconsequential to him or the general equation of power on the island.

With the death of Ecgric and Sigbert, King Anna took the throne in East Anglia. King Anna was Sigbert's cousin, and was inheriting a deeply divided kingdom which had just received its heaviest defeat, perhaps in living memory. East Anglia had spent much of its recent past looking across the sea to the continent and gathering its wealth through trade rather than war. The nation had developed a complacency towards its island neighbours which was born first from the dominance of Rædwald, and harboured by the reliance on a prepared, but deeply flawed, defensive system. Sheltered on the extremity of Britain, the East Angles were able to dedicate greater effort developing a physical culture around expert craftsmen, producing helmets, weapons, jewellery and other items of the most exquisite nature. However, their weakness had now been shown, and King Anna, Ecgric's successor, would now be in search of alliances in order to prevent any further predation by Penda and the Hwicce. King Anna, like Sigbert, was a devout Christian and he ensured that Sigbert's body was removed from the battlefield and returned to the monastery at Beodericsworth where he was interred, and eventually venerated as a Saint.

By the winter of AD 641, Penda, the 35-year-old king of the Hwicce, had killed three kings and defeated two more in Cynegils and Cwichelm. This was his fifteenth year as an independent warlord and he had established himself as perhaps the finest leader of men in combat anywhere in Britain. Over these fifteen years, Penda had earned his reputation as a feared warrior, but equally he doesn't appear to be the bloodthirsty enemy that many of the stories of the period suggest. In fifteen years he had been on a warpath only five times, two of which were not necessarily of his own volition, but required by oath. The remaining three times were not wars of destruction and conquering, but raids to gather wealth, something that was expected of all kings and thegns in this era. The record shows him to be measured in his conduct and no more aggressive than any other king of the age. What sets him apart from the majority is his success and his unwavering dedication to his ancient culture. In this age, kings were required to fight with their men and put themselves at great risk, or face the loss of their kingdom to internal forces. In large battles, this increased the risk to the king, and the opportunity for him to be struck down, ending his reign. Penda ap Pyb, the 'Son of Danger', clearly didn't shirk these front-line duties.

As kings all around him vied for power, many turned to conversion as a method of establishing internal control and external alliances. Many of these men were not true believers like Oswald and Sigbert, but instead men looking for power. Penda stands out because he never sought power or authority from any person or system, instead relying on his own abilities, while keeping closely tied to his ancestral ways. As AD 641 closed, all the nations of Britain would begin to see Penda as a threat to their power. His ability to successfully attack Ecgric and Sigbert in East Anglia showed he could reach all corners of Britain. Penda's steadfast resistance to conversion was also a concern for the converted kings, who saw Penda as a destabilizing force and a focal point for Heathen resistance in their own nations.

Chapter Ten
Oswald's Tree

While we can establish the month and day that Penda attacked East Anglia, we can't effectively determine the year; it seems that it likely occurred in AD 640 or AD 641, but a definitive answer is not presented in the historical record. By looking at future events, we may be able to align the date more accurately. Penda's raid was highly alarming to many of the nations in Britain, and he had proved that neither distance nor a well-prepared defensive system could contain him. In spite of his martial prowess and dominance, Penda had continued to live up to the commitments and alliances he had in place, and showed no outward signs of aggression directed at the Gewisse, the western Britons, nor his brother Eowa.

Oswald's reach throughout Britain would have given him precise knowledge of the events at the Devil's Dyke Gap. The king of Bernicia was no fool and he would be analyzing the East Anglian failure, and imagining how a similar raid would play out north of the Humber. Oswald was well aware of the stories of Cadwallon's invasion and predation across Deira, and he could easily imagine that Penda would bring the same destruction north of the Humber. Oswald was not willing to invite Penda north, and he probably believed pre-emptive action was the only way to keep Penda at bay.

The level of concern that Penda's foray into East Anglia generated would drive an immediate response from Oswald. Penda had been successful against East Anglia, but he still suffered some losses, and he would be keen to rest his force and replace the warriors he had lost. Since becoming a leader of warbands, and then an independent nation Penda had only once campaigned on successive years, and this was at the behest of Cadwallon. On all other occasions, Penda would conduct a campaign and then retire to Hwicce for several years before venturing out again. There is no reason to suspect anything different following the raid on East Anglia. In fact, the sheer distance the force had travelled coupled with the success they had achieved, would leave Penda and his thegns feeling comfortable with a year of rest, or at least a year of smaller scale raids in more local areas.

Oswald on the other hand saw immediate action as a distinct possibility, which would prevent Penda from rebuilding his force as one of his advantages. If he moved quickly he could catch Penda and his force in a weaker state. Oswald could not let that opportunity slip past. It would be inconceivable that Oswald would leave Penda alone in the year following the attack on East Anglia; to give Penda a window of time in which to regenerate his forces was tantamount to inviting him to invade Deira in the next campaigning season. The available records state that in AD 642 Oswald and Penda came into direct conflict, and it is for that reason that AD 641 must have been the year Penda attacked East Anglia.

Through the winter of AD 641 Oswald was planning his next actions against Penda, and trying to decide if aggressive movement or defensive preparation was the way to succeed. Oswald sought counsel from his thegns and his priests, weighing his options between attacking or preparing a robust defence. The debates would have been hotly contested at Bebbanburg and Yeavering, with many thegns siding with defensive preparations as the less risky tactic. In any of his strategic options, Oswald knew he needed to gather a larger force than he had used against Cadwallon. He could draw warriors from many of the northern kingdoms, including the Picts, and Scoti, and perhaps Britons from Strathclyde and Rheged, along with the men of Bernicia, and whatever remained of Deira's warbands. It seems likely that Eowa was also in an alliance of sorts with Oswald, and would provide some military force. Perhaps in return he would be handed Penda's lands, thus uniting the two Iclingas kingdoms. That outcome would put Oswald in near total control of the island with the exception of the south-east Saxon nations of Sussex, Essex and Kent.

From a defensive strategy, Oswald could opt to garrison the eastern route through Doncaster. This had been the more traditional avenue for armies to move north and south and was the site of many significant battles through the ages. The trouble with this defensive strategy is that it left Oswald in an all-or-nothing posture; if he lost, the route to the north was open, and a direct replay of what happened when Edwin fell to Penda's sword would occur. Penda in this scenario would be able to immediately sack York, before threatening Deira's heartland, and then push north to Bernicia. A secondary strategy would be to garrison the walled cities of Deira such as York and attempt to ambush Penda throughout Deira, before retreating north of the Tyne, and then starting the process all over again. This strategy would sacrifice Deira in the interest of Bernicia and leave the country open to unmitigated raiding, something Oswald needed to avoid in order to maintain order across the nations north of the Humber.

On the other hand, Oswald could elect to go on the offensive using aggression and surprise to tackle the Hwicce threat before it turned up on his borders. If he decided on aggression, he could move through Eowa's territory by way of Doncaster, then Lincoln, and from there move south-east along the Roman road called the Fosse Way and hope to catch Penda unaware. This would require Oswald to maintain a measure of secrecy as he moved his army south of the

Humber, something that would be difficult to do on the key north-south route. Marching a force along this busy route would attract the attention of people and his movements could not remain secret for long. Word that an army was marching down Ermine Street towards Lincoln would be broadcast far and wide, leading to a loss of surprise. Without the element of surprise, Penda would be able to select the battlefield along his route and mount a challenge against the invasion.

However, there was another less used route open to Oswald along the western shore, north of the River Mersey. The benefit of the western route was that it stood a better chance for Oswald to disguise the movements of his army's route and protect the element of surprise. From the western route, Oswald would also be able to gather a force from Eowa before moving either south against Penda, or west against Gwynedd depending on the viability of the attacks and likelihood of success. If Oswald could move fast enough and keep his movements largely unseen, he would be able to catch Penda unaware and replicate his previous success against Cadwallon. When he faced Cadwallon, Oswald was certainly the underdog, and his victory was born not through the selection of the battlefield or a pitched battle, but through speed, surprise and aggression.

Oswald would need to gather his force in a single location before marching, to protect the individual components of the army. If he allowed them to march separately to a position close to the final battle, each warband would be at risk of ambush against superior local forces. This style of conflict would grind down Oswald's force before it ever had an opportunity to face Penda in a battle between armies. For the most part, this was a simple endeavour as the majority of the army's component pieces came from the north; Eowa and his warbands were the exception. Eowa would have to move north, rendezvous with Oswald and then march south with combined force in an effort to destroy Penda. It would be entirely natural for Oswald to have had some concerns about Eowa's reliability in a fight against his brother where there had been no previous conflict. He must have also worried about Eowa's warband as a potential leak of information which could easily be shared amongst neighbours. The best way to handle these issues would be to draw Eowa and his warbands into the greater army early so that they couldn't be lobbied and swayed in the weeks leading up to the campaign. Unfortunately for Oswald, the effort to keep things under wraps failed, and Penda was able to achieve a comprehensive understanding of Oswald's plan to attack across the River Mersey and push south.

Once he gained knowledge of Oswald's plan to attack, Penda had to call his thegns in rapidly to begin mobilizing the warbands and ensure he could meet the threat presented by an invading army. We know from Bede that the Battle of Maserfield occurred on 5 August AD 642.[1] From this detail we can look backwards and see that both men must have spent the spring and early summer preparing for the battle, mobilizing men, supplies, and trying to gather as much intelligence of the other side. One of Oswald's biggest concerns was keeping his plan under wraps and to disguise his movements and mobilization, but ultimately he failed at this task. Penda kept his eye on Eowa and his people, looking for any sign that he was preparing to connect with Oswald's northern army.

At some point Eowa was compelled to gather his warbands and move north to join Oswald and his force north of the Mersey. The distance Penda would have to cover, along with the delay of getting information about the move, would put him at a distinct disadvantage, perhaps to the point that he wouldn't be able to control any part of the confrontation. It appears that Penda could have committed early on, and pre-positioned his warbands north before Eowa moved, perhaps to Chester to lie in wait. This would have been a serious gamble should Oswald choose to approach down the eastern corridor, but Penda had enough awareness of the invasion plan to feel comfortable in moving his army to cover off the western route. In reference to Penda and the actions at Maserfield, Nennius states that he gained an understanding of the actions of Oswald by using 'Diabolical agency'.[2] This could be taken literally as a reference to Penda's Heathen ways, and some support from his gods, wights and ancestors; or may have been a reference to the fact that he seemed to know things about the movements of Oswald that were supposedly concealed, allowing him to select the ground for the fight and deny Oswald the benefit of surprise.

Based on the limited information around the battle and the timing of events, Penda must have marched first to gain a positional advantage over his enemy. His deep connections with the Britons allowed him to use the western country to move quickly and relatively covertly with limited concern about being reported to either Eowa or Oswald. A Welsh poem, the 'Marwnad Cynddylan', written shortly after the events at Maserfield, seems to allude to the Britons joining Penda. The poem is a lament for the death of Cynddylan ap Cyndrwyn, a prince of a Powys sub-kingdom identified as Pengwern. Pengwern is generally placed somewhere near Shrewsbury and Wroxeter, which would be on the route Penda needed to take as he moved north to confront Oswald. The Welsh poem tells how Cynddylan responded to Penda, 'When the son of Pyd requested, he was so ready'.[3] The implication here is that Penda has gained the added weight of Cynddylan and his men to confront Oswald. Pengwern, like Powys and Gwynedd, had previously benefited from Penda and Cadwallon's defeat of Edwin's forces at Cefn Digoll, and may have felt compelled to help against the new threat from the north. The connection to Pengwern may have gone deeper, it is feasible that this was the land of Penda's mother.

Penda was now relying on both the skills he learned from Cadwallon, and the years of experience working with combined Angle and Briton armies to full use. Chester seems a likely location to establish an initial camp before crossing the River Mersey. From Chester, Penda was able to move his army directly to a crossing at the River Mersey near Warrington. This would have been a long day, marching twenty-eight kilometres, and likely at the extreme range of what was possible. Warrington, or more accurately Wilderspool, had been a Roman town and perhaps a fort at a crucial ford on the River Mersey. Wilderspool was certainly a Roman settlement, and an industrial centre focused on clay work, metallurgy, and glass.[4] It seems that the settlement's primary function was to supply the Roman forces to the north with all of the material they needed to garrison Hadrian's Wall. The site was occupied by the Romans until sometime around AD 318 when it was abandoned as the Roman Empire began to withdraw from Britain.[5] As Penda arrived here, he entered a ruined city with some stone buildings partially standing, but devoid of any Angle or Briton presence. On the north side of the river was more stonework, and a small fort to control the ford. The ruins provided a suitable location for an army to rest, as they could be used for shelter, and defence. The Angles called this place Læccford, or 'Boggy stream ford', it is the lowest fordable point on the River Mersey, and as such was a crucial strategic point. After resting at Læccford, Penda moved his army north along the Roman road and into the region of Maserfield.

Maserfield is an anglicized interpretation of the Brittonic word 'Maguir', which is 'wall, perhaps in the sense of ruins, remains'.[6] The ruins this location refers to are unknown, but may have been at Wigan and connected to the Roman fort there, or at another unidentified location to the south between Winwick and Wigan. This area includes a stretch of road extending twelve kilometres; it is along this section of Roman road that the battle likely occurred. The *Chronica Majora* gives us one more tantalizing clue about the location of the actual combat, 'a severe battle having been committed by a pagan king of the Mercians, Penda, in a disadvantageous place'.[7] This single line seems to allude to Penda having distinct advantage on the selection of the location, certainly leading to the assumption that Penda arrived first and was able to choose the battlefield to maximize his tactical advantage. A number of sites along the road may provide such an advantage.

The first place would be at Wigan, and utilizing the ruins of the Roman fortress. This approach would look similar to how Rædwald had utilized the decaying Roman fortress at Bawtry to defeat Edwin at the River Idle. Penda could anchor one of his flanks along the Roman ruins, funnelling Oswald directly to the centre of his line. A secondary option is closer to the south end of the road at a place called 'Red Bank'. At this position, the road intersects a footpath heading due east, and only one kilometre along this path is a spring called St Oswald's Well. The main road descends down into a depression and is generally surrounded by high banks. On the west side there is a small brook which forms a horseshoe bend, and surrounds some high ground, providing an excellent point to establish a front line. For the army arriving in the battlefield second, their front line would be highly constricted and unable to fully set an effective formation to advance forward. The tactical advantage of the location was acknowledged during the English Civil War, when a parliamentarian force set a pitched battle in this exact location in 1648.

As an advantageous location for a pitched battle and an ambush, Red Bank seems nearly ideal. Detaching some of his Brittonic forces into the woods east of the battlefield would allow them to pick off retreating men who may try to flee eastward along the footpath. This detachment would also provide a reserve element which could be launched into the flank of Oswald's line if they were able to establish an effective shield-wall. From Red Bank, the road is straight for one and a half kilometres, eliminating the opportunity for Oswald to surprise Penda. Additionally, Penda must have pushed a small picket north somewhere near Ashton-in-Makerfield to provide a warning of Oswald moving south. With his forward pickets properly positioned, Penda would have gained a two or three hour window to set his trap before the arrival of Oswald at Red Bank.

The opposing force had a long trek to get to Red Bank; assuming Oswald had initially set out from Bebbanburg or Yeavering, this was a 300 kilometre march in a westerly and then southerly movement. However, in order to draw in a larger force he may have been forced to march south first to Leeds or York, before turning west, and then south again; this route was around 340 kilometres. The need to absorb Eowa into the force would suggest that this later route was the more likely. The Angles measured time 'according to the course of the moon'.[8] This is important, as working backwards from the date it would seem that Oswald departed for the campaign on the July full moon, 17 July AD 642. As a matter of mobilization, such a recognizable point in time would have been beneficial and allowed all parties to get underway as needed. Without calendars at hand, the thegns would be directed to muster their men on the appropriate full moon and prepare to depart. The full army would form up in Leeds at around the end of July and then begin its move to the west and then south. If the target was to attack Penda in his territory, then this route march would have put Oswald in Hwicce territory on the full moon in August AD 642, based on covering around twenty kilometres per day. Oswald was still unaware that Penda was waiting north of the Mersey, and must have thought he still had surprise on his side.

The Roman ruins at Wigan were an appropriate location for the army to rest before crossing the River Mersey and really entering land where enemy forces may be present. The moment Oswald entered Wigan, Penda would have been made aware of the presence of the army, and was readying his forces for action. When Oswald began to move south, he would be able to see Penda about one kilometre back from Red Bank if the Hwicce were on the road, allowing Oswald to dedicate some effort and time to readying for the battle. Penda would benefit more from staying off the road and remaining partially hidden to allow Oswald to enter the killing field, and then being forced to conduct a hasty tactical set up.

Once Oswald became aware of the trap he would have had to begin drawing his force up into a shield-wall countering the position Penda had established. The Bernician king was well aware that his position was not good, but he may have been confident enough that he could face Penda's force, after all their shield-wall was only positioned on a slight rise, and the brook separating the two armies could be easily waded. Once Oswald had assembled his force into a shield-wall and began to advance against Penda, Cynddylan and his Britons could start launching ranged weapons into the flank and rear of Oswald's lines. As Oswald's combined force crossed Newton Brook, Penda pressed his line forward to take advantage of the poor footing Oswald's men would experience as they crossed the small waterway, and the confusion being caused by the Britons in their rear area. The combination of poor footing and multiple attacks from the flanks and rear of Oswald's line was swinging the battle quickly in Penda's favour.

As Oswald lost men, his line began to slowly move rearward under the weight of Penda's attack. This would prove fatal to them, as they weren't watching their feet, the brook caused men to fall, and the line started to become ragged. In quick order Oswald lost control of his army, the line started to break, pockets of men started to flee, while others attempted to stand and fight; the rout was now on. Fugitives from Oswald's army scattered, some going north, but others seeing the footpath to the west as a way out of trouble, found the woods teeming with Cynddylan's men. The Britons waited until the enemy was committed to going west before springing the ambush. Oswald's more seasoned men knew that keeping their ranks together was the best hope, but these warriors would inevitably come undone by the volume of attackers facing them.

Oswald stood with the line for the duration of the battle, before becoming wounded and unable to fight anymore,

> for when he was beset with the weapons of his enemies, and perceived that death was at hand, he prayed for the souls of his army. Whence it is proverbially said, 'Lord have mercy on their souls,' said Oswald, as he fell to the ground.[9]

Oswald may have been gravely wounded at the moment of his prayer, perhaps losing an arm in combat. Two kings died at Maserfield, 'in which fell Eowa, son of Pybba, his brother, king of the Mercians and Oswald, King of the North-men'.[10] Nennius also provides one of the crucial clues to the connection between Eowa and Oswald: 'Penda, son of Pybba, reigned ten years; he first separated the kingdom of Mercia from that of the North-men.'[11] The full political ramifications of the events at Maserfield would echo for generations, as would the stories of Oswald's treatment in the aftermath of the battle. We are told by Bede that after Oswald's death, 'the king who slew him commanded his head, and hands, with the arms, to be cut off from the body, and set upon stakes'.[12] This is a grim occasion, and while Bede reports on the event, it isn't recorded in the *Anglo-Saxon Chronicles*, the *Historia Anglorum*, the *Historia Brittonum*, *Annales Cambriae*, or the *Ulster Chronicle*. The dismemberment and display of a defeated king also doesn't appear to have any other contemporary occurrences, putting it well outside general cultural practices. Throughout all of the battles fought by Penda, this is the only occasion when such an act is claimed to have occurred.

Scholars and authors often view this event as a sacrifice by Penda to Woden, and perhaps that is the case, but then the dismemberment doesn't make sense. Sacrifice by Germanic people certainly did occur, but these highly ritualized acts occurred either by drowning, or hanging, where the body was hung in its complete state in a tree. Observation of human sacrifice by Germanic people can be found as early as the second century during a war between the Germanic tribes, including the Cimbri, and the Roman legions near the Rhone river valley, 'the horses themselves were drowned in whirlpools, and men, with nooses fastened around their necks, were hanged from trees'.[13] The Cimbri come from Jutland, and are closely related, if not in fact part of the Angles and Jutes. Human sacrifice is also mentioned as late as the eleventh century by Adam of Bremmen, who records the process at the holy site of Uppsala, where sacrificed people and animals were once again hung in the trees. The connection with Woden in hanging sacrifices is clear, and tied to his own self-sacrifice in Yggdrasil to gain wisdom and sight. The practice of sacrifice is to give something of value to the gods, portions of a corpse, or even a corpse itself holds no value, and thus would not be appropriate sacrifices. The value of the sacrifice is in the giving of the life.

If a sacrifice had been made to Woden, Oswald would have had to be alive when he left the field, and then hung in an appropriate tree, preferably an ash tree, the same tree as the world tree, Yggdrasil. The north-east corner of the battlefield is a farm field now which is called 'Gallows Croft'. The actual origin of the field name seems to be uncertain, with local references being to the hanging of soldiers during the Civil War. However, to date there have been no archaeological findings to support this. A second origin could be closer to 1066 as criminals were hung at the edge of territories as a warning. But we should not eliminate the potential that the origin is still older than this. This could be the location of 'Oswald's Tree' if he or others were hung following the battle. If he was dismembered and staked, this position would be appropriate as a warning or boundary. In the period before conversion, Heathen custom was to hang criminals at crossroads in order to confuse the spirit of the deceased; once again if Oswald's corpse was left here, it may have been a spiritual punishment.

North of the battle site is Ashton-in-Makerfield. The 'Ashton' component of the name would have related to an ash of some stature, which would be an appropriate place for a sacrifice. If we can rely on Bede about the placement of Oswald on stakes, then this was not religiously driven, but done out of rage; it was a sign marking the fall of Northumbrian power. It seems quite likely that the story is a fabrication, possibly to ensure Oswald's martyrdom was equal to those of other saints. St Alban, St Justus, St Denis, St Blaise, were all beheaded, and all were stories Bede was familiar with. Oswald's particularly gruesome ending was one that Bede thought was most appropriate for a man as saintly as the late king.

A less theological driver may have pushed the need for the story of dismemberment in order to explain how the relics of Oswald became scattered in several locations. 'Bede's emphasis should perhaps be seen as a deliberate effort to explain the fragmentation of a body, which did in fact lead to a confusing multiplicity of relic-claims.'[14]

A short document written in the mid-eleventh century lists the final resting places of eighty-nine saints. This document records Oswald's resting place as Bebbanburg, Durham and Gloucester. Interestingly only Bebbanburg seems to be original, with the latter two locations added after the document was completed. This implies that the list of saints' resting places 'seems originally to have claimed that Oswald rested at Bamburgh intact'.[15]

There is no doubt that Penda was a warrior, capable of great violence, but the events following the death of Oswald simply don't fit with Penda's previous conduct and don't hold up as a religious sacrifice. Leaving the most probable conclusion that the dismemberment and display of Oswald's corpse was a fictional addition to the story, based out of both the theological and explanatory needs of the church. Penda became a scapegoat to account for the Christian churches early 'cult of fragmentary corporeal relics'.[16] This practice included the dismemberment and display of body parts upon death of saintly figures. This macabre activity was initially a practice the early church supported, but at a later date no longer embraced and wanted to eliminate.

The usual site referenced as the location for the Battle of Maserfield is Oswestry. The key piece of evidence for this connection is the etymology of the name which is 'Oswalds-tree'. However, a number of things stand out with the setting of Oswestry as the site of the battle. For starters its location: Oswestry is miles away from the Roman road system which would form a critical part of moving armies across Britain, and played a significant role in the majority of battles in the seventh century. The second big question is why would Oswald march an army to a location where he would be surrounded by enemies? At Oswestry he would have no route of retreat and find enemies all around should there be some mishap. The location would also force him to protect his logistics corridor, which would be under constant threat from Gwynedd, Powys, and to a lesser extent Hwicce. If there were a string of battles starting in the north and moving southward it may explain how Oswald ended up in Oswestry, but that is not the case. Instead, the campaign seems to include only one isolated phase of combat, the Battle of Maserfield.

Aside from the obvious geo-political, logistic, and tactical barriers to support Oswestry as the site of Maserfield, there is also cultural reasons to dispute it. Oswald and his Northumbrian supremacy was the enemy of Gwynedd, Powys, and the future kingdom of Mercia. Why would any of these nations seek to commemorate him through a place name? The only people who would wish to memorialize him, and by extension his nation, would be Christian members of the cult of St Oswald, which did not form until long after his death. A cult site placed in Shropshire under the influence of Northumbrian power may have been used as a conversion tool, specifically directed at Powys, Gwynedd, and other Britons who still weren't directly attached to the Roman church. The connections between Oswald at Oswestry is a political and religious tool, but has no tie to the actual events.

In the year following the Battle of Maserfield, Oswald's kingdom was parted once again into Deira and Bernicia, similar to the process that followed the death of Edwin. The Bernician throne was handed to Oswald's brother Oswiu, and the Deiran throne passed to Oswine who was 'of the race of King Edwin'.[17] According to Bede, one of Oswiu's first acts as a leader was to return to the Maserfield battleground in AD 643 and recover the body of Oswald. This story lends more credence to the battle occurring north of the Mersey and not in Oswestry, Shropshire. Oswiu would have been forced to march deep into Mercian territory to recover Oswald's corpse if Oswestry was the scene of the battle, and would have faced some serious confrontation from Mercia and the Britons. However, the battle site at Red Bank would provide Oswiu with the ability to revisit the location and recover Oswald without fear of confrontation. Oswiu's recovery of Oswald is also recorded in the *Vita Sancti Oswaldi*, written in the twelfth century by Reginald of Durham. In this account, Oswiu arrives at the battle site and struggles to identify Oswald's remains. A giant bird swoops down, picks up an arm and drops it near an ash tree, which from that day is resistant to rot. The bird returns and grabs a second arm; this one is dropped in a field and a spring flows from the ground. In this tale, the ash may be the one from which Ashton takes its name. The spring, one kilometre from Red Bank, named St Oswald's Spring, must surely be the location where the second arm was dropped. This story is interesting as it has clear connections with the Angles' indigenous religion, and shows a blending of Heathen and Christian cultures.

Following the battle, Penda received the spoils from the field which were stripped from the dead, including weapons, and any silver or gold items. Penda will have seen his brother Eowa dead on the field, and now had some big decisions to take related to his future kingdom, and they needed to happen immediately. Upon the death of a king, thegns, princes in exile, and other kings all began to plot and scheme to acquire the throne. In order to unite the Iclingas kingdoms, Penda would have to move quickly and take possession of Eowa's territory in order to see off any other contenders for the throne. If he delayed, the throne would be taken by someone, likely with the backing of a foreign power. The nations north of the Humber were now trying to establish their own kings, and would not have the time to participate in the selection of Eowa's successor. East Anglia had also traditionally acted as a king maker, but they were still reeling from their defeat by Penda the year prior. The weakening of East Anglian, Deiran, and Bernician power all boded well for Penda as he sought to claim Eowa's throne, though an internal challenger could still surface and make a claim on the kingdom. Once the dead were sorted out and the riches were removed from the field, Penda turned his army south to march on Tamworth, the centre of Eowa's power, and the home of the Tomsæta. Over the next 200 years, Tamworth would become the hub of Mercian power, and was likely in use as a key power centre by the earlier Iclingas, including King Ceorl and King Eowa. Tamworth's true value was its access to the Roman road system; from this base of operation, an army was able to march on all quarters of Britain, while preventing easy exploitation of the roads by other kings.

Penda would bring his army back across the Mersey and then to Chester. At Chester the spoils of war may have been shared amongst the Britons, who then went their own way. From Chester, it was a five-day travel to Tamworth on a direct route, which passed the future site of the Staffordshire hoard. It seems reasonable that Penda's force may have set up its final camp near to the Staffordshire hoard location before finally arriving at Tamworth. In fact, stopping near the site would keep the army hidden in the woods, and make a final day of travel requiring a seventeen kilometre march to finish the trip. It could be during this moment that Penda first saw the location where the hoard would be interred. Once in Tamworth, Penda would declare himself as the king, and send messages to the thegns and nobles to join him at Tamworth. He would also send word to his own home in the south to ensure they received news of his success. Penda appears to have been successful in his claim, as there is nothing recorded which speaks to internal conflict following the death of Eowa. The lack of conflict at any point up to Maserfield between Eowa and Penda may be one of the reasons why the historical sources don't agree on the length of Penda's reign.

To consolidate his power, Penda needed to put trusted men into positions as thegns, these men would in turn project his power throughout the new land. Eowa's trusted thegns and warriors had died with him at Maserfield, leaving a decapitated nation, and an opportunity for other men to rise to the tasks at hand. Penda would be looking for a mix of supportive locals, and his own men from Hwicce to move into the vacant settlements and halls throughout the land.

The word 'Hwicce' is expected to occur in place names in Oxfordshire, in places such as Wychwood and Ascott-under-Wychwood; but the name also turns up much farther north on a general line from Wrexham to Peterborough including Wych Brook, Whiston, Wychnor, Whissendine, and Witchley Hundred. Between Tamworth and Hereford we also find Lutwyche Hall, Ledwyche, Wychavon, Wychbold, and Wychbury Hill. Only four of the places listed fall into the bounds of what is usually considered Hwicce territories. The other seven place names which are far beyond the Hwicce territory do seemingly align with the general boundaries of the seventh-century Kingdom of Mercia. The seven outliers may have been generated following Penda's accession to the throne, and the establishment of power in Eowa's kingdom through the importation of thegns from Hwicce to govern the land. These new arrivals brought with them a connection to their ancestral Hwicce home, and caused the tribal name to be attached to these more northern areas. Linking the outer limits of these Hwicce-based place names creates a territory of 17,000 square kilometres, centred on modern-day Birmingham, with Tamworth only slightly north of the centre point. This is the equivalent of 35,000 hides, 'units of assessment for taxation and other public burdens'.[18] The term itself comes from an old term for family or household, with one hide considered to be the amount of land required to support a household, about 120 acres per hide. The 35,000 hides is tantalizingly close to the hidage assigned to Mercia by the rather mysterious, but near contemporary *Tribal Hidage* document, which appears to be some form of taxation document drawn up between the seventh and ninth centuries and states that Mercia is 30,000 hides, and the Hwicce 7,000 hides, for a total of 37,000 hides.[19]

For the first time since Pybba lost his kingdom in AD 597, an Iclingas king was reigning on his own accord, without subservience to other powers. Penda's ability to link the Hwicce and Eowa's lands quickly and effectively placed him at the head of an enormous new nation, with powerful warbands, and loyal cadre of thegns. This new nation was diverse, sheltering Britons, Angles, Heathens, Christians, and various combinations of all of these cultures and languages. Leading these people was the most powerful king in Britain: Penda. As had played out so many times before, the death of one king fundamentally changed the entire power dynamic across the island. With Oswald's death, the connections between Deira, Bernicia, and Gewisse died, releasing the encirclement of Penda, and placing all the other kingdoms in orbit around Penda, but isolated and alone against his increasing power. A period of frantic diplomacy would follow as nations sought to protect themselves against their powerful neighbour, but also to increase their own authority by gaining supremacy over their neighbours. This process was made more difficult by Penda's strategic control of the primary Roman road system through the centre of Britain. From the moment Penda gained control of Eowa's territories, communication by sea became the only viable connection between the nations north of the Humber, East Anglia and the Saxon south coast.

Chapter Eleven

Cenwalh

Penda's life was truly beholden to the Norns. There were moments where he was the catalyst behind actions, where he chose a direction and brought others with him, forcing them to take steps and make difficult decisions. In equal measure he found himself immersed in events that he seemingly had no control over, events that twisted and changed, propelled by the unseen, where decisions were limited and all he could do was move in a direction. Some moments started well, and ended well; some started well, sunk into the realm of disaster, and then rebounded with riches he couldn't fully appreciate in the moment. Yet those events had thus far defined his life, and led to greater achievements. The Norns, those wise women who weave the tapestry of all things from threads of Wyrd, were never far from Penda's life.

The seventh century was a time of great upheaval in Britain; conflict was endemic, famine and disease were never far away, and for many people, disaster was just on the doorstep. In this tumultuous time, people sought stability wherever they could find it, and for many it was to grip tightly to their ancient culture. For others, they sought something new that would prevent the past from reoccurring; but the people on these paths struggled to walk together, instead turning to yet more conflict. Penda held on to the ancestral ways, and had become an inadvertent bulwark against the changing tide. He had successfully removed all of the greatest threats to his people, and had expanded the kingdom. Penda Iclingas of the Hwicce was now the king of the middle lands, the centre of power, pulling all other nations into an orbit around him. The more powerful he became, and the more successful he was in war, the more people, events, and decisions he would be faced with.

As had always been his way, Penda sought a respite following the conflict with Oswald. He had a huge nation to run now, and while his warbands took a rest and the thegns saw to their homes, Penda began travelling the land, visiting many royal halls in the same method that the kings of Deira, Bernicia, Gewisse and East Anglia had done. This world of a travelling court was new to Penda, and was likely uncomfortable to him. He had been raised as the son of a thegn and a warlord, as the Hwicce had grown he had stretched his capacity as a warlord to cover the increasing leadership demands. However, the complexities he inherited on his brother's death needed more sophisticated solutions; kingship and a travelling court. Queen Cynewise was raised in a king's household and had experience with the travelling court; she may have become Penda's guide in this new world. Her understanding of how a king should move about the land, and the tasks he needed to accomplish as part of the process, were invaluable in the early days of this new kingdom. The year AD 643 passed by in general peace across Britain, and specifically in the new Mercia. In modern times we say strange events are a 'twist of fate'; but fate or Wyrd doesn't twist, it is laid out, it is woven, and it is straight. It starts, it ends, and most of all it weaves in and out of other threads connecting people and places.

Fifteen years earlier, Penda and the kings of the Gewisse had been drawn together by Wyrd at Cirencester, with an outcome neither of them had anticipated. In that first meeting, mutual destruction seemed to be the most likely outcome, but prudence on both sides had carried the day. Instead of shield-walls clashing and warriors dying, the kings had negotiated a settlement. Neither party had walked away with gold or cattle, but instead with security, peace, and the foundations of kinship through marriages. Penda had wed Cynewise, daughter of the Gewissan king, Cynegils. In return, Penda's sister had married Cenwalh, son of Cynegils. Those marriages were the living proof of the oaths between Penda and the Gewissan kings. Penda and Cynewise had turned a matter of statecraft into an effective marriage, raising children, and running a successful smaller kingdom.

We don't hear anything from the Gewissan Cenwalh following the events in AD 628 in Cirencester; that is until AD 635 when the Gewisse began to tie their future to the powerful king of Deira and Bernicia, King Oswald. Cynegils and Cwichelm invited King Oswald south and,

> the king himself [Cynegils], having received instruction as a catechumen, was being baptized together with his people. Oswald, the most holy and victorious king of the Northumbrians, being present, received him as he came forth from baptism, and by an honourable alliance most acceptable to God, first adopted as his son, was thus born again and dedicated to God, the man whose daughter he was about to receive in marriage.[1]

Oswald becomes Cynegils' godfather, and that has connotations of Oswald's supremacy over the Gewisse followed by him marrying Cynegils' daughter. The Gewisse were a weaker nation in this period and seeking to shore up their territory and security through treaties, particularly against Penda, who they continued to fear in spite of the fact that he had never broken his oath of peace with them. At this point Cynegils has one daughter married to Penda, and another daughter married to Oswald. As long as those oaths are maintained the Gewisse seems to be in a secure position.

It seems a near certainty that Cenwalh is also baptized along with his father at Dorchester-on-Thames in AD 635, though there is some discrepancy in the available material. Bede says that Cenwalh 'refused to receive the faith and the mysteries of the heavenly kingdom'.[2] But Henry of Huntingdon tells us that Cenwalh 'held the truth, but imperfectly'.[3] The *Anglo-Saxon Chronicles* were recorded by scribes in the Gewisse successor state of Wessex and sides with Henry of Huntingdon. In the *Anglo-Saxon Chronicles*, the entry for AD 643 records that 'Cenwalh ordered the old church at Winchester to be built in the name of St. Peter.'[4] The discrepancy fits as an anachronistic inserted by Bede to address the behaviour of Cenwalh in the future, and it would seem that Henry of Huntingdon landed closer to the truth which is that Cenwalh was baptized, but wasn't the best church member. Cenwalh had as much to fear from Penda as his father had, and would surely have sought ties with Oswald to provide deeper security and ensure a relationship was started which would be capable of replacing his father's relationship with Oswald at a future date. The question that surfaces is, why did the discrepancy in the record occur, and what was Bede attempting to hide?

The answers may lie with Cenwalh's wife, the sister of Penda. As the rest of the royal household was baptized with Oswald present, had she also been baptized, or did she refuse? She was not under the same pressure to please Oswald in order to build a treaty and form an alliance. Depending on how pleasant her experience had been with the Gewisse, she very well may have held out against baptism, in much the same way that Rædwald's powerful queen had rejected baptism and held to her traditional beliefs. Penda was still her great protector, in spite of her marriage, and she may have chosen to maintain a close relationship with him, including maintaining a spiritual connection. If her relationship was not good with Cenwalh, she may also have held out against conversion as a mark of dissent and protest in an unhappy household. If she had refused baptism, then the level of discord in Cenwalh's house was deepened.

Cwichelm followed Cynegils and was also baptized at Dorchester-on-Thames, though the timing is a bit confused. The *Anglo-Saxon Chronicles* say that Cwichelm converted after Cynegils in AD 636, 'This year King Cwichelm was baptized at Dorchester.'[5] But Bede seems to suggest that both kings were baptized together: 'The two kings gave to the bishop the city called Dorcic, there to establish his episcopal see.'[6] The same year that Cwichelm converted, he also died: 'King Cwichelm was baptized at Dorchester, and died the same year.'[7] The Gewisse were now faced with the challenge of shoring up authorities and avoiding the challenges that East Anglia had faced over the last twenty years. Two Heathen kings had changed to one Christian king, who was firmly tying his future to the power of King Oswald.

The changes in Gewisse may have had a negative impact on Cenwalh's wife. She was already an outsider, but with the rejection of conversion she was pushed farther away. As Penda had gained power, she began to represent the growing fear the Gewisse had of their northern neighbour. Penda's sister was now the representation of all that the Cenwalh despised. And then in AD 643 King Cynegils died, and Cenwalh was proclaimed king of the Gewisse. Cenwalh inherited a very different throne; the security his father established was wiped off the map. Oswald had died the year previous, eradicating the connection with the northern peoples, and the agreements that Cynegils and Cwichelm had established with Penda also died, in theory. But Cenwalh was still connected to Penda through his sister Cynewise, and through his own wife, Penda's sister. The men were brothers-in-law twice over, but this had been the work of Cenwalh's father and uncle, and not of his own making. Cenwalh had been forced into a marriage, and forced to live with the defeat of Cirencester throughout his adult life. The contempt he held for his marriage, the Hwicce, Penda, and his old faith came surging to the surface.

In a brash decision, 'he put away the sister of Penda, king of the Mercians, whom he had married, and took another wife'.[8] Henry of Huntingdon uses more direct language telling us Cenwalh divorced his wife. While the nobility wanted the ability to marry and divorce for political gains, the church believed itself to be the sole authority over marriage. This moment leads us to Bede's comments that the king wasn't converted at this early stage and Henry of Huntingdon giving the more honest assessment, that Cenwalh was baptized but was selective of the churches tenets. The early church would allow for a marriage to be annulled, but only for a narrow set of reasons, including adultery, or the desire to take a vow of service to the church.

Cenwalh may have made the argument that his wife was a Heathen and unwilling to convert as his reason for rejecting her. The more secular reason was that he wanted to establish his own kingdom built on his own ideas, free from the machinations of his father and uncle. He was gambling that Penda would leave well enough alone and not take great offence to the rejection of his sister. After all, Penda was still married to Cynewise, and thus the parties were still connected. Penda's sister gathered her household possessions, perhaps a servant, and her children to begin the trek to Tamworth. She was protected by warriors who remained loyal to her as she travelled north, back to her ancestral home.

It has often been suggested that Penda's children were Peada, Wulfhere, Athelred, Cyneburh, Cyneswith and Merewalh. While most of these can be traced with enough satisfaction, the case of Merewalh cannot. The challenge arises from the Angle language itself, where familial terms which are distinct in modern English are flexible in the older language. In the case of Merewalh, earlier scholars may have misinterpreted words that defined Merewalh's relationship with Penda. For example the word 'Nef' which 'In Anglo-Saxon there was little more than a general nef which could mean nephew, grandson, or stepson.'[9] In a society which relied on oral history, it would be simple enough for the meaning of 'nef' as it related to Merewalh's connection with Penda to be lost or misinterpreted by future generations. This misinterpretation could result in a stepson eventually being understood to be a grandson; there would be no way of knowing that such an interpretative mistake had occurred. One common theory is that Merewalh was an adopted son, or perhaps a stepson to Penda, which would also fit the term 'Nef' really well. The challenge with this theory is, why did Penda adopt him, or how did Penda come to be attached to a stepson? The adoption avenue could have come about through fosterage, and does seem plausible. In the future, Merewalh becomes a king in his own accord, and it would be quite a noble thing for Penda to give a nation to an adopted son. The stepson avenue seems less plausible as there is no reference to Penda taking a second wife at any point in his life.

But the third option which has gone unassessed is that Merewalh was the nephew of Penda. This theory also closely fits the term 'nef'. The question this theory drives is through what parentage line was Merewalh, Penda's nephew? There are two clues which lead us to understanding that relationship. For starters, is the practice of using culturally important naming principles of alliteration and variation to mark familial relations.[10] Until the Normans arrived in 1066, the Angles and Saxons used these two principles extensively. Alliteration is the process of sound at the beginning of the name; for example Peada was the son of Penda. Variation was the 'practice of so forming one name that it differs from another through the change of a name theme, e-theme (as in Eadgar and Eadweard or in Ælfthryth and Æthelthryth), through the addition of a new element to an uncompounded name (as in Gode and Godgifu), or through the transposition of both name-themes (as in Beorhtwulf and Wulfbeothrough)'.[11] The latter part of the name 'Merewalh' is unusual and very rare, however, in this period there is one other person who carries it and that is Cenwalh. The second clue is that Merewalh doesn't turn up until after AD 643, when Penda's sister is disposed of by Cenwalh.

It seems most likely that Merewalh was not Penda's stepson or adopted son, but rather his nephew, who Penda took in along with his sister, following their abandonment by Cenwalh. Cenwalh was happy to dispose himself of Merewalh, as this eliminated the threat to his throne from the Ætheling, and the threat of the Gewisse being drawn closer to the influence of Penda's court. In AD 643

Merewalh would have just started to enter the period of his life when he would begin travelling with the warbands and honing his skills as a warrior, something Penda would be happy to oblige.

Penda inherited a new challenge from the actions of Cenwalh. Aside from the obvious political attack that Cenwalh's actions carried, there was also a very personal attack. The abandonment of Merewalh and his mother was a direct afront to Penda and his kin, and one that could not go unpunished. Kin and the bonds of family were the single most important link that people of the seventh century had. Kinship had a deep cultural resonance to the Angles and the Saxons, and was the foundation for all other relationships. The importance of kinship can be seen in Beowulf, where upon the hero's arrival at Heorot he recites his ancestors in order to determine his kindred:

> The presence of Beowulf's party is then announced to Hrothgar, the Danish king, who says that he knew Beowulf, when he was a boy, and that he knew both his father and his mother. The Danish messenger from court is able to report back to Beowulf that all is well, that his æthelu, his kindred, is known.[12]

At a time when tribal affiliations were flexible and nations were still fledgling associations of diverse settlements, kinship provided the only unflappable link to the past, and a protection against future calamities. As a member of a kinship group, an individual owed loyalty to the members of that group, to protect them and to prosecuting a feud against an enemy.

Penda's challenge lay in the fact that he was married to Cenwalh's sister Cynewise. She was the link between the men, and the living embodiment of the peace between the nations. On the one hand Penda was compelled to protect his sister and the honour of the Iclingas. On the other hand, he had an oath to his wife that he must maintain. As he weighed the options, Penda accepted that peace with the Gewisse, and the treaty that he had negotiated with Cynegils and Cwichelm died with them. Cynewise, for her part, sided with her husband, and was probably appalled by Cynegils' treatment of his wife and son. She may have asked Penda to restrain his attack against the nation of the Gewisse, and focus only on Cynegils, but otherwise she supported action against her brother.

The timing of all of these events is difficult to discern. Both Bede and Henry of Huntingdon don't attach dates to Cenwalh's actions in abandoning his wife, or to Penda's retaliatory activities. In both sources, the two items are treated as multiple and related components of a single story arc, with a timeline that is implied to have occurred in immediate procession. From Bede we get the following story:

When the king died, his son Cenwalh succeeded him on the throne, but refused to receive the faith and the mysteries of the heavenly kingdom; and not long after he lost also the dominion of his earthly kingdom; for he put away the sister of Penda, king of the Mercians, whom he had married, and took another wife; whereupon a war ensuing.[13]

Henry of Huntingdon largely echoes Bede. 'Cenwalh, who held the truth, but imperfectly; for having divorced his wife, who was the sister of Penda king of Mercia, and married another, he was conquered'.[14] The *Anglo-Saxon Chronicles* deviate and break these events into separate occurrences spaced over two full years, however, the chronicles fail to mention that Cenwalh divorced his wife. The chroniclers may have been trying to protect the sanctity of the house of Wessex by redacting elements which were not particularly noble, virtuous, or glorious.

Penda had never been a rash man and had always considered his actions deeply before committing to a course. He had traditionally rested his army for a year or more between great campaigns, when he could. In the case of Oswald, he had no choice but to march north, but in the case of Cynegils he had time. There was no immediate threat from the Gewisse, and in any case his feud wasn't with the nation or its people, but with the king alone. Penda would look for quick success which inflicted the minimal amount of damage on his own warbands. To hastily march off would put his own nation at risk. He would prepare himself and his warbands for the task first. For this reason, it seems that there was a delayed response between the events, but they were all linked, and would all happen in a sequential series as identified by all of the sources. With a lack of any further detail to go on, it's reasonable to accept that Cenwalh began his reign as king of the Gewisse in AD 643. The follow-on actions started to occur between when Cenwalh began his reign and perhaps AD 645 when the *Anglo-Saxon Chronicles* record that Penda attacked the Gewisse, which was his response to Cenwalh for abandoning his wife and her son Merewalh.

Henry of Huntingdon's chronology does deviate from this sequence of events in a number of areas where he writes, 'Cenwalh who held the kingdom of Wessex 31 years as his father had done. The same year was slain the Holy King Oswald...Cenwalh in the fifth year of his reign was attacked by Penda.'[15] This recording of events places Cenwalh on the throne in 642 A.D. and Penda's attack on the Gewisse in AD 647. The chronology is clearly different, and more importantly is the gap between Cenwalh taking power and the long wait for Penda to march south. While Henry of Huntingdon got details of the story correct, it appears he missed the mark on the chronology of events.

Following his divorce, Cenwalh married Seaxburh of Wessex as his second wife, but we know virtually nothing about her, not even where she came from, or if they had any children. Seaxburh of Wessex rises to prominence much later when she replaces Cenwalh after his death in AD 672 as the queen of the Gewisse. There is, however, another Seaxburg in this same era who also rose to prominence as the consort of the king of Kent, and then retired to an abbey; this is Seaxburg of Ely. Duplication of names is quite rare in Angle and Saxon culture of this period, so it bears examining this case, especially as both women share connections. In both cases there is a variety of spellings for their name, which can be examined through the Prosopography of *Anglo-Saxon England* database maintained by the University of Cambridge. This database is an attempt to list and record information on all recorded inhabitants in England between the sixth and eleventh century. Inside the prosopography, Seaxburg of Ely is recorded three times, twice with the spelling 'Seaxburg' and only once with 'Seaxburh'. In light of no other evidence it seems plausible that the correct spelling of her name was Seaxburg. For Seaxburh of Wessex there are six entries, two for 'Seaxburg', one for 'Seaxburh', one for 'Sexburgae', and two for 'Sexburh'. Unfortunately this analysis results in an even split; however, it is reasonable to eliminate the version of 'Sexburgae' as it comes from a charter, and stands out amongst the others as not originating from a chronicle, in which case 'Seaxburh' is the appropriate spelling. In both of these cases that interchanging nature of the name cannot fully be addressed.

Accepting that the names of these two remarkable women are similar but not identical, along with the chronology of their lives, it seems possible that the naming is a matter of alliteration between mother and daughter, with Seaxburh-of-Wessex being the mother and Seaxburg-of-Ely being the daughter. King Anna of East Anglia has a daughter named Seaburh or Seaxburg, who it is believed married the king of Kent, but this could be a moment of confusion in the recording of the chronicles some 200 years after the events. For Cenwalh to burn the bridge with Mercia by abandoning his wife suggests he must have had a plan in place to build links with another kingdom. A marital alliance with a nation that is similarly predisposed to mistrust Penda would be highly beneficial to Cenwalh. In the south, that left him two options: Kent and East Anglia. Kent had been able to mainly avoid large-scale conflict since the time of Hengist and Horsa, and instead relied on its direct connection with the Franks and the continent for wealth; its kings had no concern with the petty squabbles of the island. East Anglia on the other hand had been a major power for generations, right up to the death of Rædwald, and it had also been recently attacked by Penda. Both East Anglia and the Gewisse shared borders with Penda, and could both benefit from collaboration.

King Anna could have been born as early as AD 600, but didn't become king of East Anglia until AD 636. King Anna had five children, with Seaxburh being born perhaps around AD 625. She would have been in her late teens or early twenties when she was wed to Cenwalh, and would have produced a daughter very early in the marriage, giving birth to Seaxburg in AD 643. It has been suggested in the past that Seaxburh and Seaxburg where one and the same, but the length of time they are in the chronology of events seems too long; however, a matrilineal connection would fit the timeline. This theory does create time pressure for Seaxburg, based on when her husband King Erconbert of Kent dies in AD 664, and that they had four children. But even without adjusting the provided chronology, this is still possible.

By AD 645 Cenwalh has established a marriage and an alliance with East Anglia, and was beginning to feel more secure and less concerned about retribution from Penda. But Penda had not forgotten about Cenwalh's slight against the Iclingas, and he launched an attack on the Gewisse. Unfortunately we only have fleeting references to this series of events. Bede says that after Cenwalh abandoned Penda's sister, 'a war ensuing, he [Cenwalh] was by him [Penda] deprived of his kingdom, and withdrew to Anna, King of the East Angles, where he lived three years in banishment'.[16] Bede's comments provide yet more clues to the connection between East Anglia and the Gewisse. Henry of Huntingdon adds that Cenwalh was 'conquered and driven out of his kingdom'.[17] Finally, the *Anglo-Saxon Chronicles* provide no additional details, just stating that in AD 645 'Cenwalh was driven from his dominion by King Penda.'[18] The reconstruction of the assault on the Gewisse and the location of battles is purely theoretical as there are no sources to turn to. What is possible is to look at the road system and make educated estimates as to the route that armies may have taken, and from that attempt to discern how Cenwalh fled to East Anglia and the protection of King Anna.

By the time he attacked Cenwalh in AD 645, Penda had been able to rest his warbands for a year or two and felt confident that his skilled warriors would be able to handle anything the Gewisse could throw at him. Since his first conflict with the Gewisse at Cirencester, Penda had fought in sieges, pitched battles and ambushes; he had fought in well-prepared situations, hastily drawn together positions, and most importantly he had fought at great distances from his home. Against Edwin, Oswald, Sigbert and Ecgric, Penda had marched his army hundreds of kilometres, fought, succeeded, and returned home. The ability to reach so far from home was an incredible strategic asset which opened up the options for Penda.

From the outset of the campaign, Penda was likely travelling from Tamworth, which provided him with excellent access to the Roman road system. Penda was now able to draw a force from a much larger area than any of his previous campaigns with the inclusion of Eowa's land. Although the entire area was likely not called Mercia by Penda, it is the only term that is useable in the post Maserfelth era. With his Mercian force, Penda began marching south against the Gewisse. The lack of a record of this campaign may imply that Penda's attack was surgical in nature, which in turn would suggest that he had a clear understanding of where to find Cenwalh. This knowledge would come from travellers and merchants, or someone in Gewisse with an intimate knowledge of the general routine of Cenwalh. This person could have been someone who was put off by Cenwalh's actions in AD 643. Perhaps more realistic is that the winter quarters for kings of the era were well-known and routine. If this is the case, then the attack must have come very early in the spring to ensure Cenwalh had not moved to a new location. By waiting at least a year to launch his attack, Penda had gained the element of surprise as Cenwalh began to relax and believe there would be no repercussions from his actions.

The route could have taken one of two ways depending on the target. If Cenwalh was out in the western part of his country, then Penda would march south through the old Hwicce lands and Pebworth before marching on Cirencester and then pressing west through Gewisse territory. This route would be difficult as much of the Gewisse land would need to be crossed by footpath and the ridgeway. Penda perhaps had the benefit of a local guide to help the cross-country portion of the movement; one of the warriors who had protected his sister perhaps. Entry from the west, though, would alert Cenwalh as the army would be forced to move a long distance through his territory, and it is likely that it would have led to a series of skirmishes across the landscape.

The second and more logical route was from the north. This route would be utilized if Penda believed that Cenwalh was at Sutton Courtenay, which was only ten miles from the Gewissan northern border. Coming from the north, Penda would arrive in about five days. The final hurdle the Mercian army had was crossing the Thames, which was perhaps done at Oxford. Oxford was the northern gateway controlling access to Gewisse lands, and it must have been monitored by Cenwalh. An approaching army would have sent a rider south to warn the king and the people of Sutton Courtenay. If the fording of the Thames occurred immediately after the army was seen, then Cenwalh had at best three or four hours before Penda was on his doorstep. At this moment the king of the Gewisse had some difficult decisions to make. He could abandon his royal hall and move inland to begin a defence in depth; he could set a defensive position at Sutton Courtenay maximizing his time to gather warriors, but also putting the entire settlement at risk. He could march northwards and establish a position at Boars Hill and oppose the Mercian army two miles after it forded the river; or he could flee.

If he fled, he would certainly lose his kingdom in the short term, and then no doubt lose it forever as the thegns and nobles would never again support a coward who hadn't done his duty and stood against the aggressor. Such was the system of kingship in the Angle and Saxon kingdoms that, without broad support, the king would be unable to maintain his reign. Cenwalh had to fight, but wouldn't want to bring the battle to his doorstep, so he must have gathered what warbands he could and hastily set out to meet Penda, attempting to put as much ground as he could between Sutton Courtenay and the battlefield. Penda was pushing his force across the ford at Oxford, and was now so close to Cenwalh's royal hall that he must have pushed on. There would be no point in resting here and allowing the Gewisse to organize their defences. The initiative was with Penda, and once the Thames was crossed he would be pushing the army to move as quickly as they could. Penda and Cenwalh would send small parties to scout ahead of their main forces to prevent ambushes and establish the location of the enemy. These scout parties were also searching the land for appropriate locations to set up the shield-walls, and hopefully lure the other side into a fight.

Both armies were now on the march and destined to meet halfway to their objectives, somewhere on the backside of Boars Hill, or the northern outskirts of modern-day Abingdon. As the armies formed up, it quickly became evident to all that the advantage was Penda's. He would have brought a larger force with him than Cenwalh had been able to raise. Bede is quite clear that a war occurred between Penda and Cenwalh, but there is no mention of a specific battle site, similar in fact to Penda's attack on Ecgric and Sigbert of East Anglia. A confrontation must have occurred between the armies, but as occurred at Cirencester and Exeter perhaps it ended before blood was spilt. With the armies ranged against one another, Cenwalh could see the writing on the wall and sought treaty instead of death. At the conclusion of the battle, or the treaty, Penda let Cenwalh walk away into exile. This moment is peculiar as no other king is afforded this opportunity by Penda. In all other cases Penda presses on until the king is dead, which is the only way for a war to end in this period. Penda must have been held back in his response by something, the most obvious thing would be Cynewise, his wife, and the sister of Cenwalh. At this moment the king of Mercia could have killed Cenwalh and ridden roughshod through the Gewisse territories, but he didn't. Instead, he was content with defeating Cenwalh and allowing him to flee Gewisse and head to the protection of East Anglia.

Penda must have sacked Sutton Courtenay, and turned his success into a limited raid before retiring from the land of the Gewisse. At this point the Gewisse were left without a king, and operating with the localized leadership of nobles and thegns, much as occurred in Deira after Cadwallon's success. Unlike

Deira, the Gewissan king was still alive, and no one seems to have threatened his throne in his absence, which implies that his exile was honourable in some manner, and he was still revered as the rightful king of the Gewisse. Had he fled immediately and offered no resistance, it would be hard to accept that others wouldn't come forward and challenge him for the throne. Cenwalh's connections to King Anna of East Anglia provided him with the safest place to buy time before he could return to the Gewisse.

The story of Cenwalh is picked up by Bede where we are told that following his defeat by Penda, he

> withdrew to Anna, king of the East Angles, where he lived three years in banishment, and learned and received the true faith; for the king, with whom he lived in his banishment, was a good man.[19]

Henry of Huntingdon disagrees slightly on this account as he says that while in East Anglia Cenwalh was 'restored to the faith'.[20] This minor variance is important as it suggests that he was already converted before he fled, which may have been one of the leading factors or at least an excuse in his abandonment of his first wife, the catalyst of his exile.

The events around the defeat and return of Cenwalh are interesting as they paint a different picture of Penda from the bloodthirsty Heathen and enemy of all that is right, as Bede and subsequent authors would have us believe. Instead, we see a restrained and thoughtful Penda, who utilized a minimum amount of force to achieve a response to a personal attack on his kin. Penda in this event is not after territorial gain, and doesn't appear to have aspirations as an all-conquering king. He is also not moved by anger, otherwise he would have been swift with his retaliation against Cenwalh. Penda instead waits, organizes, and then strikes at a moment that is most advantageous to him. In the aftermath of the fight he doesn't pillage the unguarded lands, but instead takes a reward from the local area and then retires home, the opposite of how Cadwallon had carried on following Edwin's defeat in the north. Archaeological surveys at Sutton Courtenay have never identified any fire damage to the buildings. If we can assume that Penda was here, this fact also speaks to the restraint he demonstrated in his feud with Cenwalh. It would have been nothing to level the site of the royal hall, and yet that didn't happen.

Closer to home for Penda, the attack on Cenwalh offered an opportunity for his older son and nephew to gather valuable combat experience. Peada and Merewalh would have been in their late teens at the time of the battle, and it was an ideal opportunity for them to begin their indoctrination to the skills of fighting in a shield-wall. Both had probably earned some experience raiding, but a shield-wall would have been a very different experience. Against Cenwalh the young men had the opportunity to watch Penda lead from the front, and this exposure likely impacted how they would lead in the future. Based on their future achievements both Merewalh and Peada must have performed well in the eyes of Penda on this occasion.

Cenwalh's three year exile means he returned to the Gewisse in AD 648, and must have been with the blessing of Penda. Penda had achieved such power that he was now able to decide who ruled where. Bede uses the term 'Bretwalda' as the most powerful king in Britain, and he provides Rædwald, Oswald, and Edwin with this title, but not Penda. By AD 645 the king of the Mercians had defeated seven kings, and martyred four of them; clearly he was the most powerful king in Britain by the mid-seventh century. There must have been communications between Penda and Cenwalh, and Cenwalh would have been forced into some oath with Penda in return for his kingdom following his exile. Without those steps it would be nothing for Penda to back an Ætheling and replace Cenwalh on the Gewissan throne. Once again all of these decisions may have taken place with the help and guidance of Cynewise.

It seems possible that Penda was unaware of where Cenwalh had ended up in his exile early on, but by the time the Gewisse have their king back, Penda knew that King Anna had provided shelter and support to Cenwalh. If Penda was going to maintain his authority and dominance, he needed to demonstrate that support for his enemies placed a target on those supporters. In the case of East Anglia, he would need to show King Anna that he was not immune from the reach of Mercia and had to be punished for supporting Cenwalh for three years. Once again though, Penda would be thoughtful in his future actions, seeking preparation over haste.

Chapter Twelve

Cnobheresburg

One of the primary characterizations of King Penda is that he is an aggressive warmonger, terrorizing the land and bringing conflict to all corners of Britain. This is certainly the picture that is painted by Bede and taken up by generations of scholars afterwards. Penda never shirked from his responsibilities on the battlefield, and had gained a reputation which was well-deserved as both a warrior to be feared, and a great leader of men. But this reputation blurs the reality of Penda's conduct. The decade following AD 640 provides an interesting cross-section of his conduct, starting with his attack on East Anglia and the death of Ecgric and Sigbert. This invasion seems to be aggressive in nature, but certainly a raid where wealth is the prime objective and not territorial gain. The next major action is in AD 642 which is a defensive battle fought against the aggression of King Oswald. In AD 645 Penda attacks Cenwalh in Gewisse as a matter of honour and protection of his sister. After the attack on the Gewisse there is no other recorded action by Penda on a battlefield until AD 649, showing nine years where outright aggression occurs only once against East Anglia. The other two cases are in response to the actions of other kings and nations, and wouldn't have been conflicts which Penda had sought out.

Looking even further back, we have the campaigns for Cadwallon in AD 630 and AD 633, which Penda was sworn to support after his failure at Exeter in AD 630. The attempted sacking of Exeter is the only moment of outright belligerence on a major scale by Penda between AD 630 and AD 640. All told, in almost twenty years, Penda can be seen as culpable in the waging of an aggressive war only twice in the historic record. In an age where kings were expected to fight as a matter of territorial expansion, territorial protection, and the acquisition of wealth, Penda hardly seems like a warmongering monster. That is not to say that he didn't show a willingness to be an aggressor, and there are a number of occasions when a reason for a campaign can't be tied to an external force and must be accepted as militarily aggressive actions by Penda. Penda's success in offensive warfare was very much a mixed bag; he had experienced negotiated success against Cwichelm and Cynegils, negotiated defeat at the hands of Cadwallon, and total success against Ecgric and Sigbert.

For the people ruled by Penda, he had become the great protector. Since Penda took control of the Hwicce and shored up the southern boundary with the Gewisse, they hadn't faced a notable invasion in over twenty years. This level of stability was only shared by the south-eastern kingdoms of South Saxons and Kent. Following Eowa's death and the uniting of the Iclingas thrones, Penda had perhaps doubled his nation geographically, but also militarily. He would now leverage this power to see off would-be aggressors and continue to ensure relative peace for the people he ruled. Under the leadership of Eowa, it seems his people had not had the same general safety. To achieve security Eowa had tied his nation's protection and well-being to the authority and power of Bernicia and Deira. In the Welsh poem *Marwnad Cynddylan* there is a reference to a raid on Litchfield, which would have been at the heart of Eowa's nation,

> Grandeur in battle! Extensive spoils Morial bore off from in front of Lichfield. Fifteen hundred cattle from the front of battle; four twenties of stallions and equal harness. The chief bishop wretched in his four-cornered house, the book-keeping monks did not protect. Those who fell in the blood before the splendid warrior.[1]

It is a testimony to Penda's effective use of both war and statecraft that he was able to provide security to his people for so long, particularly in an era of endemic warfare. On the warfare side, Penda used raids to keep his warriors appeased and stocked with riches, these were internal benefits from external activities. He had also used war as a defensive tactic, but seemed hesitant to use it as a tool for territorial expansion. Statecraft and negotiated settlements had done more for Hwicce and Mercian security than war had, and this is perhaps one of the most overlooked skills which Penda had. The equal measures of war and treaty made Penda a truly dominant figure by AD 649. This decade had seen him rise and achieve the pinnacle of power, and as the decade closed another campaign was needed to restock the wealth of the nation, and ensure his dominance south of the Humber, would not be eroded by the actions of other kings.

The return of Cenwalh to Gewisse in AD 648 may have occurred with some level of approval by Penda as there was no further war aimed south. However, it may have also occurred by force of arms. There are no recorded battles for this event, but the *Liber Eliensis*, a monastic chronicle written in the eleventh or twelfth century from the Isle of Ely, may provide some lesser known details. The *Liber Eliensis* speaks of Cenwalh's exile in East Anglia and how Cenwalh, 'returned to West Saxony with his auxiliaries, and obtained his paternal kingdom powerfully from the enemy'.[2] This material is interesting as it demonstrates that Cenwalh was not alone in his exile, he had brought some warbands and warriors with him. If Cenwalh had been able to retreat with some of his army it may be another reason why Penda had not pursued him into East Anglia.

Whatever components he fled with though was not a full army. If Cenwalh had fled with the majority of his army there would have been no reason to wallow in exile for three years.

The truth of Cenwalh's return is likely somewhere in the middle. He did return to the Gewisse with part of his army still intact, but Penda was also willing to let it happen. His return was in the interest of Penda as the two kings were still linked through Cynewise. Cenwalh may have needed the use of the warriors he had with him to see off any claimants to his throne. Penda, however, had to address King Anna's willingness to support the fugitive Gewissan king as a direct attack on his authority and Mercian dominance in Britain. If he took no further action, other kings would read this as weakness in Mercia and potentially look to exploit it. In order to maintain Mercian dominance and keep the other nations and their kings under control, Penda needed to punish King Anna.

King Anna must have known he faced the wrath of Penda for offering shelter to Cenwalh. In his calculations he surely realized his forces were no match for the dominant Mercian warbands. The inclusion of Cenwalh's warbands that had fled Gewisse with him may have placated King Anna's nerves a bit, but not by much. There are local folk stories and hints in the *Liber Eliensis* that connect King Anna with the town of Exning. This location is perilously close to Devil's Dyke Gap and the location of Ecgric and Sigbert's defeat. If this was Anna's town, then it is not outside the realm of the impossible that he had been at the battle led by Sigbert. King Anna was fully aware of Penda's capacity for war and the damage that had been inflicted upon East Anglia during his last raid, which culminated with the deaths of King Ecgric and Sigbert. That King Anna was still willing to shelter the exiled King of the Gewisse, in spite of the danger of Penda's vengeance, seems to support the theory that the connection between King Anna and King Cenwalh went beyond that of nobility. There was a more personal connection between the men, the kinship connection through King Anna's daughter Seaxburh and granddaughter Seaxburg. By supporting Cenwalh, King Anna was protecting his daughter, his granddaughter, and any future claimants to the throne of the Gewisse.

Penda once again relied on his patience and careful consideration before acting. He hadn't chased Cenwalh, and he hadn't attacked East Anglia in the subsequent three years in search of Cenwalh. Even at the moment that Cenwalh returned to Sutton Courtenay, Penda hadn't moved. In the wake of Cenwalh's return, Penda began to consider his next move against King Anna in the following campaign season. Assuming Penda had allowed Cenwalh to return, he would have perhaps stipulated that Cenwalh's return could only occur late in the autumn. This protected Penda from the outside chance that Cenwalh would launch a hasty attack on Mercia. This insurance policy came at a cost, and that was the delay in punishing the East Anglian king. Penda would have to wait for the winter to pass before he once again marched to the east. As he had always done, Penda used the winter to prepare his warbands for the hard march across Britain to attack a distant enemy. Penda's ability to attack long distance successfully speaks to his capacity to generate sound strategy, and in particular the need for effective logistics to support his movements. He used the periods between his major campaigns to prepare these details and ensure his success, and the winter of AD 648 was no different. As the winter gave way to the spring, Penda called his thegns and warbands together to begin their march east, back to East Anglia.

The conversion of East Anglian kings had been accomplished in a relatively short period of time. Rædwald was the first of the East Anglian kings to convert, though the results seem spurious at best. Bede tells us that Rædwald 'seemed at the same time to serve Christ and the gods whom he served before; and in the same temple he had an altar for the Christian Sacrifice, and another small one at which to offer victims to devils.'[3] This process of absorbing another amongst a pantheon of gods and goddesses was nothing new to the Heathens, and would not have been seen as an out of place process to them. However, for the Christian missionaries this was seen as a failed conversion.

The next four kings of East Anglia, Eorpwald, Sigbert, Ecgric, and Anna, all fully embraced the new religion. Sigbert and Anna in particular had provided huge investments in the new faith through the construction of churches, monasteries, and abbeys. For example, Sigbert had spent years in exile in Gaul, and upon returning to East Anglia, 'being desirous to imitate the good institutions which he had seen in Gaul, he founded a school wherein boys should be taught letters'.[4] Along with the infrastructure came the material wealth based on patronage and tithing, so that the church in East Anglia steadily grew and became a powerful cornerstone of that nation. In AD 633 Sigbert was able to attract monks from Ireland to preach, convert and teach the East Anglians. Amongst these religious men from Ireland were three brothers: Foillan, Ultan and Fursa, all of whom would become canonized by the Catholic Church. These three men played a crucial role in the establishment and teaching at the religious school Sigbert established, and the development of the monastery at Beodericsworth, which would eventually take King Sigbert in as a monk when he abdicated the throne and Ecgric began his reign as the East Anglian king.

Upon their arrival, the Irish monks, led by Fursa, were given a disused Roman castrum or fort on the North Sea coast of East Anglia in which to open a monastery. The Angles called this place Cnobheresburg. 'This monastery was pleasantly situated in the woods, near the sea; it was built within the area of a fort.'[5] This fort started life as the Roman castrum of Gariannonum. Typically, the Roman castrum was a square or rectangular fort ringed by an external ditch and a wall. The castrum would have four gates, one centred in each of the walls. Along the East Anglian coast, Gariannonum castrum formed a key deterrent against the predations of the sea-going Angles and Saxons; it was one of the forts of the Saxon Shore. The castrum at Cnobheresburg is roughly a rectangle 200 metres by 100 metres, and enclosed by a stone wall, with roughly six acres of space inside. The walls, which are still standing, were an imposing defence standing over fifteen feet high and eleven feet wide at their base. In an age without siege weapons, the only way to take a fort with stone walls was to get over the wall, or get through an open gate. There were no machines which could breach a well-constructed stone wall.

In the Roman period, this castrum would house a legion, or more likely auxiliaries and Foederati, with a capacity of around 1000 men.[6] The castrum would have been fitted with all the requirements of a Roman military unit including a canteen, barracks, administrative buildings, sanitation facilities, stables, and a small temple. In general the Roman castra were designed to be nearly self-sufficient, and if the buildings or sections of the buildings remained in AD 633, Cnobheresburg would be an ideal setting for a monastery. Repurposing the barracks into cells for the monks would be a simple enough task if they were still standing, and any stone foundations could have been easily built upon to construct new wooden buildings. The nearby Roman fort at Caister was likely built and designed by the same people who constructed Cnobheresburg. At Caister the foundations of buildings can still be seen. The buildings were formed with 'low flint wall footings, timber-framed walls and a tiled roof'.[7] Archaeological exploration of Cnobheresburg in the 1950s identified signs of a wooden church in the south-west corner of the fort along with a cemetery containing 144 graves which were interpreted as being comprised of Christian burials.

Under the reign of King Anna, Cnobheresburg was further developed. 'Anna, king of that province, and certain of the nobles, embellished it with more stately buildings and with gifts.'[8] Fursa would leave East Anglia following the attack by Penda which killed Sigbert and Ecgric, but his brothers continued to see to the growth of the monastery at Cnobheresburg. By the latter part of the 640s the site at Cnobheresburg was a renowned religious centre, drawing both clergymen and laymen from across Britain. King Anna, as Bede remarked, had a particular affinity for this monastery, and aside from providing it with wealth and patronage, also likely spent ample time within the walls of Cnobheresburg.

As Penda planned the campaign against King Anna, he was preparing himself for another battle at the nearby Devil's Dyke. This location was still a crucial defensive work, even though it hadn't prevented Penda from successfully defeating

Ecgric and Sigbert. In all likelihood, the East Anglians would try to reinforce this location if they gained word of Penda's movements. As he had done in AD 640, Penda would seek to use surprise as best he could to attack the gap before his enemy was able to fully establish a defensive position. In his previous venture, the East Anglians had received enough warning of Penda's approach to draw together warbands and pull Sigbert out of the monastery at Beodericsworth to help lead them. In the nine years since those events, Penda's authority and reach had grown so much that many of the small nations between him and East Anglia were now fully within his sphere of influence, and in many cases under his direct rule. This drastically lowered the risk of King Anna receiving any early warning of the approaching army.

The trek to and from East Anglia was long; to ensure he maximized the value of the raid, Penda would set out as early as possible. The Spring Equinox and the celebration of Eostre provided an ideal opportunity to draw his force together and begin the move to the east. This timing could also be advantageous to him as it may catch the East Anglian defenders unaware as their Easter festivities fell sixteen days after the Eostre celebrations. Penda could march his army in a more direct route than he was forced to use nine years prior. With the addition of Eowa's lands and the dominance of the smaller Middle Angle sæta groups, Penda could move his army through Leicester, Cambridge, and then across the border into East Anglia. This route was about 160 kilometres long, and would take the Mercian army around eight days to complete. However, it is likely that another day was added on to ensure the force had a rest before pushing on to the Devil's Dyke. The final camp was set up at Worsted Lodge, or Six Mile Bottom. After one final rest, the army marched to the frontier with East Anglia, fully prepared for another battle at the Devil's Dyke, but it seems from the lack of any record that a battle didn't happen. Perhaps the East Anglians had recognized the failure of their defensive strategy and had left in place only the capacity to send a warning of the incursion.

At this point, Penda needed to identify where King Anna was, and would be seeking information from any locals he could find, though it is fair to assume that most of the public would be fleeing their homes as a foreign army approached them. The kingdom of East Anglia was around 9,200 square kilometres in size, and Penda was at one extremity of it. Many of the East Anglian power centres were along the coast, which was 85 kilometres to the east and to the north, and 110 kilometres to the north-east. Without clear intelligence on the location, Penda would be forced into a monumental task of tracking down King Anna, which would provide the East Anglian king with time to further ready himself and his army for an eventual clash. Time and the landscape were on the side of King Anna, unless Penda could figure out quickly where he was.

There are virtually no records on this campaign, save for a few remarks about its outcome. This is partially due to the fact that neither East Anglia nor Mercia benefited from the authorship of chronicles, and so they both tend to be only occasionally mentioned in Bede, Henry of Huntingdon or the *Anglo-Saxon Chronicles*. However, had there been an early clash of the armies, one would expect to find some mention of it, and that doesn't occur, nor do we see mention of Penda roaming East Anglia for a long period of time, suggesting that he was able to narrow down King Anna's position in fairly short order. King Anna, it seems, was celebrating Easter at Cnobheresburg, another 100 kilometres from the Devil's Dyke. This was deep inside East Anglia, and Penda would be in a bad spot if he suffered any setbacks on the march or at the destination. From this point he was marching through enemy land and would need to ensure all of his camps were well selected with an eye on defence. In East Anglia this was a serious challenge as the land didn't offer any heights, instead fords and woods would have to suffice as defensive positions. The march to Cnobheresburg could be completed in five days, but moving through enemy territory, where the route of retreat could not be maintained, warranted a slower and more methodical approach. Additionally, the need to properly establish a camp that could be defended each night required more time to set up and tear down each day. Moving fifteen kilometres a day would put Penda at his target in seven days.

King Anna must have been aware that Penda was moving against him by this point, and was doing his best to draw together a force to confront the Mercians. The challenge that King Anna faced was the remoteness of Cnobheresburg which delayed communications, slowed warbands from arriving, and may have given thegns cause not to send troops. For some thegns, the risk of losing at such a remote spot meant that the rest of the country would be open for Penda to raid at will. The fear of this happening may have kept some thegns from answering the call to arms, instead seeing to their own local defence over that of King Anna's. After so many years of political instability in East Anglia, it is logical that many power holders would not readily jump to the aid of King Anna. The kingdom of East Anglia was still very divided, with multiple factions at play. King Anna did have some advantages working in his favour; for starters, Penda had to travel a long distance, potentially tiring his warbands. Secondly, the Roman defences at the Cnobheresburg.

After travelling over 260 kilometres, Penda and his army had reached the North Sea coast. He had crossed East Anglia without meeting a concerted attempt to stop his army, and now he was preparing to take Cnobheresburg. He was camped near enough to the castrum that the monks could see the Mercian army and they began to prepare for an inevitable defeat. King Anna had been unable to gather an effective force in time to meet Penda, and now had limited options remaining. He could take to the field and die at the hands of a superior enemy, or he could attempt to hold the castrum and force Penda into a siege. The Roman fortifications were well constructed, and depending on their state of repair could still present a serious barrier for Penda to overcome.

However, a siege did not occur, likely because it simply wasn't a viable strategy for the East Anglians, for any number of reasons. King Anna may have had insufficient men at hand to hold off an enemy. Additionally the site didn't have sufficient food to keep the defenders in place long-term, or perhaps the defensive works were already too damaged to hold off an attacking army. King Anna and his retinue chose to flee in the face of the superior force. If a vessel was available, King Anna's best chance of escape was by sea. As Penda watched the vessel depart he knew now was the time to sack Cnobheresburg.

As the Mercian force entered the castrum they found undefended monks along with some gold items still at hand. There are a number of Christian accounts of the event, which all seem to differ slightly. In one account, Penda attacks Cnobheresburg and is about to slay the monks including Abbot Foillan, but King Anna, hearing of the attack, raises an army and 'the heathens heard of the approach of King Anna and were afraid. The monks were redeemed from captivity and the holy relics were found.'[9] Abbot Foillan then takes the relics, texts, and monks off to Gaul. This version of events seems completely incorrect, after all it implies King Anna successfully saw off King Penda, but if that were the case, why did the East Anglian king end up in exile, and why was Penda allowed to live?

A second account has Abbot Foillan arriving on a ship after the attack. The abbot had been away visiting his brother Fursa in Gaul, but arrives in time to save the monks of Cnobheresburg by paying a ransom for them and the relics to Penda. Foillan loads his ship with the rescued monks and sails back to Gaul. This second account is perhaps closer to the truth, though it would seem incredibly fortuitous that Foillan would arrive in the nick of time. As the attack may have occurred around Easter, it also seems unlikely that Foillan would be away from the monastery, especially if the king was present for religious services. What seems more likely is that Abbot Foillan and King Anna departed together, fleeing by ship with those members of their retinue that they could carry. The rest were left behind at Cnobheresburg. The stories of rescue were likely crafted after the events to add more nobility to the decision and actions of powerful individuals, in particular the Abbot Foillan and King Anna.

None of the accounts, however, allude to the sacking of the monastery as a particularly violent event. It seems as if Penda and his force were able to take the monastery with very little resistance, gather wealth from it and leave. Penda doesn't seem to have spent a long period of time in East Anglia, as there are no records of the Mercian army decimating the country. As he had done with the Gewisse, this attack was meant to directly impact King Anna.

In most stories of the raid, King Anna is pushed into exile, and in some versions he ends up in the territory of the Magonsæta. However, both the exile and the connection to the Magonsæta seem unlikely. If Anna had been pushed into exile, Penda would have been able to place a friendly king on the East Anglian throne, but he didn't do that. This fact alone seems to suggest that Anna had not fled into exile. After fleeing from Cnobheresburg, King Anna only had to sail south sixty kilometres to be back in his primary township of Rendlesham. From this point he would be able to re-establish his control of East Anglia and draw together an army. The east Anglian coast and their mastery of sea provided King Anna with a capacity that Penda simply couldn't match. The East Anglians could freely move military forces anywhere on the coast to contend with Penda, once they were mobilized. The ship burial at Sutton Hoo gives a clear example that the East Anglians were still mariners, perhaps the last of the great Angle and Saxon seafarers that had so terrified the Roman author Sidonius Apollinaris in AD 480.

With King Anna on the loose, Penda was now at a greater disadvantage. While he still had some time to gather wealth from East Anglia, he needed to begin the process of retreating westward to prevent King Anna from establishing ambushes or a pitched battle. Penda's whole purpose was to de-throne King Anna; that was the point of the raid, but he hadn't been able to accomplish that.

Penda could have turned his force south in pursuit of King Anna, but he didn't. This may be a reflection of the fact that he didn't know where Anna had moved to. Equally though this could be another sign of his disciplined strategic approach to combat. He had prepared his army and logistics to attack King Anna, complete the raid and return home. He was ill-prepared for a prolonged occupation and hunt. Having made a fulsome assessment, Penda took his failure to deliver on his primary objective of his campaign and began the process of getting his army home. Any of the East Anglian settlements that were along the route would have been targeted by the Mercian army and stripped bare of any mobile wealth including livestock.

King Anna kept his kingdom, and more importantly his life, but Penda had made a very public demonstration of his authority. He was capable of reaching any point on the island, and capable of responding to any king who felt brave enough to challenge his dominance and authority. King Anna lost more than the monastery at Cnobheresburg; he also lost the wealth housed there both by the predations of the Mercians, and also the items that were removed by the fleeing monks and taken to Gaul. Perhaps more concerning for King Anna was the loss of security across East Anglia. No invading army had entered East Anglia in the past nine years, and no army had ever pushed so deep into East Anglia. Penda's attack in AD 640 had shown the failure of the east Anglian defensive system, and the ensuing peace had lulled King Anna into a false sense of security. The East Anglians had utterly failed to understand the political landscape across Britain, and had paid a heavy price.

For King Anna, the sobering reality of Penda's attack on Cnobheresburg highlighted the vulnerability of East Anglia, and how limited his own power was. This was not the East Anglia of King Rædwald the 'Bretwalda'. For decades East Anglia had looked to the continent, ignoring the events of the island, and seeking to emulate the kings of Gaul and Frankia. They had invested heavily in the church, neglecting to look at the nations around them and to understand how they fit into the power structure on the island. What King Anna needed now was to shore up alliances with other nations, and to prepare for the next time Penda turned up on his doorstep. King Anna already had connections with the Gewisse, but they were now firmly dominated by Penda and would be of little help to the East Anglians. If he was to survive as a king, he needed to send envoys out to more of the island's kingdoms and to seek alliances wherever he could find them.

By the end of AD 649 Penda was unquestionably the most powerful king in Britain. He had direct control over a growing Mercian nation which formed the centre of the island. From this location he controlled the network of Roman roads linking other nations. With this strategic grasp of the roads, Penda owned the primary method of communication between nations, the movement of goods, and the ability of kings to make alliances with one another. In the south, the Gewisse had survived the actions of their king, but were firmly subservient to Mercia. The other traditional power south of the Humber, East Anglia, was still outside Penda's direct dominance but it was teetering on the verge of collapse, and demonstrably weak. East Anglia no longer looked like it could threaten any nation. The Saxon south-east remained largely aloof to the games of nations on the island, instead focusing their attention to the continent.

AD 650 is often referenced as the earliest likely moment when the Staffordshire hoard was buried. Depending on the nature of the hoard and its original purpose, this date fits neatly within the story of Penda. On his return from East Anglia, Penda would be able to claim success on the battlefield for nearly twenty years. His last setback had been against Cadwallon at Exeter, and was at this point long in the past. Penda had amassed fantastic personal wealth, and had been able to supply his thegns and warriors with gifts of weapons and gold. The continued and regular success, however, did put him in possession of more objects then he had necessity for. Kings did not have the option of investing their wealth in the future of the kingdom. Penda could give more of it away, but that came with the risk of driving greed and envy amongst his thegns, leading to destabilization. Another option was to sit on the wealth and keep it for himself to demonstrate his power, but this may also lead to confrontations with the thegns who expected the king to be a giver of gifts. Finally, he could remove it from middle-earth and give it to the gods.

Hoards are often placed for one of a number of reasons; the simplest interpretation of them is that they are placed for safekeeping and recovery at a later date. These type of hoards can be broken down even further into founder and merchant hoards,

> 'Founders' hoards comprise material that was collected for its intrinsic value. Such hoards are characterized by scraps and broken pieces that might be refashioned for a new use. 'Merchants' hoards, on the other hand, tend to contain complete pieces, often with numerous examples of a single type.[10]

This definition is interesting as the Staffordshire hoard appears to fulfil both options, but this assumes that it was placed to be recovered. There are global examples, many of them from the Germanic people of sacrificial hoarding. A sacrificial hoard is never intended for recovery, it is a gift to the gods, spirits or ancestors. This may appear to be a strange thing to do with such a rich composite of material, but it may have had a more earthly driver in the sacrifice and removal of the material from circulation. Ritual hoards have a long history in Northern Europe, and were developed by the culture over thousands of years. The removal of these outward signs of wealth supported the stability of the nation, tribe or kinship group,

> where differences in wealth and prosperity exist, resentment and rebellion may grow despite fears of spiritual retribution. The offering ritual, as reflected in the hoards... helped to ameliorate these tensions. It consisted, after all, of burying wealth and status symbols. The ritual thus allowed high status individuals to demonstrate their power by making the appropriate gifts to the gods. At the same time, it served to remove wealth and sumptuary goods from the elite's control. When the offering ritual was over, the elite were reduced in wealth and lost control of the very sumptuary goods that had set them apart from the general population. Tensions would be eased, yet the hierarchical ranking would remain clear.[11]

The sacrifice of the abundant wealth also removed the material from circulation, thus ensuring the value of objects remained high. This was particularly important when a king was extremely successful, and when the arrival of new objects occurred with regular frequency. On a spiritual level, the hoard allowed the king or the giver to lavish his gods with high-value items, and in turn expect their continued influence. For the people, the sacrifice of rich goods demonstrated the king's continued devotion to his people. He was their protector, and the sacrifice showed to them his willingness to do whatever it took for them.

Aside from the size of the Staffordshire hoard, it is the selection of items that truly sets it apart from other found hoards. This is a hoard of war; all of the material can be linked in one way or another to war, including the Christian items which likely came to a battlefield with a marching army. There is no jewellery or coins in the hoard. This fact also pushes the purpose of its interment towards one of sacrifice. Had this hoard been a true-to-form founders' or merchants' hoard, one would expect to see a variety of other items. Penda had been successful on the battlefield for twenty years, he was the most powerful king in Britain, and thanking the gods would be an appropriate spiritual and cultural motive for the construction of the hoard. By AD 650 Penda was a great warrior, and so he chose to sacrifice war goods, interred for the use of Woden. At the same time, he needed to keep his thegns and nobility supporting him, without elevating them to a point where they would begin conspiring against him.

Removing the gained wealth was a move toward stability at the highest levels of Penda's kingdom. The great Heathen king's nation was much larger by AD 650 and while he had many successes, there were most certainly undercurrents of dissension in his nation. There were those he had conquered, perhaps there were still remnants of Eowa's followers, and most certainly there were plots being hatched in the other nations of Britain. Assassination and political intrigue were well within the playbook of the other kings and even the church at this point. Any of these people could seek to leverage a discontented thegn within Mercia. Any action Penda could do to maintain a balance within the nobility of Mercia was time well spent.

In the poem Beowulf, the namesake king is faced with the same struggle in the latter part of his reign. A hoard is disturbed and a great dragon brings havoc on the kingdom. Beowulf is forced to fight the dragon and in the end the king dies. The hoard that the dragon was guarding was never meant to be removed; it was a sacrificial hoard protected by the dragon. The Staffordshire hoard was Penda's sacrifice, and the dwelling place of his dragon. All of those items were selected because they were gained in combat; they represented the defeated kings, and the power Penda now held across Britain.

The hoard was interred to remove the wealth out of circulation in order to help stabilize the upper ranks of his kingdom and spiritually as sacrifice to his Heathen gods. Such a hoard would undoubtedly attract scavengers, so Penda must have done the work of interring the hoard alone, or with a trusted confidant, perhaps his sons. The selection of the burial location was not random; he had chosen a place that was difficult to get to, hidden, and connected to the landscape and the other worlds through the presence of the tumuli. Penda had selected the location extremely well, and even after the tumuli was eroded away by the work of men ploughing the field, building roads, and placing fences, the hoard remained hidden for 1,400 years.

Chapter Thirteen
Bebbanburg

The attack on Cnobheresburg is usually referenced as occurring in either AD 649 or AD 650, with little evidence to push us in one direction or another. However, Penda's habit of resting his forces for at least a year following a major campaign would seem to point towards AD 649, as we know from Bede and other sources that AD 651 was a campaigning year for Penda. Meaning, in the year AD 650 Penda was able to dedicate time to his family, resting his warbands and maintaining his enlarged kingdom. Like all kings in Britain, he had royal halls spread out across his land, which he travelled on a circuit to maintain his connection with the nobility of the area and ensure his rule was still obeyed. There is very little archaeological evidence for these royal townships, but they may have been in locations near mæthel sites. Some of these places can be identified by place names such as Mayfield, or Matlock, while others may have a connection to the future sites of the hundred courts.

With the Mercian territory expanding, the demand for leadership and command from the king grew in complexity and increasingly required more of Penda's time. Without dedicating time to the maintenance of his kingdom, it would inevitably come apart as a consequence of external pressures, but also internal tribal and kinship based conflict. Mercia was especially challenging as it was made up of many disparate groups, only recently drawn together, with no traditional connection to tie the nation together. By AD 650 Penda's land included the South-Humbrians, the people who had been ruled by Eowa, the Hwicce, the Middle Angles, and scattered smaller groups of Angles and Britons. Alongside these groups, Penda held sway over the Gewisse, and perhaps to a lesser extent East Anglia, though he had no formal tie to them.

As Penda travelled his lands, he was also collecting food and bounty from the land, a type of taxation, and at the same time giving gold and weapons to his thegns and warriors. This mutual exchange of gifts maintained the bond between Penda and his warbands. During these trips, Penda met the new youth who would join the warbands, and they may have sworn oaths to him, or to the thegns in his presence, thus starting the process of bonding between the warriors and the king. Oath rings appear in the archaeological record of Denmark dating back to the Bronze Age 1700 BC. The culture around these items continues on through the Viking age until at least AD 1000. However, there is no evidence of them being used within the Angle or Saxon cultures, which seems a strange deviation from the broader Germanic cultures of the time.[1] The process of swearing an oath to a king or thegn was occurring, but it may have been sealed with another item, perhaps an exchange of a weapon instead of the arm ring.

For Penda, more warriors also meant a greater need for raiding and wealth; however, small targets would no longer suffice for him. He was now hunting for entire nations. East Anglia had been successfully raided, and while he could return there, it would not be worthwhile unless he was intending on subjugating the kingdom into a greater Mercia, which had never been Penda's primary goal in combat. He could target Kent and the south-west, there was plenty of wealth there, but there was no history of attacking those people. A raid on Kent may draw in the other southern kingdoms, leading to a much larger conflict, and one that Penda wasn't sure he could succeed at. The Gewisse were still maintaining peace, as were the Britons to the west. Penda's only legitimate target was to push north of the Humber, as Cadwallon had done years before. Cadwallon had stripped Deira of its wealth, but his attack on the north had ended on the southern border of Bernicia. The northern Angle kingdom had been largely unscathed for generations, making it a plump target for Penda. It's likely that Bernicia was relying on its remoteness to defend against incursions from the south, but Penda's attack on King Anna had proven that he could move an army a great distance and succeed. What was needed was effective planning and logistics, something Penda had become a master at.

When Deira and Bernicia were united under a single king, they were the most powerful nation in Britain. However, in the wake of Oswald's defeat, the nations were once again caught in a cycle of animosity, discord, and violence as the two kings who replaced Oswald competed directly with one another for greater power north of the Humber. The growing conflict between Deira and Bernicia following the fall of Oswald provided an optimal moment for Penda to raid the great northern power. Penda had spent the winter of AD 650 working out a plan for the campaign against Bernicia, and had determined there were two routes available to him. The decision on the route would be guided by the complicity of either the King of Deira or the King of Rheged in Penda's plans.

The Brittonic nation of Rheged is nearly mythical, so little has been left behind in either the archaeological or historical record. This nation was on the west coast, bordered to the north by the River Esk, and in the south by the River Kent. The exact limitation of the nation and influence over other local populations could have stretched a great distance in either direction, perhaps as far south as the River Mersey. Rheged had been subjugated by a number of Deiran and Bernician kings, but had maintained some level of regional power, as can be seen in the marriage between the Rheged princess Rheinmelth and

Oswiu. However, this marriage ended near the point when Oswiu ascended to the throne following the death of Oswald. Upon taking the throne, Oswiu divorced Rheinmelth and quickly wed a Kentish princess, providing him with southern links. The record doesn't provide us with any satisfactory answers as to what happened to Rheinmelth, however, there are potential links between her and an abbey recorded in a ninth-century document which lists donors names.[2] If the Durham *Liber Vitae* is correct and Rheinmelth can be connected with the abbey, then it seems Oswiu divorced Rheinmelth by sending her to an abbey, which was one of the very few avenues available for the new king to divorce his wife.

This was a serious strategic blunder, however, as the king of Rheged wouldn't look kindly on Oswiu and his new bride, after he had lost a direct connection with the king and the power of Bernicia. Oswiu was gambling on Kentish power being more useful to him in the long run than Rheged support. Here was a serious weakness to Bernicia's frontier which properly managed could be exploited by Penda. The disintegration of the connection between Bernicia and Rheged at the hands of Oswiu likely drew Rheged into Penda's orbit, or at the very least opened Rheged up to Penda so that he could march unchallenged to the north. The spurning of Rheged by Oswiu put his frontier much closer to Penda than Oswiu had clearly considered.

In the years following the defeat of Oswald, the formerly united kingdoms of Deira and Bernicia had been tossed into a period of sustained strife driven by dynastic fighting. Oswiu, the brother of Oswald, had ascended to the Bernician throne, but had designs on reuniting the provinces north of the Humber. On the other hand, Oswine, who held the Deiran throne, seems to have had no such motivation, and was likely engaged in the continued recovery of his nation following the devastation of Cadwallon's invasions years prior. Deira was surrounded by insecurity and aggressive neighbours, threatened by Oswiu in the north, and also from the south by the growing strength of Penda. Oswine was generally in a terrible spot, he must have made it a point to keep the peace with his neighbours to the south as the general animosity across the Humber evaporated in the years following Oswald's defeat.

In AD 651 the animosity between Oswine and Oswiu came to a head, and Oswiu launched an invasion of Deira. Oswine raised a force and proceeded to confront the Bernicians in Deiran territory but

> Oswine perceived that he could not maintain a war against his enemy who had more auxiliaries than himself, and he thought it better at that time to lay aside all thoughts of engaging, and to reserve himself for better times. He therefore disbanded the army which he had assembled, and ordered

all his men to return to their own homes, from the place that is called Wilfaraesdun, that is, Wilfar's Hill, which is about ten miles distant from the village called Cataract.[3]

Wilfar's Hill is likely the spot now known as Diddersley Hill which is, '686 feet high. This has a small Roman fortlet to its west, a British earthwork (Scots' Dyke) to its east, and a medieval fortification (Grange Castle) to its north. For over a thousand years it had evident strategic importance.'[4]

The position at Wilfar's Hill was tactically dominant, and it says something about the mismatched nature of the forces that Oswine felt compelled not to stand and fight. With his army disbanded, Oswine went into hiding, hoping to bide his time before raising the army again and attacking Oswiu with a superior force. Unfortunately this tactic utterly failed Oswine who,

> with only one trusty thegn, whose name was Tondhere, withdrew and lay concealed in the house of Hunwald, a noble, whom he imagined to be his most assured friend. But, alas! it was far otherwise; for Hunwald betrayed him, and Oswiu, by the hands of his reeve, Ethilwin, foully slew him and the thegn aforesaid. This happened on the 20th of August, in the ninth year of his reign, at a place called Ingetlingum.[5]

Oswine was betrayed by his own thegn; the power of Oswiu must have been significant for a man to betray his own king. This could also have been caused by Oswine's own actions. His timid attempt to confront the Bernician would have sat poorly with many of his thegns who had to rely on him to protect their nation.

In the early part of AD 651 Penda had two strategies available to him in his northern advance. First, there was an opportunity for Penda to work alongside the Deiran king to march through Deira against Bernicia. The second strategy was to work with Rheged and march north along the western route which crossed the River Mersey, past the battlefield of Maserfield, and then north along the west coast. This second route was through more wild land, with a variety of small polities including Brittonic settlements and small kingdoms. These people would have no love lost with the Bernicia, and could be a valuable partner for Penda, providing him with a safe ingress and egress to Bernicia. The people and nations of the west coast, including Rheged, could provide valuable guides through the country, and perhaps a supply of warriors eager to join the raid.

From Tamworth, Penda would have to move his army almost 450 kilometres to attack the key towns of Bernicia. Such a march with no significant delays caused by ambushes, river-crossing, foul weather, or other issues would take twenty-two days at the pace expected of well-drilled armies of the era. However, the addition of a baggage train and logistics supplies would slow the movement of the army. Assuming Penda was maintaining a friendly disposition with Rheged to protect his route in and out of Bernicia, he would need to bring his own supplies north, and wouldn't be able to rely on raiding along the way to feed his army. Forced to protect his own logistics, the army may have only been capable of fifteen kilometres per day meaning the march north directly to Bebbanburg could have taken as much as thirty days. If the western route through Rheged was the selected route Penda could expect to be on the border of Bernicia on the twenty-first day of the march. From this point he could set up a protected camp and begin conducting quick strikes against local settlements if a pitch battle wasn't offered by Oswiu.

Through the Deiran route Penda could cross into Bernicia on the twentieth day, but this line of attack was much less stable than the Rheged route, and Penda could expect some level of resistance through Deira. This area had been torn apart by Cadwallon years earlier, and many wouldn't have forgotten the role Penda had played in Cadwallon's success. The route through Rheged seems the safer option for Penda's army. Moving through the safe territory of Rheged would maintain a level of surprise which the Deiran route would not be able to provide for the advancing army. Deira and Bernicia may be at odds, but the familial connections were close enough to almost guarantee there were watchful eyes ready to report the movement of armies on both sides. When Penda emerged from Rheged he would find himself and his army placed perfectly to launch attacks against the Bernician countryside, Yeavering, and Bebbanburg, like a wolf on the edge of pasture, lurking and ready to pounce on its prey.

It seems likely that the Rheged route was the one Penda selected. Oswiu's inept statecraft left him facing dissent and grievances emanating from Deira, whose king he had killed, and replaced with his own person, and Rheged who he had spurned early in his reign. Effectively Oswiu had destabilized the buffer between him and Mercia, allowing a golden opportunity for Penda to march further north than any previous attack had ever been able to do.

For Penda, the normal process of mobilizing the army at a prearranged time and place occurred, but the added logistics needed may have added a few days of delay once the army was formed up. Marching through safe territory allowed the army to move and camp without the need of establishing fortified positions each night, significantly decreasing the workload of the force. Moving north through the western route, Penda passed the site of Oswald's defeat at Maserfield. North of this point he was entering largely uncontrolled territory before moving into Rheged. In both cases the size of his force, and the support of Rheged, meant the march north was conducted with no enemy action.

Following twenty-one days on the move, Penda and the Mercian army arrived somewhere east of Carlisle on the Roman road designed to service Hadrian's Wall, the Stanegate Road. Penda entered Bernician territory, north of the River Tyne with the benefit of an open road to the east around 20 August AD 651. This timing was much to the benefit of Penda, as an act of Wyrd had put Oswiu on the march home having confronted Oswine. Oswine was now dead, and the Deirans without a king would be of little concern to Penda during his attack on Bernicia. The surprise of the attack had been maintained by using the Rheged route; had Penda used the eastern route his army would have stumbled into the Bernician army marching home from Wilfaraesdun. As this didn't happen, it is clear that the armies were moving across the landscape on different routes, supporting the theory that Penda had moved north through Rheged.

Oswiu would have disbanded his force as soon as they returned to Bernicia, releasing the men back to their homes and whatever work remained in the running of their estates. This was common practice as none of the kingdoms in Britain maintained standing armies. The sooner the army was disbanded the sooner the cost of feeding and maintaining it would disappear. The timing of the demobilization of the Bernician army was very much to Oswiu's detriment, as he was still unaware that the Mercian army was lurking in his country. By the time Oswiu became aware that there was a threat in Bernicia, it was too late and he was unable to recall his force in time to confront Penda, instead withdrawing to defensive quarters in the north of Bernicia. This was similar to how King Anna had dealt with Penda's aggression, believing that distance was a barrier that could provide some protection. With no direct conflict, Penda was able to move rapidly through the countryside, looting as he went.

Penda may have received word of the death of the Deiran king, and seen both an opportunity and a new threat. The nations north of the Humber had never acted aggressively to their southern neighbours, except when they were united under a single crown. Penda could all but guarantee his northern security while Deira and Bernicia were individual nations, but would most certainly be drawn into conflict the moment they were reunited, as had occurred under Æthelfrith, Edwin and Oswald. However, the death of Oswine did provide an opportunity for Penda to strike at Bernicia without fear of the Deirans riding north to support Oswiu. The loss of their king at the hands of Oswine provided another opportunity for Penda to draw the Deirans closer to him, and perhaps provide military support, or tacit support by allowing Penda to move freely through their lands as he attacked and withdrew from Bernicia. The wealth of Bernicia had not been under serious threat for most of its existence, save for the attacks by Cadwallon. Yet, even the great Cadwallon had been unable to get to Bernicia having been crushed by Oswald at the River Tyne.

Penda and the Mercians faced no serious defensive actions by the Bernicians early in the campaign, largely due to his own good fortune, and the poor timing of Oswiu's demobilization following the death of Oswine. As Penda pushed north he was able to send out small foraging parties from the main army which would bring back raided goods from the local area. This process continued as the force moved north and targeted Yeavering, one of Bernicia's most important royal townships. Yeavering has had human settlement dating back to the Neolithic period and continuing into the seventh century in varying degrees and methods. In the pre-Roman era, a hill fort stood above the site on top of Yeavering Bell. Yeavering Bell hill fort is the largest hill fort north of the Humber encircling some thirteen acres.[6] To the north of the Yeavering Bell, down in the valley bottom along the River Glen, was where the Berncian kings constructed their royal township of Yeavering.

Yeavering itself was developed over centuries, with new additions and new building methods used between the sixth and perhaps as late as the eighth century. The township site contains signs of Brittonic-style buildings which slowly give way to Angle-style buildings, including the second largest great hall surpassed only by the one at Sutton Courtenay. Yeavering included several halls, the grandstand, and the great enclosure, which looks defensive in nature, but was most likely used for the mustering of livestock. The site, like many royal townships in the Angle and Saxon lands, was not built to be defended. There were no palisades or earthworks surrounding it. This site was not a permanent residence for the kings of Bernicia, but used throughout the year to support the governance of the land, and the consumption of resources. Yeavering

> fulfilled in general respects the customary function of a royal estate and the king resorted to it with his entourage only in the course of such progresses as Bede illustrates. At other times the township would presumably be left in the charge of a reeve or praefectus; and the halls set aside for the accommodation of the king and his company probably remained unoccupied more often than not.[7]

During his excavations in 1955 and 1962, Brian Hope-Taylor believed that the halls at Yeavering had been destroyed by fire at multiple times, potentially aligning with Cadwallon's attacks in AD 633, but this assumes that Gwynedd's king was able to make his way into Bernicia, which seems unlikely. Excavations in the mid-twentieth century identified significant destructive events in the seventh century. 'The second destruction of the township may follow as the result of Penda's burning and pillaging the district in 651.'[8] The dating of these destructive forces that impacted Yeavering could easily be off by twenty or thirty years, placing the earlier destruction closer to Penda's AD 651 invasion and the latter destruction nearer to AD 670, or later. As there is no definitive connection to Cadwallon and Yeavering, it seems possible that the first and more significant destructive event at Yeavering may have been under the watchful eye of King Penda.

There is no historic record which speaks of a serious military encounter at Yeavering, which surely implies that King Oswiu was not at the site when the Mercians entered the valley of the River Glen. With King Oswiu and his court not at the site when Penda arrived, it seems unlikely that much material wealth would be available for the raiding army to take away. The consolation for Penda was the destruction of the township at Yeavering. This, however, was not wanton destruction, but an attempt to slow down Oswiu's development of authority, and perhaps make it more difficult for him to control both Bernicia and Deira, the union of which had always been the major threat to their neighbours. Yeavering had been a traditional power centre of Bernician kings, and with it had gone their entire Kingship system which needed to be redrawn and rebuilt. This may decrease the threat that Bernicia could project as the king would be forced to focus his efforts at the internal structure of Bernicia. The burning of Yeavering may also have served to inspire the Deiran Æthelings to rise against King Oswiu, and return balance to the power structure of the north. Until now Penda's actions against other nations had been driven by the need for wealth, and some had been punitive in nature driven by kinship feuds; but Yeavering was an attempt to degrade the infrastructure that supported the power structure of a kingdom. With the Royal township of Yeavering burning, Penda would begin to turn his attention on Bernicia's de facto capital Bebbanburg.

Bebbanburg had been the home of Bernician kings since the arrival of the Angles. The site sits directly on the coast on a rocky outcrop which rises forty metres around the surrounding area. In the 100 years between the arrival of the Angles and the rise of King Ida in AD 547, the Angles and Britons traded control over Bernicia with regularity. King Ida was eventually successful in gaining and maintaining control over Bernicia, and he placed his throne on the rock outcrop at the coast. The *Anglo-Saxon Chronicles* say, 'This year Ida began his reign; from whom first arose the royal kindred of the Northumbrians…Ida reigned twelve years. He built Bebbanburg Castle, which was first surrounded with a hedge, and afterwards with a wall.'[9]

Bebbanburg had a longer history, and was originally called Dynguoaroy by the Britons of Goddodin. King Ida's grandson Æthelfrith continued to develop the site and improve its defences; he 'reigned twelve years in Bernicia, and twelve others in Deira, and gave to his wife Bebba, the town of Dynguoaroy, which from her is called Bebbanburg'.[10]

Bebbanburg was only twenty-five kilometres from Yeavering, and King Oswiu was certainly alerted by this time of the destruction of his royal town on the River Glen, and the danger that Penda and his Mercian army presented. Oswiu was acutely aware that Bebbanburg would be targeted by Penda in the coming days but he was short on options at this moment. He could choose to flee as King Anna had done, perhaps to Deira and raise a force to cut off Penda's retreat. It would be easy enough to bring boats ashore at Bebbanburg, load them with all of his valuables and move south along the coast to safety, though this would likely cost him his northern crown. Or he could trust that the fort at Bebbanburg could hold off an attack by the Mercians, and that Penda would be unwilling to sit through a protracted siege. Bebbanburg was strong, but in a siege it could be easily cut off from the land, eliminating any resupply. If Penda had the supplies and the will, he could force a siege which would compel Oswiu to either sally forth and face the Mercian army, or surrender.

While Oswiu debated his next action, Penda put his force on the road and began moving eastward from Yeavering. The force picked off small towns and hamlets as it moved searching for livestock, gold, weapons, and any other items of value. Penda arrived in front of Bebbanburg in late August AD 651, confronted by the strongest fortress in all of Britain. Penda had been faced with sieges before, and relied on his own good fortune, and the poor judgment of others, to pull through them. The best case scenario for taking the position would be to draw Oswiu out and fight him army to army. Penda formed his army into a shield-wall outside the fortress, but Oswiu was unwilling to entertain him. The Mercian army began looting the town outside the fortress and set up camp to begin the siege.

It seems that Penda may have tried to storm Bebbanburg early in the siege, likely with camp-made ladders to get over the walls. This was risky to say the least, as the defenders could hurl missiles from above, strike downwards with spears, or seek to knock the ladders over. An assault like this over a wall could decimate an army in no time. If Penda tried this route, he prudently withdrew when he saw that the assault would accomplish nothing but to drain his forces. An alternative technique would be an attack on the Bebbanburg gate. In this scenario, Penda would seek to pull the gate apart using ropes and horses. All attempts to attack Bebbanburg failed as Bede tells us that Penda had not been 'able to take it by storm or by siege'.[11]

The Mercian King had to come up with a new approach to break Bebbanburg open. Penda

> endeavoured to burn it down; and having pulled down all the villages in the neighbourhood of the city, he brought thither an immense quantity of

beams, rafters, partitions, wattles and thatch, wherewith he encompassed the place to a great height on the land side, and when he found the wind favourable, he set fire to it and attempted to burn the town.[12]

The gathering of material must have occurred quickly, and Penda was not forced to wait long for the weather conditions to favour him and the lighting of the great pyre. Unfortunately the wind shifted direction, causing the flames and embers to drift landward, scattering Penda's army and allowing the fortress of Bebbanburg to survive. Bede attributes this to the actions of St Aidan who was watching the assault on the city from the Farne Islands, three and a half kilometres to the west:

> When he saw the flames of fire and the smoke carried by the wind rising above the city walls, he is said to have lifted up his eyes and hands to heaven, and cried with tears, 'Behold, Lord, how great evil is wrought by Penda!' These words were hardly uttered, when the wind immediately veering from the city, drove back the flames upon those who had kindled them, so that some being hurt, and all afraid, they forbore any further attempts against the city.[13]

Bebbanburg had lived up to its reputation, and Penda had been unable to punch his way in, but there were still opportunities for success in the local area. The connection with St Aidan and his prayers helps establish the timeline of events a bit. St Aidan died shortly after Oswine, the king of Deira was murdered: 'Aidan himself was also taken out of this world, not more than twelve days after the death of the king he loved, on the 31st of August.'[14] This means that Penda was moving fast and the assault, and the attempt to breach by fire occurred before 31 August AD 651. After entering Bernician territory Penda had moved quickly to take Yeavering and then attack Bebbanburg in a rapid series of events. The fact that he was able to move so quickly shows a lack of an organized defence in Bernicia, which was caused by the disbandment of the army just before Penda launched his surprise attack from Rheged.

After the fire failed to breach the walls, Penda turned some of his attention to the north, the holy island of Lindisfarne. Lindisfarne is a small island measuring about five kilometres by two and a half kilometres and encompassing around 1,000 acres. The island can be reached over a narrow causeway, 'as the tide ebbs and flows, is twice a day enclosed by the waves of the sea like an island; and again, twice, when the beach is left dry, becomes contiguous with the land.'[15] The island had been given to St Aidan in AD 635 by King Oswald, for the establishment of a monastery. Oswald's vision was the creation of an Eastern

Iona, the island that he had spent part of his exile on, and where he had found his Christian spirituality. Saint Aidan was an ideal man for the task, as he had spent much of his life on Iona, and understood how a remote religious order should be developed and run. In the ensuing fifteen years since it was established, Lindisfarne became a centre of Christianity north of the Humber with a church, cells for monks, a library, and all the other peripheral supports for the site to largely be self-sufficient.

King Oswald was a man of deep religious conviction, and his reign was relatively successful; both of these factors would have greatly benefited the religious order at Lindisfarne. Throughout Oswald's reign he funnelled wealth and prestige on St Aidan's episcopal see, making the site extremely wealthy, and a target that Penda, or any other raiding party, couldn't pass up. Gold in particular was the primary target for Penda. The churches had always had plentiful supplies with which they made religious regalia. The island's safety was bound to the cycling of the tides, and the shifting sand bars which tied it to the mainland. Penda would be keen to keep his intentions of attack unknown in the hope that it would prevent the people of Lindisfarne from fleeing with the islands riches by boat. He also needed to keep Oswiu engaged, and incapable of seeking assistance, so the main part of his force was required to maintain the siege at Bebbanburg, while a smaller raiding party was sent to take Lindisfarne.

When the tide was still dropping and the sands were exposed connecting Lindisfarne to the mainland, Penda's warband launched the raid. This had to be done quickly to prevent the monks from fleeing with the monastery's valuables out to sea. As the place was likely not protected by warriors, Penda's small and mobile force on horseback would make quick work of the action. As soon as the tide dropped low enough, the mounted warband hurried across the sand flats and rode hard for the centre of the monastery. The raid was partially successful, but it is fair to assume some of the precious objects were safely hidden by the monks. Bede records the attack on Lindisfarne, but the dates he gives are very loose, and suggestive of a second attack in the following years after the assault on Bebbanburg. But this doesn't fit well with the chronology of future events. It also seems doubtful that Penda would be capable of launching another raid so deep into Bernicia without them having established a fortified position in the north. Had Penda launched multiple annual attacks which pierced so far north with little or no defence from Oswiu, it would seem almost impossible for Oswiu to maintain his reign. His failure to defend his nation against Penda in such a scenario would surely lead to him being deposed. The attack on Lindisfarne and the destruction of the church must have occurred during a single campaign, and that was Penda's AD 651 invasion.

Penda is often accused of conducting a war against Christianity with the attack on Lindisfarne being held up as a prime example. But this opinion simply isn't true, he saw a weakness and sought to exploit it. Within his cultural and moral compass, a church or monastery was a viable target, and if a king was foolish enough to place his wealth in the hands of those with no weapons and no defences, then it was his fault if it was taken by his competition. This exact same scenario played out again in AD 793 when the first Viking raid arrived off the coast of Northumbria. In fact the *Anglo-Saxon Chronicles* entry for AD 793 could easily have been written for Penda's attack on Lindisfarne, 'heathen men made lamentable havoc in the church of God in Holy-island, by rapine and slaughter'.[16] In the attacks against Lindisfarne it was the failure of the kings of Bernicia to protect the holy island which led to the raids. Raiding was endemic across northern Europe and formed a critical part of the warrior culture, and the king's role as the provider of wealth to his people. The kings of Bernicia seemingly forgot, or ignored, the cultural setting, choosing instead to base their decisions on a foreign culture, which didn't account for the realities of northern Europe since the dawn of the Roman Empire right through to the conclusion of the Viking era at the turn of the eleventh century. In both Penda's attack in AD 651 and the Viking raid 140 years later, the attackers had no concern over religious difference; they were merely conducting culturally appropriate raids. It is the future interpretation through Christian eyes that cast the raids on Lindisfarne as acts of religious war pitting the ancient Heathen religion against the defenceless Christians.

Penda still had the upper hand against Oswiu, and could set in a siege against Bebbanburg, eventually starving the king and his people out of the fort, but he didn't. Instead, it would appear that the kings reached a settlement which goes unrecorded, other than an interesting marriage which is recorded by Bede offhand in a passage assigned to another topic. Bede is speaking of Peada, the son of Penda in AD 653 and tells us, 'King Oswiu's son Alhfrith, who was his [Peada's] brother-in-law and friend, for he had married his sister Cyneburh, the daughter of King Penda.'[17] It is an odd marriage to have occurred in the year after the attack on Bernicia, and is more than likely part of a peace settlement that saw Penda withdraw from the northern nation. Oswiu would swear some form of oath, and the end of hostilities would be bound by the wedding of Alhfrith and Cyneburh. What this scenario truly says is that Penda was ready to hold the siege, but was not as bloodthirsty as his reputation suggests, choosing instead to find another way to end the campaign.

Penda had succeeded in setting back Oswiu's authority, destroying some of his infrastructure, and removing plenty of wealth from Bernicia for redistribution in Mercia. This was one of Penda's most successful raids. He had suffered minimal losses and achieved maximum results. His ability to seemingly reach any quarter of Britain gave all kings reason to consider their future actions. Penda may have exited Bernicia through Deira, and helped place the Ætheling Æthelwald on the throne. Æthelwald was the son of King Oswald, who had fallen at the hand of Penda. The newly established king of Deira was a devout Christian, much like his father had been, but neither his father's death nor his religious beliefs held him back from accepting the support of the Heathen King Penda. This further highlights the fact that the animosity between religions was much lower than the pictures painted by the limited records of the time would have us believe. What was more important than religion was the traditional ideals of kingship, which were focused on the security of the people through the power and protection of the king.

For King Penda, the establishment of Æthelwald on the Deiran throne was a major success. He now had a reliable partner north of the Humber, who could act against Northumbrian unity, and keep Mercia's northern border free from security threats. Æthelwald benefited from the arrangement as well; by gaining the support of Penda, he was able to guarantee the wellbeing of Deira against the biggest military threat in Britain, and could focus his attention on other matters of state, including the threat posed by Bernicia. By providing support of Æthelwald, Penda had taken on the role of kingmaker in Britain, something that Rædwald, Edwin, and Oswald had all enjoyed during their reigns, placing Penda amongst the most powerful kings to rule between the evacuation of the Roman Legions and the establishment of the Danelaw in the ninth century. Penda had developed from the role of destroyer of kings, to maker of kings, and had entered the period of his greatest power and influence. Through prudent military actions and astute statecraft, Penda had brought stability to Mercia on all of its frontiers. The greatest military threat had always come from north of the Humber, but that threat was now under control through the devastation of the centre of power in Bernicia, and the placement of a subjugated king in Deira. To the east, the traditionally dominant East Anglian kingdom was a shadow of its former self, and to the west Penda continued to enjoy a reliable relationship with the Brittonic kingdoms.

The attack on Bernicia was remarkable for the distances covered by Penda. The direct route to and from Bebbanburg was almost 900 kilometres. Marching home through Deira and seeing to the establishment of Æthelwald in York put the triumphant Penda back home at the end of September, just in time to prepare for the winter and enjoy the spoils of war. Along with King Penda, his son Peada and nephew Merewalh also returned home having experienced what a campaigning king was required to do, and learned how to move an army across the landscape, as well as using the art of statecraft to ensure long-term solutions to security and power.

Chapter Fourteen

Pendingas

Mercia in the seventh century was still a nation divided by many boundaries formed by divergent cultures and competing groups. The effort to keep all of them together must have been all-consuming at times for King Penda. We know a little about Penda and his activities writ large, but close to nothing about how he ran Mercia. Throughout his time as a warlord first, and then as an established king, Penda was keeping Britons and Angles of many tribal affiliations, and even more kinships groups together as a single national entity. The variance in culture was most striking from east to west as the balance of Angle and Briton changed the local demographic. In AD 652 and AD 653, Penda would continue acting as a kingmaker, supporting Æthelings and helping to establish new kings. But, rather than looking beyond Mercia, he was now focused on the cause of internal state management and establishing Peada and Merewalh in positions of power. This was smart organization of leadership, as it would decrease the potential for internal strife amongst the brothers, lessen Penda's workload trying to manage such a large territory, and still maintain his external authority over Britain.

Succession of the crown was perilous business in the seventh century as factions internal and external vied to place their favoured Æthelings on the throne. There was no formal process to pass the throne between kings, and the Æthelings themselves would be in direct competition with one another vying for position and favour in the hopes of achieving the position of king. This competition would increase with age as the reigning king continued to succeed and hold the throne. Should one of the Æthelings reach a point where they saw their opportunity to rule slipping past because the king simply wouldn't die, it could certainly spill over into armed revolt or assassination. To avoid these issues, most kings sent viable claimants into exile, something the kings of both Deira and Bernicia had used frequently since the sixth century. While this method eliminated the immediate risk to the king, it produced an ongoing risk of usurpation and drew other nations and other kings into the internal politics and governance of particular kingdoms. In turn, this drives future issues and the risk of revolt supported by foreign kings. When an exiled Ætheling was finally able to succeed to the throne, he owed something to the nation that had sponsored him in exile and supported his claim. This naturally placed the new king automatically under the control of another party, something that could directly impact the longevity of that king and impact his freedom to act. In the modern day this is not unlike what occurs with lobbyist and campaign funding in much of the democratic world. A special interest group supports the election campaign of a person through donations, and in return gains certain access and support from the individual once they are elected.

Penda seems to have had no inclination to utilize exile in his own court, and had done a remarkable job of containing any of the dynastic threats inside his own house. It could be that Penda had no reason to suspect there were any threats from within his own family but he was keen to ensure the ingredients needed for a dynastic struggle were removed from the equation. Penda was motivated to address any opportunity for discord within the ruling Iclingas both from a self-preservation perspective, but also wanting to see his sons succeed, something many kings would never be afforded.

His plan was relatively simple: he would place his eldest son Peada and his nephew Merewalh as kings of Mercian sub-kingdoms. By AD 652 Peada and Merewalh were in their early twenties, and in the eyes of Penda, ready for the responsibility of leadership. In his own life, Penda had taken on the role of a warlord and thegn at a similar age. While he had to wait a number of years to eventually rise to the position of king, he clearly saw that the time was right for his son and nephew. Penda had learned his craft largely on his own, as he had never known his own father as a king, only as a thegn. He had been granted good fortune in life, and the influence and guidance of his wife Cynewise likely played a part in his education as a king and the occupation of ruling. What set Penda apart from the cohort of kings in Britain is that his methods and skills had been learned through experience first and foremost, and a gradual increase in authority where he was able to use what worked and dispose of what didn't. He was able to mix this real world experience with the culturally appropriate court components, through the guidance of Cynewise, who had been brought up in the household of a king.

Peada and Merewalh had been afforded the opportunity to learn the methods Penda had developed and blended over his lifetime, giving them a head start in their future roles. Peada would be expected to govern in the same manner as Penda, as that was what he had been exposed to for his entire life. Merewalh on the other hand had a variable background to draw from. While he had certainly learned many important lessons from Penda, he could also rely on the exposure to court life he had in his father's house in Gewisse, though this wasn't a king's household. The way Cenwalh had treated Merewalh's mother, it could very well be that Merewalh was not well liked by his father, and may not have been given the education he needed to one day be a ruler. However, even that experience could be beneficial for him as he moved forward and matured.

Kings of the seventh century were required to not only employ sensible statecraft, but also be capable of leading men on the battlefield. The martial aspect of the role was formed through experience and the demonstration of bravery and skill in the face of the enemy. The martial obligation had slowly been eroded by the Saxon and Angle nations of the south-east, much to their own detriment. Penda on the other hand had built his career on his skills as a warrior. It was a foundational block of his success, and something he would surely demand of both Merewalh and Peada. Both men must have proven themselves as capable warriors and leaders on the battlefield for Penda to see them as viable rulers in their own right. They were old enough to take part in the campaign against King Anna, and the attack on Bernicia; both of these campaigns had shown the young men the value of proper logistics, and the balance between aggression and prudence. These two lessons were crucial if they were to become campaigning warrior kings. The one thing that was missing from these campaigns was the use of a large set-piece pitched battle between massed shield-walls. Nonetheless, the time had arrived for the two young men to be promoted and begin ruling.

Peada, the son of Penda, was given the kingdom of the Middle Angles to rule. This was the eastern flank of Mercia. From this position Peada would be able to counter any future aggression from East Anglia, though in their current state that would seem a long way off. The Middle Angles were a non-homogenized group of traditionally smaller sub-kingdoms which had survived as buffer states between the more powerful nations. Peada now had the task of trying to draw all of them together into a single stable nation. He would also need to contend with subversive activities emanating from the East Anglians, who would see a serious threat from a united polity near their border. None of this was easy, but Peada could still count on the power and support of Penda, which would go a long way in the early days of his reign. Nation-building in these turbulent waters would take a man of intellect and empathy. Bede records that Peada, 'Being an excellent youth, and most worthy of the name and office of a king, he was by his father elevated to the throne of that nation.'[1] If he was a capable warrior like his father, Peada could look towards Lindsey and even Elmet as areas of expansion.

Upon ascending to the throne of the Middle Angles, Peada needed to find a wife. Penda would be keen on using the opportunity of his son's ascension to continue tying other nations to him, but the match would need to be from a nation which had stature and power. For Penda, the clearest need and most suitable option remained in the north. Bebbanburg had saved Oswiu and Bernicia, and would continue to be uncrackable by force; only statecraft would open those gates. Word was sent to Oswiu by Penda asking for a suitable wife for Peada, and Oswiu, keen on reciprocating the marriage between his son Alhfrith and Penda's daughter Cyneburh, (and perhaps under some duress from the power of Penda) agreed to allow Alhflæd to marry Peada, but on one condition. Oswiu stipulated that Peada

> could not obtain his desire unless he would receive the faith of Christ, and be baptized, with the nation which he governed. When he heard the preaching of the truth, the promise of the heavenly kingdom, and the hope of resurrection and future immortality, he declared that he would willingly become a Christian.[2]

Peada was the first, but not the last, of Penda's children to convert to Christianity. Had Penda been the religious zealot that he is portrayed, this event would be expected to cause serious discord between Penda and his son, but it does not. Penda didn't care about a person's religion, not amongst his nation, kin, or children. Instead, Bede records that Penda 'hated and despised those whom he perceived to be without the works of faith, when they had once received the faith of Christ, saying, that they were contemptible and wretched who scorned to obey their God, in whom they believed'.[3]

Aside from establishing Peada in the east, Penda also had work to complete in the west. The sequencing of events here is unknown, but it would seem appropriate for Penda to first establish his son Peada, and then turn to Merewalh. Very little is known about Merewalh, and his name is recorded in a few scattered hagiographies and the *Liber Eliensis*. He is recorded as the first king of the Magonsæta, a nation along the River Severn bordering Hwicce in the east and the Brittonic kingdoms of the west. What goes unrecorded is how he gained the territory. This area had been under the control of the Iclingas since Penda's grandfather, and was a stable area built on the foundation of solid relationships between the Iclingas and the Brittonic nations, primarily Powys but also Gwent and Brycheiniog. The people here were both Britons and Angles, and the leadership of them required skills in both cultures and languages.

Theories around the rise of Merewalh often centre round an interpretation of him being a Briton of noble birth who was being rewarded with a sub-kingdom following the events of Maserfield. This interpretation is based almost entirely on the reading of Merewalh's name; in particular the second portion of his name, 'walh' which can be interpreted as 'foreigner'. This was the vernacular term used by the Angles for Britons, and the forerunner of the word 'Welsh'. While this may be an accurate understanding, it fails to assess all of the other clues around him including the connection to Cenwalh. This interpretation is also peculiar, if Merewalh was a Briton, why would he have a name that is clearly an Angle name formed by Angle words?

By the end of AD 653 Mercia had been divided into three parts, ruled by King Peada, King Merewalh, and King Penda. The Magonsæta were likely a mixed group with both Heathens and Brittonic Christians present. Mercia was still a Heathen nation, but with smaller isolated groups of converts scattered through the nation. The kingdom farthest to the east had nominally converted with Peada. The conversion of Peada was not an event driven by goodwill and a desire to spread the faith, but politically motivated. Oswiu was using conversion as a weapon and a method of influence and control. Peada's conversion under the guidance of Oswiu was a significant political victory for the Bernician king, as it increased his ability to influence events within the lands of the Middle Angles.

Oswiu then turned to the East Saxons and began their conversion in AD 653, 'At that time, also, the East Saxons, at the instance of King Oswiu, again received the faith, which they had formerly cast off.'[4] This story is more interesting in that King Sigbert of the East Saxons travelled north to Bernicia to meet Oswiu and be baptized 'by Bishop Finan, in the king's township above spoken of, which is called At the Wall, because it is close by the wall which the Romans formerly drew across the island of Britain, at the distance of twelve miles from the eastern sea'.[5]

In this event we see the shadow of a subservient relationship where Oswiu is the power broker. Penda was watching these manoeuvres and most certainly began to suspect that Oswiu was encircling Mercia with a loosely allied group of nations, using conversion and Christianity as a diplomatic tool.

The connection between Sigbert and Oswiu shows that the transportation routes running north and south along the eastern seaboard remained open and accessible to all, in spite of the fact that Mercia had control of the most important ones. Mercian dominance of the road system had great strategic benefit to Penda who could gain word of messengers travelling north and south, allowing him to maintain at least some awareness of what was going on across Britain, particularly in the case of a king moving across the land as Sigbert had done. Sigbert's retinue was able to move on the periphery of Mercia, on a north-south route straight to the Humber, but at some point would have crossed Mercia or a Mercian dominated sub-kingdom before entering Deira and then heading to the Bernician border.

In the middle of this period of expanding Bernician power and influence through diplomatic channels, Penda's attention was drawn back to East Anglia. The exact cause of Penda's next actions is unknown, but he launches another deep-striking campaign against King Anna in AD 654. Based solely on the proximity to events surrounding Oswiu, it seems likely that the kings of East Anglia and Bernicia were in contact perhaps through the baptism of King Sigbert. A coalition between Bernicia and East Anglia would pose an extreme hazard to Penda and Mercia, and such an alliance couldn't be allowed to develop any further. Penda would have to attack Bernicia or East Anglia in order to derail this threat. If he went north against Bernicia it may impact his son Peada, who had connection through marriage with Oswiu. Peada's reign was so new that shaking it with a contentious attack north may cause massive internal instability. Moving against East Anglia, however, didn't create any of these same problems, and would at the same time eliminate the current threat. The East Anglians had also twice failed to deal with Penda's warbands, and there was no reason to think they would be able to tackle them a third time. Penda would launch another attack against East Anglia, with the primary focus being on regime change. He needed to put a friendly king on the throne to maintain security in the east and to isolate Oswiu in the north.

Penda's calculations to attack must have taken into account the security of Mercia if he moved his warbands eastward. He had a subservient king in Deira, blocking Bernicia, King Merewalh in the west, and King Peada in the East. Through his efforts to establish friendly kings, he had encircled his own nation with a cordon of trusted nations providing a barrier between him and the other powerful kingdoms of Britain. In effect he had established a series of marches, which prevented direct contact between Mercia and the other dominant nations. Although he may not have had a name for this strategy, it is precisely the same one that would be employed by Charlemagne and the Franks 150 years later.

Attacking East Anglia this third time would still require a long-range attack, but the lands had been subdued in the previous attacks, so the march to the border may have been quicker. There was no need for Penda to use deception in his movement, from Tamworth it was an uncomplicated trip along the Roman roads in a south-east direction towards Cambridge and the East Anglian border. This route would push the force back through the Devil's Dyke Gap. The major challenge with East Anglia was that the majority of the nation was hinterland, with the developed areas mainly being coastal. This meant an attacking army now had to move 100 kilometres through enemy territory to reach the coastline and the critical settlements. The depth of the nation provided King Anna with the opportunity to buy time and draw together a defensive force as soon as he received warning that Penda was on his border. A more skilful warrior king, however, would have sought to establish ambushes, or a pitched battle at a favourable location, but King Anna seemed to have done neither of these things.

At some point Penda was able to zero in on King Anna's location, near the coast and the present day town of Southwold. This location was strategically advantageous for King Anna, as it maximized the distance Penda had to travel, and made travelling much more difficult. The Roman road system had no direct links between Cambridge and the Southwold area, and using it would increase the travel distances required to reach King Anna. The Mercians would be forced to use footpaths and ancient roads, and cross-country travel to reach the general area. This was difficult travelling involving effective reconnaissance and well-selected locations for camps which could be defended. Each day that Penda was travelling was a day King Anna was gifted to continue forming his army and preparing his defensive position. There is once again no record of a multiple skirmish campaign, only a single act of combat near Bulcamp. While a series of battles and skirmishes can't be eliminated, it seems that King Anna had decided to set a defensive position deep in East Anglia, drawing Penda in. Such a strategy did create a significant advantage for King Anna, provided he could find an appropriate spot to host a pitched battle, and that he could draw a force equal to the Mercians.

Penda would need six or seven days to push north-east once he entered East Anglia. His route would bring him to Halesworth on about the fifth day of marching through East Anglia. The area around Halesworth is a likely location for a final camp before facing King Anna. By the time the Mercians arrived here they would have a good understanding of the location of King Anna. Both sides would be sending out riders to watch the other side and get an understanding of the strength and disposition of the opposition. King Anna had selected a defensive position which placed the River Blyth south-west of his front line, with his main force on the high ground at the crossroads on the north shore of the Blyth estuary. King Anna's position had the advantage of height, though it was only about twenty metres, and his rear was protected by the woods. His left flank was partially secured by the estuary. King Anna had multiple routes for retreat should that be needed. His strategy was to draw Penda onto the high ground, and then push him south wedging him between the River Blyth and the estuary were Penda would have no place to retreat from.

There are a number of alternative locations for King Anna's position in the local vicinity which can't be outright rejected. For starters there is Land Hill which is north of the crossroads. This position would provide more elevation, though it would seem to not match the idea that the king was killed to the south as this route of retreat would be covered by Penda's force. Alternatively, King Anna may have had his force farther west, perhaps in the vicinity of the old holloway called King's Lane, which in local tradition is named for King Anna. At this western point he could effectively use the River Blyth and the swampy ground around it to protect his left flank. Any of these options, along with the ground in between them, are all viable locations for the battle, and until archaeological evidence uncovers material which points to a battle site, all of the locations must remain as possibilities.

On the day of the battle, Penda moved east out of Halesworth with his force following the footpaths on the north side of the River Blyth. Near Bulcamp, King Anna's position was sighted. Penda set up his shield-wall and finally began a westerly approach. In the final moments, Penda may have wheeled his line around the right flank to change the angle that the two forces would meet and give the Mercians some advantage. The shield-walls came together, the tide once again turned in Penda's favour.

> Fierce as a wolf, by hunger rendered in bold, O'erleaps the fence, and ravens in the field, mangling the fleecy flock, besmeared with blood; His jaws, his shaggy hide, reek in the gory flood. Some he devours, insatiate; some he tears; nor one of all the quivering crowd he spares. So mighty Penda, dealing furious blows, prostrates the foremost of his cowering foes.[6]

The *Chronica Majora* also provides some colour to the conduct of Penda in the battle of Bulcamp: 'Penda king of the Mercians, who was all Furious in arms, none but blood spilled. He rejoices to have his ways. He invaded Anna, king of the East Angles, a well-religious man, in war, and in a moment broke in pieces all his army.'[7]

This passage corroborates the destruction of the East Anglian army, and suggests that the Mercians were overwhelming in their dominance. There is nothing recorded to suggest that the force King Anna had drawn together provided any sort of test for Penda's force.

King Anna's army crumbled under the weight of the Mercian attack, and was now caught in its own trap being pushed back against the Blyth estuary. As the East Anglians were mauled by the Mercian army, a few warriors were able to flee, but most fell on the field. King Anna withdrew with a small force along the road to the south where he eventually fell. 'King Anna and his army fell quickly at the edge of the sword, and there was scarcely one who survived.'[8] Local legend places the point of King Anna's death along the modern road at a location called the 'Bulcamp Oddity'. This is a peculiar early nineteenth-century brick traveller's shelter built into the embankment on the road. The local legend is that the shelter was built over the site of a spring which miraculously formed on the spot that King Anna died.

King Anna's son Jurmin also perished at Bulcamp. Both of them were recovered from the field at a later time buried at Blythburg one kilometre south from where they fell. Penda's mission in East Anglia was regime change; he hadn't come for wealth or territory, but to ensure Oswiu's influence was slowed in the east and the south. Penda used his prerogative as the most powerful king in Britain to place Anna's brother Æthelhere who 'succeeded to the kingdom. He was made a friend to King Penda, who was to reign under him, and then received the throne'.[9] Like so many others, we know very little about Æthelhere other than his lineage. He was the brother of Anna, and a son of Eni, who had been the brother of Rædwald. Æthelhere would have seen the drastic change in East Anglian fortunes over the years, and had perhaps turned to Penda in search of a more secure future for East Anglia.

The removal of King Anna placed Penda in a position where he had influence over five kings, with only Bernicia, Kent, East Saxons, and the South Saxons as major power centres not connected in some way with him. The King of Mercia was very much operating within the boundaries of cultural norms in his conduct with other nations and established thrones. Rather than absorbing and dominating the nations, he sought out an Ætheling that needed support, and in return would owe something to him. Had Penda deviated from this, he very well may have put the idea of 'England' much further down the road, rather than waiting until the rise of Wessex in the ninth century.

Æthelhere must have taken the throne with some level of trepidation. No East Anglian ruler had faired particularly well since Rædwald in AD 624. For the East Anglians, political, religious, and external strife had consistently ended the reign of kings early and frequently. In the past thirty years there had been five rulers of East Anglia, an average of six years for each. Three of the kings had fallen at the hand of King Penda, and one had been assassinated by an East Anglian dissident. All of the previous rulers had failed to understand the broader political landscape of the island along with the cultural issues associated with conversion. Æthelhere had additional challenges related to the support of Penda. The East Anglian nobility had suffered greatly at the hand of Penda in three invasions, and for many there must have been unwavering hostility towards the Mercian. The challenge faced by the new king of East Anglia was to keep Penda happy, and at the same time bring the thegns of East Anglia on to his side. Failure with either of these tasks would result in another invasion by King Penda, or an internal political challenge from rebels within East Anglia, as Ricbert had done against Eorpwald the successor of Rædwald. On top of these issues, Æthelhere was likely exposed to overtures from Oswiu, perhaps via the East Saxons. These conversations in particular were high risk to the East Anglian king, as they had caused Penda to dethrone King Anna.

Æthelhere had to choose a side against a backdrop of competing religious influences, political pressure, personal preservation, and the needs of his people.

Penda withdrew his force back to the Icknield Way, and then from Cambridge to Tamworth. As he returned home he would have passed through the land of the Middle Angles and his son Peada. The men were able to share stories, and the court of Peada, with his connections to Oswiu, was able to pass on the message of what had happened in the east. The news of King Anna's defeat, and the establishment of a Penda-backed king in East Anglia was surely received as the worst of news by King Oswiu. While he still had tight enough connections to the East Saxons and Kent, neither of these nations were capable of competing against the Mercian warrior king. Bernicia could no longer count on the support of Deira, and had no chance of a relationship with the nations of the Brittonic west. This left King Oswiu with only one option, and that was to turn north to the Britons and Picts for support and mutual defence. Bernician kings had maintained deep connections to these northern nations, going back to the exile of Edwin and in particular Oswald and Oswiu. The brothers had spent most of their exile in Dal Riata, and had deep cultural and personal links to that nation. Through Dal Riata, Oswiu had connections with Gododdin, Strathclyde, Pictish kingdoms, and the Irish lands, and it was to these nations he now focused his attention.

The relationship that Penda had with the western Brittonic nations of Powys and Gwynedd, along with Oswald's and Oswiu's connections to the northern Brittonic and Pictish nations, certainly draws into question the idea of ethnic conflict between Britons and Angles. Instead, we see people with a variety of cultures closely connected to one another, and using those connections to benefit their tribal groups. There is in fact no difference between how Brittonic nations treaty with one another, or with how Angle nations compete and collaborate together. In the seventh century there was no surety of power, and the rise and fall of nations and kings was a regular feature of the age. Kings were in a constant state of competition with one another and when a king was outcompeted he sought the protection of more powerful nations, regardless of the language, religion, or culture of the more powerful king. Religious zealousness or tribal affiliation was a luxury that would be dismissed when security and safety couldn't be guaranteed.

The ideas that Bede and future writers provide about the rift between competing characteristics of nations and individuals were simply not relevant in AD 654. In fact, genetic research of the modern population of Britain seems to support the idea of intermingling, rather than outright replacement of Britons by Angles,

> Two separate analyses show clear evidence in modern England of the Saxon migration, but each limits the proportion of Saxon ancestry, clearly excluding the possibility of long term Saxon replacement. We estimate the proportion of Saxon ancestry in England as very likely to be under 50%.'[10]

Had there been broad ethnic conflict one would expect for the genetics to be much more separate than they clearly are.

With Peada and Merewalh successfully established in their own kingdoms, Penda's house was a little emptier, though he still had three of his children at home. Wulfhere and Æthelred, both of which were Penda's sons, were around thirteen and eight years old. They still had many years before they would need to establish their own homes, and perhaps own kingdoms. Of his two daughters, Cyneswith seems to still be at the hall of Penda. His other daughter Cyneburh had been betrothed to Oswiu's eldest son Alhfrith in the immediate aftermath of Penda's victory in Bernicia. Often it is assumed that this marriage followed that of Peada and Alhflaed, but Bede makes it clear that isn't the case as he references Alhfrith's part in the conversion of Peada prior to his marriage. 'King Oswiu's son Alhfrith, who was his brother-in-law and friend, for he had married his sister Cyneburh, the daughter of King Penda.'[11] Alhfrith and Cyneburh's marriage may well have been an attempt by Oswiu to ensure he had a treaty with Penda, though none is recorded. On the opposite side it may have been forced upon Oswiu by Penda as part of the ending of hostilities.

Alhfrith's mother was the Rheged princess that Oswiu had put aside when he took power. If Alhfrith held any animosity toward his father this marriage was perfect for him, as it opened opportunities to work with Penda against his father. There is no proof of any tension between Oswiu and Alhfrith in the immediate years following the union between Cyneburh and Alhfrith. However, they would eventually fall out with one another. Penda had relied on the tacit support from the Rheged King during the attack on Bernicia, it was the free access to pass through Rheged lands that had allowed the attack to occur without warning and without direct defensive action by the Bernicians. This marriage would also be seen as a positive bond between Mercia and Rheged, from who Alhfrith could claim some descent through his mother.

Cyneburh had been raised by one of the finest Queens of the age, and she would no doubt seek to replicate the courage, intelligence, and loyalty her mother had shown. Because of this, it can be expected that Penda had no illusions that he would have even the slightest influence over the affairs of the Bernician court through Cyneburh. Instead, he would expect her to serve her family and her king as Cynewise had done when she left the Gewisse and married Penda. No doubt that Alhfrith was reminded of his duties and the oath he now had to his wife, and was under no misconception that Penda would launch nation-on-nation conflict in the interest of his kin, as he had done with Cenwalh.

Chapter Fifteen

Winwaed

In AD 655 Penda would find no rest from the complications of kingship and the challenges of the battlefield. He had improved the internal governance of Mercia through the establishment of both Merewalh and Peada as kings in sub-kingdoms of Mercia, and he had removed the last major southern threat in King Anna. AD 655 should have been a year of rest for Penda, with a focus on the internal needs of Mercia, but unfortunately it wasn't. Perhaps as early as the winter of AD 654, Penda had decided to deviate from his usual approach of resting between campaigns and set his mind to finally removing the threat of Oswiu and Bernicia. What drove this decision is unknown, but it seems likely that it was still connected to the diplomatic manoeuvring of Oswiu, which continued to present a threat to Mercia. This attack was to be the largest and most complex of his career, and shows signs of significant planning based on the number of participants Penda was able to draw together. This campaign was not a hastily put together operation, and must have had its roots deep in the winter of AD 654 with the messaging from Penda to his partners.

Throughout the winter Penda was sending messengers to all corners of Britain, asking some, and perhaps telling other kings to prepare for war and to meet him with their warbands at a specified location and time. He may not have shared the target with them, but they could all work out that this must be a push against the north. By AD 655 Penda had spent nearly thirty years as a leader of warriors; there was no other king with the same level of combat experience as he had gained. Penda had experienced the breadth of combat, sieges, failures, pitched battles, raids and ambushes. He had on countless times demonstrated contempt for his personal safety and continually led his men from the very front, earning the nicknames 'Penda the Strong' and 'Penda Son of Danger'. For many of the subservient kings, and certainly for their young warriors, the opportunity to march with Penda was not a tough sell, but rather a great opportunity to expand their skills, reputation and wealth.

Penda's motivation to go against his usual trend of resting a year between campaigns is puzzling. Throughout his life, only during the Cadwallon years had he campaigned in back-to-back years. Either he was compelled to react to something, or he was hopeful that one more campaign would allow him to finally secure the entire island. Oswiu may very well have continued his diplomatic pursuit to form a broad coalition against Penda, perhaps even courting kings that were firmly resigned to Penda's authority such as the Gewisse in the south. Oswiu was also likely targeting the South Saxons to ensure he could influence the south-east corner of Britain as a single block of action. Far to the north he was certainly continuing the effort to create a more formal relationship with the northern Brittonic and Pict nations. Oswiu may also have been working on swaying Peada into a more hostile position against Penda. All of these actions would have run counter to a formal agreement that Penda and Oswiu had established through the marriage of Cyneburh and Alhfrith, compelling a retaliation from Penda. When other nations' kings had opted to turn away from an oath with Penda, or acted against him through diplomacy he had attacked them, but let them flee into exile as punishment. This method of combat and exile had occurred with King Cenwalh and King Anna. While the case of Cenwalh seems to have worked to put him in his place, the case with King Anna had forced Penda to launch a secondary attack.

As Penda prepared his plan for the march north he took a decision not to allow exile as an appropriate outcome; this attack was for total regime change and to bring the northern threat under the overlordship of the Mercian King. Bede adds more flair to this objective stating that Penda 'had resolved to blot out and extirpate all his nation, from the highest to the lowest'.[1] This is a pretty drastic measure, but if Penda killed King Oswiu, and destroyed his nobility he would in fact cease the existence of Bernicia. Then, through his own patronage, he could rebuild the nation and its leadership on his terms. To ensure a complete result in the north Penda would pull together the largest army he had ever led. This army was formed by warbands from Mercia, East Anglia, Deira, Rheged and Gwynedd. Interestingly neither Merewalh nor Peada seem to have participated in the attack. It is impossible to understand why, but perhaps it was a moment of charity from Penda, ensuring that his two most powerful heirs would have an opportunity to take over Mercia if he fell in combat. The fact that neither Merewalh nor Peada supplied men to the campaign may also have compelled Penda to rely on the warbands of other nations to augment his own force. This must have weighed heavy on his shoulders as he simply couldn't guarantee the quality of the men he would receive.

Penda was allowing a number of strategic deviations in his preparation for the campaign, and taking risks he had never taken before. The first was back-to-back campaigns, and the second was the reliance on other nations for warriors. This type of deviation and increased acceptance of risk appears common as kings of the era reach the zenith of their power, with King Edwin being a prime example in his final battle at the River Idle. Part of this change may have been driven by ego, but it could also be that to maintain their power, overlord kings were simply required to act. For a king to keep a grip on power he couldn't allow transgressions to go unpunished, lest those contraventions invited even more rebellious actions in future, and inevitably eroded the king's authority. Penda had always been a prudent leader, and must have taken the decision for action cautiously and with the support of counsel from his thegns, and certainly Cynewise.

The route for this expedition north would be significantly easier for Penda than the campaign of AD 651, where he had moved his force through Rheged. Instead, this time around he would be able to move first to York, and then due north along the Roman roads through Deira thanks to his control over King Æthelwald. Until Penda reached the Bernician border he would be able to move his force in a non-tactical manner, as the territories were all friendly to him. This would speed up his ability to move a large force and its logistics, perhaps achieving twenty kilometres per day. Much of his force would be mounted, but the speed of the transit would be dictated by the supply train and the unmounted warriors. If Penda didn't encounter any obstacles he could expect to be at the gates of Bebbanburg around twenty days from the moment he departed Tamworth. Of course, twenty days would only occur in a perfect world with no challenges along the route. Penda had moved large forces great distances on a number of occasions, and was well aware that a perfect transit wasn't likely and that they would surely meet some challenges and forced delays.

As a young warlord Penda had watched Cadwallon draw together a disparate force and move them a great distance against a powerful enemy. Cadwallon had overcome barriers with language, culture, religion, and kinship affiliation to lead a successful campaign, for a time. The lessons from this experience had not been lost on Penda. By AD 655 the Mercian king was one of the few kings of Britain after Cadwallon who had the experience of operating in a multi-national army, and he would put the lessons to good use in the coming months as he moved against Bernicia. Tamworth was an ideal location for the Mercian, Gwynedd, and East Anglian warbands to form into the army before pushing north and picking up the Deiran warbands and perhaps Rheged warriors at York. As soon as the warbands were mobilized Penda pushed them north on their long journey.

On the fourteenth day of the campaign King Penda crossed into Bernicia and 'King Oswiu was exposed to the cruel and intolerable invasions of Penda, king of the Mercians.'[2] Once the River Tyne was crossed, the travel would slow down as there was a risk of ambush and enemy action at any moment. Penda assumed that Oswiu would be holed up in his coastal fortress at Bebbanburg, and this would be the first target for the invading force. With a large army behind him, Penda would be sending out raiding parties as they moved north, drawing in any wealth that could be removed from the land. After five days moving north through enemy territory, Penda arrived at Bebbanburg. In his last foray north Penda had been unable to crack the fortress, so what changed this time? With his superior force he knew that Oswiu would not be willing to engage in open combat; he also knew that breaching the fortress was nearly impossible and would be very costly in the lives of men. Penda must have been prepared for the protracted siege of the city this time around, banking on the fact that he could seal off Bebbanburg and starve Oswiu out. With such a superior force he could still detach elements to prowl the country without risk of failing at Bebbanburg.

As the southern force approached Bebbanburg, it became clear that something was off. Oswiu and his warbands were not at the fortress; the site was under the control of a reeve and perhaps a small garrison. The emptiness of Bebbanburg may be a sign that Penda's actions had not been predicted by Oswiu, who had expected a year of peace in which to continue his drive to solidifying military alliances with the northern nations and taking tribute from those nations which were already subservient to him. An alternative, but unlikely interpretation is that Oswiu was aware of the force marching against him and he knew he couldn't defend Bebbanburg against them, so he withdrew from the fort. Penda could have launched an attack on Bebbanburg at this moment to destroy the site, as he had done against Yeavering previously, but this would come with risk, and would take time. Infrastructure and wealth were not Penda's targets this time round; he wanted to end Oswiu's reign, and so he turned away from Bebbanburg after learning that the Bernician king was farther north.

From Bebbanburg, Penda first moved his army west, and then north along the Roman roads. The route he was taking put him back in the destroyed royal settlement of Yeavering after a hard day of riding along regional paths. This location was a safe place to encamp the army, either on top of Yeavering Bell, or down along the River Glen. If any new construction had happened then these buildings would have been used by the senior men of the army for rest. The next day the march would arrive at the River Tweed and the boundary between Bernicia and the Brittonic kingdom of Gododdin. This was a Brittonic kingdom loyal in some degree to Oswiu, likely as a vassal kingdom owing tribute and service to Bernicia. Penda was still in enemy territory and would need to move cautiously across the land. Each night, he drew together the leading men to discuss the army's movements for the following day. Æthelhere King of East Anglia, Æthelwald King of Deira, Cadfael ad Cadfan King of Gwynedd, and King Penda of Mercia represented the breadth of Britain, and the army they had formed under Penda was certainly a mighty sight as it continued its progression north.

Oswiu clearly knew by this point that Penda was in Bernicia with one of the greatest armies of the time. He was spending his days drawing in warriors and setting up a defendable position at a place called Iudeu. The exact location of Iudeu is still unknown and has been debated for generations based primarily on some passages written by Bede:

> two broad and long inlets of the sea lying between them, one of which runs into the interior of Britain, from the Eastern Sea, and the other from the Western, though they do not reach so far as to touch one another. The eastern has in the midst of it the city Iudeu.[3]

Bede's description seems to place Iudeu along the Firth of Forth, a heavily fortified location, based on the Latin Bede used to describe the location: 'This place was an urbs, a stronghold fortified by native, rather than Roman ingenuity'.[4] Since the 1950s, Iudeu has generally been placed at Stirling. However, this hypothesis is primarily based on the assumption that the location of modern Stirling is so strategic in nature as the north-south corridor that a fortress must have been there. It is hard to argue with the clear need of some type of fortification at Stirling, but it provides little clear evidence that Iudeu was at Stirling. A second major strike against placing Iudeu at Stirling is that Bede clearly places the location on the sea, and not inland.

Adding to the confusion around its location, Iudeu is recorded by a number of name variations including Giudi, and Giudiu. The etymology is unclear but in all likelihood, 'the place-name is ultimately British in origin, and that it means "place of a king"'.[5] While this doesn't provide any geographic clues, it does show how important the location was. There are three clear possibilities for Iudeu which match the description from Bede: Carlingnose Battery, Cramond Island and Blackness. Each of these are not perfect fits, Cramond Island for starters is an island, something Bede didn't mention. However, Cramond Island is tidally connected to the mainland, not unlike Lindisfarne. The causeway to reach it is over one and a half kilometres, providing an excellent defensive position. Cramond Island is sited at the sea, and on the eastern body of water as Bede had described. Blackness, which is further to the west is an alternative site for Iudeu, and is formed by a rocky promontory jutting out into the Firth of Forth. Finally, Carlingnose Battery on the north shore of the Firth of Forth is an excellent defensive promontory.

Both Blackness and Carlingnose Battery fit the general geographic characteristics favoured by Brittonic fort builders, 'builders of native coastal strongholds in northern Britain in the Early Historic period preferred sites on craggy promontories.'[6] However, to accept Carlingnose Battery as the location of Iudeu implies that Oswiu held lands which have usually been attributed to the Picts, of which there is no evidence. The natural boundary between the

Picts and the Britons occurs at the Firth of Forth. Without archaeological evidence, it is impossible to tie Iudeu to one location or another, but Cramond Island seems the most likely candidate. The importance of Cramond Island was known by the Romans as well, and much to Penda's delight they had built a road leading directly to it.

While Oswiu had confidence that he could hold off a direct assault on the island, if Penda attacked across the tidal causeway, he must have also known that without relief or escape by sea, a prolonged siege here would lead to an inevitable defeat. In the days leading up to Penda's arrival at the causeway, Oswiu had been stockpiling food and other necessities into Iudeu, in an effort to withstand a siege, but it wasn't enough, and he knew it. Trapped at Iudeu with Oswiu was a fortune in tribute he had been collecting from Gododdin, Caertrick, Strathclyde and other parts of the north. While wealth had not been Penda's primary reason for the campaign, it was always a welcome outcome. Once Penda's army arrived at Iudeu, he set about establishing a siege posture which would prevent Oswiu from departing or sending for help. It's fair to assume that Oswiu was not universally adored by the northern Brittonic nations which were forced to pay him tribute, and the fact that he was on the ropes may very well have drawn more warriors into Penda's camp. Men from Strathclyde, Gododdin and Caertrick were now adding their weight to the Mercian army.

Oswiu was in a terrible spot, and he could see the writing on the wall. If he was to survive he needed to sue for peace. In a process that would be normalized during the Viking age, the besieged king sought to purchase his way out of danger. Oswiu sent a message to Penda across the causeway, 'compelled by his necessity, he promised to give him countless gifts and royal marks of honour greater than can be believed, to purchase peace; provided that he would return home, and cease to waste and utterly destroy the provinces of his kingdom.'[7]

There are some interesting discrepancies in how Penda received this proposal. Bede reports that Penda refused this overture, and would only be placated by the death of Oswiu and the destruction of Bernician power. Nennius, on the other hand, provides us with an opposite account: 'Then Oswiu restored all the wealth, which was with him in the city, to Penda; who distributed it among the kings of the Britons, this is called the restitution of Iudeu.'[8]

The siege of Iudeu may have gone on for some time before Oswiu offered up what was effectively a Danegeld, and a hope that it would be enough to placate Penda. It is interesting that Penda opted to distribute the wealth while the army was still in the field, rather than waiting for the moment of demobilization to give shares of the riches as was the more regular cultural norm. Yet, something made him accept this as the appropriate step to take in the moment. It could be that Penda believed this initial burst of wealth would draw the kings in even closer, perhaps with promises of greater riches once the Bernician king was defeated and Iudeu and Bebbanburg were taken.

As the campaign ground to a close, Penda was forced to take his loot and his army and begin the march back to the south. For the nations south of the Humber, this was a sensible action, as they may be cut off by the winter weather if they didn't leave enough time to return home. This was likely an unpopular decision for the nations north of the Humber who would be faced with reprisals from Bernicia the moment Penda was back in Mercia. These northern nations felt betrayed by the southern warlord and likely departed the encampment at Iudeu immediately, though Penda was still in control of a significant force with the Mercians, East Anglians and the Men of Gwynedd. Penda the great warlord, departed Iudeu around 31 October AD 655, and began moving his army back to their homes south of the Humber.

On the fifteenth day of the march, the army reached the River Winwaed. Until 1966, the location of the Winwaed was believed to be west of Leeds, but it has since been identified as the River Went. Penda and his force were following the Roman road south. This road is north-west of Doncaster and parallels the Humber estuary. When they finally reached the ford at the Winwaed they were met with a thoroughly disheartening scene for any army long on the campaign trail and trying to get home. The usually fordable River Winwaed was in a serious flood, spilling its banks and appearing almost impossible to cross. The army had been in the north for so long that the winter weather had set in and heavy rains had caused major flooding. The flood plain at this point on the Winwaed was very large, as the land is generally low and flat allowing the river to inundate the area at fairly regular intervals. Penda placed the army into a camp on the north side of the river at a location with some elevation, perhaps near the modern Ackworth water tower to rest while he worked out a way forward. This point was the highest point of land overlooking the River Winwaed, and provided protection from ambush, but more importantly from rising waters.

Penda would draw together a war cabinet, a Witan of sorts, and discuss the challenge with the other leaders of the campaign. King Æthelhere of East Anglia, and Cadfael ad Cadfan King of Gwynedd, were certainly still with him in his formation, but Æthelwald remains questionable. The records suggest that Æthelwald King of Deira was also still with them, but this makes no sense as his territory was to the north. It seems that Penda had already shared portions of the fortune from Iudeu, and as he had quit the nation without further action against Bebbanburg, there was little reason for Æthelwald to continue marching south, where he would then be forced to turn back north. However, perhaps Penda had decided to share the rest of the spoils once they were safely back in Tamworth, forcing Æthelwald to continue on the march. If that was the case then he would have some disapproving thegns and warriors with him desperate to get home and shelter from the winter.

The discussions on how to proceed must have been robust and emotional amongst the kings and their trusted advisors. The men gathered around a fire, or perhaps in a tent, as men on the land had done for thousands of years, and continue to do in battlefields today. The concern about the river was certainly in the forefront, and was the almost sole focus of the leadership. It is entirely possible that they had weighed the risk of enemy action as nearly zero, and had looked at the current issues only through the prism of logistics and transportation, completely ignoring the need for a defensive strategy at such a dangerous crossing. Although they attempted to shelter the warriors from the discussion, there can be no doubt that the men could see there was disharmony growing between their leaders, and this would translate down into the rank and file. Penda was confronted with some heated debate on what was the most appropriate action. For many of the kings, spending the winter outside of their territories was unacceptable as it could very well lead to dynastic challenges.

The debate on what to do next dragged on late into the night as the kings and thegns argued their cases. For the Mercians, they wanted to get home, and the most obvious choice for them was to take the ford at the Winwaed and move slowly. The men of Gwynedd also wanted to get home, but they were in favour of moving quickly. There is no source material to point to their route, but heading west and seeking a different ford seems the most likely. It could be that they went as far west as Læccford and crossed the Mersey. This route, though, could add another five days of travel at best, and potentially more under the poor weather conditions, and the River Mersey may be as impassable as the Winwaed. The Deirans wanted no crossing; they wanted to be released from service and head home, for they had watched as their homes passed by, and they were slowly beginning to edge closer towards mutiny. Finally, the East Anglians, like the Mercians, wanted a quick route home; they still had the longest route back to their nation. Eventually Penda weighed the options and directed that the force would use the ford over the Winwaed and continue the march south.

For Æthelwald this decision was tantamount to a declaration of revolt. How could he force his thegns and men to cross an incredibly dangerous river, when their route home didn't require it? Furthermore, how could he leave his lands ungoverned over the winter when the threat of Oswiu was still present? Æthelwald had every reason to be concerned about Oswiu as the Bernician was being left an open invitation to take Deira the moment the Deiran warriors crossed the Winwaed. There can be no doubt the Deira were not a homogenized nation, having spent generations as part of a united kingdom with Bernicia, and there were elements still that would welcome Oswiu over Æthelwald. This moment was quite dire for Æthelwald. He may have sought a private moment of counsel with Penda to discuss all of this. Penda had always been a prudent man, and not one to waste lives with undue risk. It could be that he relented on the movement of the Deirans seeing the implications and risk posed by Oswiu. Instead, he would have the Deirans act as a rear guard while the force crossed the ford in the morning. Once the army was across, the Deirans could return home. This was the best solution for both the men who had to ford the river for the Deirans, although some amongst their ranks would still be bristling at the idea of standing around while Penda and the army crossed.

Cadfael, the king of Gwynedd, may have learned that Penda had relented his position with Deira, but was unwilling to listen to the arguments of the Britons. Incensed by a perceived sleight from the Mercian king, Cadfael opted to move unilaterally in the night. As the evening wore on, Cadfael ensured that his men were camped at the extremity of the army. When most of the fires in the camp had dwindled to embers and it seemed that no one was stirring, he slowly and cautiously woke his men and then led them out of the encampment. Nennius says, 'Cadfael alone, king of Gwynedd, rising up in the night, escaped, together with his army, wherefore he was called Cadfael the Battle-Shirker.'[9]

Cadfael's only route was to go west following the higher ground. Around seventeen kilometres to the west is the town of Bretton; the etymology is 'Britons' Farm'.[10] Perhaps Cadfael was able to shelter here with his fugitive warbands before continuing the journey west. That Cadfael was able to steal his force away in the night without setting off any alarms says much about the conditions of the camp. For starters, the camp was not a tactical camp with defences of any kind. Nor was the camp being patrolled at night by any guards, insinuating that Penda felt completely secure at this location with no concern about possible combat with Oswiu or anyone else.

At dawn, the camp began to awaken and the force became aware that Cadfael had left them unannounced. Penda was surely irate that Cadfael had abandoned the force, but was likely more angry that he had done so against the expressed wishes of the Mercian king. However, all of that would have to be put aside while Penda prepared for what would no doubt be an incredibly dangerous and difficult day trying to get across the river. Once he was secure in Tamworth he could spend the winter deciding on how to address Cadfael's fleeing. For now, the camp was packed up, and the men began to move towards the ford. Æthelwald and the Deirans would stay on the higher ground overlooking the road, somewhere near the modern Rigg Lane. From this position the Deirans would have a good view of the crossing and the northern approaches. The extent of the crossing can be estimated based on the Ordnance Survey which calls the location 'Standing Flats'.[11] The 1852 Ordnance Survey map even provides a label on the standing flats which says 'liable to floods'.[12] Based on the Ordnance Survey, and the topography of the land, in full flood Penda was looking at crossing 150 metres of water from the north bank to the south bank of the Winwaed.

The crossing would see the deepest and fastest water encountered on the south side of the ford, with the shallower and hopefully slower water encountered on the near shore. This meant the men would be faced with an ever increasing risk as they attempted to wade the river. The pathfinders who went ahead of the main force needed to ensure they stayed along the road's trackway in order to have the shallowest water to tackle. Once they were across, the main force could begin to move in earnest. This was a painfully slow process, as men started to wade into the river, but were forced to stand still while others negotiated the deeper water. As the fording went on, the nervousness on the north bank was ever increasing, and the tension must have been immense for each man waiting to get across.

Only a handful of warriors were across the river, others were struggling with their footing as they entered the strongest current and deepest water at the end of the crossing; yet others were piling up in the water waiting for those before them to finish the crossing, and finally more were still on shore with King Penda and King Æthelhere waiting to start the process. Suddenly, and without any warning from Æthelwald, an army led by Oswiu and composed of warriors from Bernicia, Goddodin, Strathclyde, Dal Riata and the lands of the Picts came thundering down the road. The Deirans did nothing to protect the men in the ford. In the eyes of Bede, Æthelwald was already a traitor, working with Penda against his fellow Northumbrians, and now he turned on the Mercian warlord, 'Æthelwald, who ought to have supported them (Bernicia), was on the enemy's side, and led them on to fight against his country and his uncle (Oswiu); though, during the battle, he withdrew, and awaited the event in a place of safety.'[13]

King Penda turned to the threat and started to draw together a defence against the Bernicians. He expected the Deirans to move to support him, but without compassion or compunction they sat idly by and let the Mercian and East Anglian defenders confront Oswiu alone. Æthelwald had shown utter contempt for his oath, and towards the man who had made him king, perhaps expecting that his treachery would put him in good stead with Oswiu when he regained his authority. Penda had now lost two critical components of his army, and was down to the Mercian and East Anglian warbands, but half of them were in the process of crossing the river. No doubt the sudden attack sowed panic amongst the ranks, a particularly perilous addition to the current circumstances. 'The battle was fought near the river Winwaed, which then, owing to the great rains, was in flood, and had overflowed its banks, so that many more were drowned in the flight than destroyed in battle by the sword.'[14]

The final scene of Penda's time on Middle-Earth was as dramatic as the ending of any of the tales of Penda's gods or the heroes that were told in the dark of winter huddled around the hearth as the lyre was gently plucked and strummed. Penda and a handful of his finest thegns stood facing the north with shields linked and swords drawn, their feet soaked by the rising waters. Ahead of them, Oswiu and his men dismounted and formed a counter-wall, much larger than the one Penda was able to piece together. As the walls met, the advantage held by Oswiu quickly destroyed the defenders one at a time, each man compelled by his culture and his oath to not outlive his king. In this setting, perhaps King Penda was the last of the line to hold out before being hacked and stabbed by a myriad of attackers.

As had happened to other great warlord kings, it was the edge of a river that defeated King Penda. The last defenders were slaughtered at the edge of the river, and many countless others drowned in the panic of the attack. A very few made it across and passed the word of Penda's death. Alongside him died the King of East Anglia, and as Bede records it, 'the thirty royal commanders, who had come to Penda's assistance, were almost all of them slain; among whom was Æthelhere, brother and successor to Anna, King of the East Angles.'[15]

There is no clear record of Penda dying on the battlefield at the Winwaed, but nor is there proof that he had survived it. Instead, Bede leaves us with a troubling sentence and no clear indication of who it is in reference to: 'He had been the occasion of the war, and was now killed, having lost his army and auxiliaries.'[16] It seems that this is a likely reference to Penda's death, though it may also point to Æthelhere. The *Anglo-Saxon Chronicles*, however, are quite clear on the fate of King Penda: '655 A.D. This year Penda was slain at Winwaed and thirty royal personages with him.'[17] Finally, Henry of Huntingdon states 'Penda was slain by Oswiu near the river Winwaed'.[18]

Put together, the scant records seem to show that Penda didn't flee, and didn't drown, but instead died fighting. It is also telling that he had waited on the enemy side of the ford while his men crossed. He could have just as easily been in the vanguard of the crossing, but had chosen to stay in a point that he could continue to command the totality of the operation. This was the end that all great warrior kings expected and accepted. As he was cut down his body may have drifted away on the current of the Winwaed, along with many of his men. Loaded down with weapons and armour most of them sank rapidly in the rain-swollen river. A few may have washed upon the shores, but many more would be buried in the silt. For Oswiu there was no great pay-off at the

Winwaed. What treasure was with the army perished in the waters, though some small portions may have been recovered on the northern bank.

In the immediate aftermath of the battle, Oswiu wasted no time in turning on Deira, and King Æthelwald vanishes from the historic record. Oswiu installs his son Alhfrith on the Deiran throne by the end of AD 655, meaning Æthelwald was only able to maintain his kingdom for a matter of weeks before Oswiu dethroned him. Deira had been a broken land since the ravages of Cadwallon, and Æthelwald had been faced with division and revolt since he was placed on the throne by Penda. The Mercian king alone was the only thing keeping Deira apart from Bernicia, and at least nominally as an independent kingdom. Effectively it was Æthelwald's own inaction, cowardice, misjudgment, and failed ethics which led not only to the defeat of his sponsor, but almost inevitably to the collapse of his own house and the fall of Deira as an independent nation.

Cadfael fares no better following the battle at Winwaed. His cowardice and breaking of his alliance allows him to survive the river crossing and the battle, but he soon disappears from the record. It is possible that he was killed by his own men, or died in a subsequent battle with Oswiu, but by AD 656 the crown of Gwynedd has passed to Cadwaladr, a son of Cadwallon. Cadfael's cowardice leads to him receiving the epithet 'Battle-Shirker' and a quick exit from the seat of power.

The power vacuum left by the felling of Penda was immense, and directly impacted every corner of Britain. In Mercia, Peada, Merewalh, and others had to quickly establish power before that confederated nation was torn apart by its own internal divisions. East Anglia, traditionally one of the most powerful nations, is now without a king, but also free from the control of Mercia. Deira was once again a province of Bernicia, and that meant a reformed northern powerhouse capable of vast dominance. Even in the distant south the reverberations of Penda's death were felt, primarily by the Gewisse. For the first time Cenwalh was free from the chains which bound him to Penda. For the kings of Kent, the South Saxons, and the East Saxons, the fear that Penda would show up on their doorstep was finally over. In the west, Penda had always been a trusted partner and connection between the Brittonic Kingdoms and the Angle nations, with his death that connection no longer existed, and the wild western frontier, the march, would be open to raids and conflict once again.

Unfortunately we don't know what happened to Cynewise in the aftermath of the Winwaed. Cynewise was an enormous influence on Penda, and a seemingly amazing woman who kept Mercia together when Penda was on campaign. She deserves as much credit as Penda in the success of the early Mercian nation. Her importance is captured by Bede in a single sentence where we learn that Oswiu's son, 'Egfrid was then kept as a hostage at the court of Queen Cynewise, in the province of the Mercians.'[19] The hostage which Oswiu had been forced to give at some point before the invasion that ended at Iudeu was not under the care and control of Penda, or his sons, or a trusted thegn, but the Queen.

Until conversion, it was common practice for the new king to marry the previous king's wife. This could have been her fate if Mercia had been able to maintain its independence under a king who was unrelated to Cynewise, but that is not how things played out. The other option was for her to turn to the security of an abbey and retire in the care of the church, but we see no record of that either. In fact, her religious affiliation is completely unknown though it seems most likely that she remained a Heathen throughout her life. It is unlikely that the last great Heathen Queen would be welcomed by the abbess and sisters at an abbey. It is, however, interesting that two of her daughters did join abbeys and were later canonized by the Church as Saint Cyneburh and Saint Cyneswith. It's a tragedy of the historic record that we don't know what became of Cynewise. Perhaps she fled south to the Magonsæta and the protection of her nephew Merewalh with whom she shared the dual connections of Mercia and Gewisse.

What of Cynewise's son, Peada? Penda was a man with whom the cultural rules surrounding oaths where iron clad. It does seem that if Peada held an oath with Oswiu after marrying his daughter, that Penda would never force him into a position where that oath would be broken. In that scenario Peada's involvement in the invasion of Bernicia, the siege at Iudeu and the Battle of Winwaed make sense. But it could also be that he had betrayed his father and was waiting for an opportunity to seize the Mercian throne on the death of Penda with the backing of his father-in-law Oswiu. There is no clear answer to this puzzle, but Bede gives us the final story of Peada after Oswiu,

> gave to the above-mentioned Peada, son to King Penda, because he was his kinsman, the kingdom of the Southern Mercians, consisting, as is said, of 5,000 families, divided by the river Trent from the Northern Mercians, whose land contains 7,000 families; but Peada was foully slain in the following spring, by the treachery, as is said, of his wife, during the very time of the Easter festival.[20]

It seems treachery was never far away from the Bernician kings. With hindsight it is clear where Penda's final campaign went astray. Throughout his career Penda had never been successful in siege warfare, when the opposition was unwilling to sally forth and wage a pitched battle. The inability to crack the defences at Bebbanburg and Iudeu led Penda to retire from campaigns without having met his primary objective. In the case of Bebbanburg this had largely worked out for him, but the second time around it turned out to be his final demise. It seems Penda did not fully comprehend the threat he was leaving at Iudeu. A deeper assessment would have forced him to garrison Deira to protect against incursions from Bernicia before launching another campaign to unseat Oswiu. It shares many similarities with the ultimate fall of Cadwallon who had failed to understand the threat presented by Oswald and the Bernicians.

Penda had opportunities to succeed against Oswiu at Iudeu. He could have forced the siege by attacking the fortress, but he opted against this, perhaps fearing that an attack across the causeway would have led to heavy losses, but he may have been able to break Oswiu in one single concerted effort. Alternatively, he could have committed to a winter at Iudeu and starved the Bernicians out. If he still had the support of Merewalh and Peada he could have turned to them to protect his kingdom in his absence. By the time he retired from the north the weather had already turned, and Oswiu may have had only a few short weeks left before he was desperate and out of options. As Penda withdrew from Iudeu he must have known the campaign was a failure.

Penda's defeat at the Winwaed was a product of treachery, timing and his own deviation from a series of general strategies that had served him so well throughout his life. The first was the utilization of a rest year between campaigns. This had allowed Penda to refresh his warbands and prepare effective strategies for the following year. The second was the reliance on his own loyal Mercian forces as the stalwart of his army. When he split the Middle-Angles and the Magonsæta from the larger Mercia, he lost access to a pool of manpower that he was forced to replace from other untested and unreliable sources. Following the 'restitution of Iudeu' Penda portioned out the treasure immediately, rather than waiting for the conclusion of the campaign. He did this trusting that the oaths between kings were strong enough, but they weren't. Laden with wealth, Cadfael, Æthelwald, and a few unnamed northern Briton leaders had no incentive to maintain the unity of the army, nor continue their service with Penda. Finally, he treated the withdrawal south without the tactical care it deserved. This final error was driven by fatigue, disharmony within the army, and a desire to quickly get home after a long campaign.

Epilogue

Inside the mound designed by wisemen they laid arm rings, gems, trappings taken from the long lost hoard. They left earth to guard the gold where to this day it still lies fast underground, safe from men's hands and eyes.

Beowulf [1]

King Penda has no tomb, no site like Sutton Hoo which we can turn to as a memorial for a key figure in the birth of England. More problematic is that Penda has been painted by scholars since the Venerable Bede as a bloodthirsty tool of evil who stood against the glory of Christianity and cultural advancement. It has been his lot to be a man of the Dark Ages, and even more damning, a Heathen man of the Dark Ages who actively chose not to convert at a time when the overwhelming tide was one of conversion. In England, and thus the Anglo-sphere writ large, there is tendency to see the early Middle Ages as a time of backward thought, an interlude between the civilizing worlds of the Roman Empire and the Norman invasions. These views neglect to examine the impact that the age had on the development of the modern United Kingdom and the foundation myths of all of the home nations.

Penda was the first powerful king to rise to prominence without a tie to another nation or the backing of a powerful king. Kent had relied on its connections to the continent to drive its success. East Anglia drew on its contacts to the near continent and further to the ancestral homelands of the Angles. In the north, Bernicia's rise was built on the Celtic connection to the Picts and Ireland. Penda, on the other hand, had risen to his position and created his nation without linkages and support of other nations. While he had created linkages with the Britons of the west, this had not been the reason he was able to rise to the position of king nor to the importance of his kingdom. Penda and the subsequent rise of Mercia can be seen as the first embodiment of an Angle nation that was born from within Britain, with no external focus.

The Staffordshire hoard contains the components of at least seventy-four swords.[2] It is commonly asserted that swords represented a rare weapon in this era. Examinations of grave goods of this era show the majority of weapons interred were spears, with only 12 per cent containing swords. One survey identified that, out of 3,814 graves, 702 contained weapons.[3] The majority of these graves, about 85 per cent, contained spears while 45 per cent of them contained shields.[4] The shield is important as it serves only one function, and that is war; whereas the spear could serve as a hunting implement and can't be assumed to mark the grave of a warrior. If the graves with shields can be interpreted to be of warriors and members of warbands, this makes 315 warrior graves, of which an estimated 37 would contain swords. These numbers show that the sword was less rare than is often assumed, with one in eight warriors carrying one.

There is no doubt that a sword was an expensive tool, but at a ratio of one in eight warriors carrying a sword it could very well be that it was less a weapon of wealth, but instead a weapon of authority and command. In most modern militaries, the lowest common denominator for a military unit is the section. A section is made up of a leader and between seven and ten soldiers. The size of a section has been shaped by the concept of span of control, which is ideally between five and seven people. In modern leadership theory, it is felt that effective command and control begins to degrade when the span of control exceeds seven people. The great Prussian military theorist Carl von Clausewitz believed that eight was the ideal span of control, though he doesn't use the term specifically.[5] It seems entirely possible that the sword represented a leader, starting with the smaller components of the army and moving up to the king.

Throughout the period of Penda's life, when an army was defeated it was totally wiped out. Returning to the 74 swords of the Staffordshire hoard, they may represent the defeat and death of 592 warriors. There is no doubt that Penda retained many weapons from defeated armies throughout his life, and would have gifted these to his own men. The question remaining is: what percentage of the total weapons recovered from defeated enemies was placed in the hoard? If the hoard represents 10 per cent of Penda's defeated enemies, then his successes could account for the death of some 5,920 enemy warriors across his life.

In the seventh century, it is estimated that the average population of Britain hovered around a million people.[6] Based on the presence of shields in graves, it would seem that roughly 8 per cent of the population may have been warriors. The ratio of warriors has analogues in the modern world during periods of conflict. By the end of the Second World War, Britain had a population of nearly 50 million, and a military of over 4.6 million people; by percentage, that is 9 per cent of the population. In 2023, Ukraine's military makes up 4 per cent of the total population.

These numbers clearly show the impact Penda had on the population and politics of Britain in the seventh century. If 8 per cent of the male population were engaged in warfare, then there may have been as many as 32,000 warriors in Britain in the mid-seventh century. Assuming Penda's activities account for the death of nearly 6,000 of them, this means he participated in the defeat of nearly a fifth of all warriors. It is an astonishing number from a military standpoint.

Off the battlefield, the example set by Penda is worth remembering in the polarized modern world where topics such as Brexit are seen as finite turning points. Britain and its many composite polities have waxed and waned since the Roman invasion on the topic of continental engagement. The East Angles and Kent continued to hold close trading ties to the continent in the seventh century. The converted kings in the Saxon and Angle nations also began developing cultural ties to the continent. Penda, and many of the Brittonic nations, turned away from these ties seemingly stepping away from the advancing world. Over time many of the kingdoms would turn away from the continent, until the Norman invasion brought England back into the European fold.

Penda led Mercia from a group of divergent sub-kingdoms and tribes to the single largest power broker in Britain. The nation was the first to utilize the strategic benefits of the Roman road system to control and draw together an enormous nation constructed out of a myriad of cultural, religious, linguistic, and tribal affiliations. Mercia should never have been able to rise as it did, surrounded by competitors on all sides. Without the military prowess of Penda, Mercia likely wouldn't have gained the stature that it did. However, Penda was more than a great warlord; he was a man who fit all of the characteristics of a great classic hero, similar in all ways to Beowulf, Sigurd, Tiw, and even Woden. Like Woden he had never shied away from conflict, but he had always used sensible thought and prudence to choose the most appropriate action. This skill had been developed over time, and grew from failures he experienced in life. From the moment of failure at Exeter, Penda had learned and never stopped improving as a military commander or statesman.

In the Western world, pluralism is often rejected for homogeneity and seen as a point of weakness. This belief was born out of the great western march of Christianity brought to Europe by the Roman Empire, but taken up by other men of power who sought to control nations through its use. In this school of thinking a nation can only be successful under one dominant culture, with one language, one religion and one god. Unfortunately for greater humanity these ideas led to numerous crusades, religious conflict, colonialism, and a post-colonial world left to pick up the pieces. Penda proved to be the great contradiction, and perhaps that is part of why he was left in the past; he was inconvenient to the ideals of a homogenous society. Penda used pluralism as a completely successful tool to run his nation, to form unlikely alliances, and ultimately to provide stability and security for Mercians for an entire generation, something which was nearly unheard of at the time. Penda's willingness to support a pluralistic society is really captured by a single sentence in the *Ecclesiastical History* written by St Bede:

> Nor did King Penda forbid the preaching of the Word even among his people, the Mercians, if any were willing to hear it; but, on the contrary, he hated and despised those whom he perceived to be without the works of faith, when they had once received the faith of Christ, saying, that they were contemptible and wretched who scorned to obey their God, in whom they believed.[7]

Penda's importance to history is the same as other indigenous heroes the world over who turned away from the perceived advancement of society brought by the importation of foreign ideals and culture through the suppression of local cultures and knowledge. The great warlord of Mercia is deserving of remembrance as the final example of Angle kingship which is embedded in the traditional cultures of the European north. The culture that Tacitus had encountered in the first century at the edge of the Roman Empire was already ancient, and would continue through to the death of Penda. Penda was the last powerful Heathen King in Britain, and perhaps one of the last opportunities for that ancient culture to survive on the island.

Following the death of Penda, King Arwald of the Wihtwara on the modern-day Isle of Wight would be the final kingly holdout of Heathenism in Britain. King Arwald is eventually assaulted by Caedwalla of the Gewisse who

> had obtained possession of the kingdom of the Gewisse, he took also the Isle of Wight, which till then was entirely given over to idolatry, and by merciless slaughter endeavoured to destroy all the inhabitants thereof, and to place in their stead people from his own province.[8]

With the invasion of the Isle of Wight, Heathenism as a major religion in Britain is destroyed. The Heathen culture dwindled in Britain over centuries, eventually becoming tangled in regional folk tales and traditions. However, the ancient culture continued to the end of the Viking age in Scandinavia before eventually being overcome by Christianity.

Penda is important because he provides the opportunity for one last look at a culture before it goes dormant, replaced by new ideas from distant lands. Within the Heathen Germanic traditions, the veneration of ancestors and tales of heroes which helped record stories that otherwise would have been lost. These tales developed over time as new events occurred and new heroes surfaced. Had that culture continued, one could imagine the saga of Penda being told alongside the story of Beowulf. Both of them were warlords who rose to be kings and ultimately died as kings in combat. Over the last century there has been a resurgence in Heathenism, built around the few recorded sources available to help regenerate this indigenous spiritualism. Many people refer to the stories recorded in Iceland by Snorri Sturluson or the Viking sagas to help recreate the connection. Penda can be added to the list of heroes. Exploration of Penda's life and telling his story provides modern Heathens with one more connection, and can help build a resurgent Heathen community which, 'is a possible religious philosophy for a pluralistic, multicultural society'.[9] There are groups who have sought to taint Heathenism with racist ideologies, but these run tantamount to the actions of the last great Heathen king who built a secure, stable, and powerful nation on the very ideals of pluralism, multiculturalism and freedom of religion.

In 2007 the United Nations adopted the Declaration on the Rights of Indigenous Peoples. This declaration was a reflection of the rekindling of indigenous cultures around the globe in the wake of the failed colonial system. The slow decomposition of colonialism has exposed many nations, in particular those in the Anglo-sphere, to traditional indigenous ideals centred on the related nature of all things, the power and importance of nature, the value of deep culture, the acceptance of plurality, empowerment of individuals in a spiritual system, and the maintenance of traditional knowledge. All of these characteristics are found in the spiritualism which Penda held, and which modern Heathens are breathing fresh life into. Reconnecting with the understanding and of Wyrd as a core cultural concept will help us address the outcomes of colonialism and the existential threat presented by climate change.

Penda's life reminds us that the world is plural and filled with countless pathways. In his life he saw the end of a culture that was flexible and open. Penda's culture bent and warped with the events around it; it was organic and in a constant state of regeneration. For Penda, the spiritual world was all around him, constantly developing and interacting with people. These ideas were part of the reason Christianity was so successful. Penda, like many others, didn't see competition or a threat from other gods or ideas. Unfortunately, the Church was in direct opposition to those ways of thinking and only had room for singularity; a single church, a single source of power, and a single culture. Penda was the last of England's great Heathen kings, but he wasn't the bastion of Heathen ideals and belief driven by religious zealotry. King Penda Iclingas is a reminder that there are other pathways to take, though our own modern world is only now rediscovering that truth.

> The scene of a warrior's last stand remains a mystery. He never knows if after the battle he'll sit drinking mead with friends again. – Beowulf [10]

Notes

Prologue
1. *Maxims II*, Exeter Book, https://www.sacred-texts.com/neu/ascp/a15.htm

Chapter 1
1. Martinon-Torres, Marcos, Fern, Chris; Dickinson, Tania; Webster, Leslie (2019), *The Staffordshire Hoard: An Anglo-Saxon Treasure*, Society of Antiquaries of London.
2. ibid.
3. ibid.
4. Allan, J.P. (1984), *Medieval and post-Medieval Finds from Exeter 1971–1980*, Exeter City Council and The University of Exeter.
5. Maltby, Mark (1979), *Faunal Studies on Urban Sites. The Animal Bones from Exeter*, Department of Prehistory and Archaeology, University of Sheffield.
6. ibid.
7. Gildas, Translated by Giles, J.A., *On the Ruin of Britain*, Project Gutenberg Ebook.
8. ibid.
9. Bede, St (673–735), *The Ecclesiastical History of England*, Christian Classics Ethereal Library.
10. Gebühr, M. 1996: Angulus desertus? In: Hans- Jürgen Hässler (eds.): *Die Wanderung der Angeln nach England*. Studien zur Sachsenforschung.
11. Ejstrud, B; Hunnicke, T; Husum, C; Korre, A; Maarleveld, T; Vafeiadou, K (2008), *The migration period, Southern Denmark and the North Sea. A workbook in relation to the Gredstedbro find*, Maritime Archaeology Programme, University of Southern Denmark.
12. Bede, St (673–735), *The Ecclesiastical History of England*, Christian Classics Ethereal Library.
13. Manco, Jean (2018), *The Origins of The Anglo-Saxons*, Thames & Hudson Ltd, London.
14. Gildas, Translated by Giles, J.A., *On the Ruin of Britain*, Project Gutenberg Ebook.
15. Sidonius Apollinaris, *Letters*. Tr. O.M. Dalton (1915) vol. 2. pp. 138–175; Book VIII.
16. Ejstrud, B; Hunnicke, T; Husum, C; Korre, A; Maarleveld, T; Vafeiadou, K (2008), *The migration period, Southern Denmark and the North Sea. A workbook in relation to the Gredstedbro find*, Maritime Archaeology Programme, University of Southern Denmark.
17. Sidonius Apollinaris, *Letters*. Tr. O.M. Dalton (1915) vol. 2. pp. 138–175; Book VIII.
18. Tacitus, Translated by C. W. Eliot ed. (1910), *Voyages and Travels: Ancient and Modern, with Introductions, Notes and Illustrations*. New York: P. F. Collier and Son, [c1910] The Harvard classics, [vol. XXXIII].
19. Procopius, Translated by H.B. Dewing (1962), *History of the Wars*, book VIII, chapter XX, section 31, Harvard Press, London.
20. Berge, R; Jasinski, M; Sognnes, K (2009), *N-TAG TEN Proceedings of the 10th Nordic TAG conference at Stiklestad*, Norway 2009. Published by Archaeopress, Oxford.
21. Myhre, B. and I. Øye 2002. *Norges landbrukshistorie I. 4000 f. Kr. – 1350 e. Kr.*, Oslo, Det norske samlaget.

22. Sidonius Apollinaris, *Letters*. Tr. O.M. Dalton (1915) vol. 2. pp. 138–17; Book VIII.
23. Jones, Michael and Casey, John (1988), 'The Gallic Chronicle Restored: A Chronology for the Anglo-Saxon Invasions and the End of Roman Britain', in *Britannia*, Vol. 19, pp. 367–398.
24. ibid.

Chapter 2

1. Tacitus, Translated by C. W. Eliot ed. (1910), *Voyages and Travels: Ancient and Modern, with Introductions, Notes and Illustrations*. New York: P. F. Collier and Son, [c1910] The Harvard classics, [vol. XXXIII].
2. Bede, St (673–735), *The Ecclesiastical History of England*, Christian Classics Ethereal Library.
3. Edwards, K.J. (2017), 'Recent Developments in the Study of Place-names and the Anglo-Saxon Settlement', in Kent Archaeology Society.
4. Smith, A.H (1956), *English Place-Name Elements*, Part 1 (Á-Īw) [hereafter EPNE], Cambridge: Cambridge University Press.
5. Giles, J.A; Ingram, J., trans. (1996), *The Anglo-Saxon Chronicles*, reproduced by the Gutenberg project.
6. A. J. Church and W. J. Brodribb, trans. (1877), Tacitus, *The Agricola and Germania*, London: Macmillan, 1877.
7. Tremblay, M; Vezina, H (2000), 'New Estimates of Intergenerational Time Intervals for the Calculation of Age and Origins of Mutations'. In *American Journal of Human Genetics* Vol. 66 Iss. 2 pp. 651–658.
8. A. J. Church and W. J. Brodribb, trans. (1877), Tacitus, *The Agricola and Germania*, London: Macmillan, 1877.
9. Giles, J.A; Ingram, J., trans. (1996), *The Anglo-Saxon Chronicles*, reproduced by the Gutenberg project.
10. Jones, Michael and Casey, John (1988), 'The Gallic Chronicle Restored: A Chronology for the Anglo-Saxon Invasions and the End of Roman Britain', in *Britannia*, Vol. 19, pp. 367–398.
11. Giles, J.A; Ingram, J., trans. (1996), *The Anglo-Saxon Chronicles*, reproduced by the Gutenberg project.
12. ibid.
13. Minter, Faye; Plouviez, Jude; Scull, Christopher (2016), 'Rendlesham Survey 2008–2014: Assessment Report', Suffolk County Council Archaeology Service.
14. Tacitus, Translated by Jackson, J. (1937) *The Annals of Tacitus*, Published in Vol V. of the Loeb Classical Library edition of Tacitus.
15. ibid.
16. ibid.
17. Talbot, J (2018), 'The Die is Cast: Investigating Icenian Coinage', in *Current Archaeology*, Vol 341, 16 July 2018.
18. Geiriadur Prifysgol Cymru (2023), *A Dictionary of the Welsh Language*, Geiriadur Prifysgol Cymru (welsh-dictionary.ac.uk), accessed March 5 2023.
19. Sayer, Duncan (2020), *Early Anglo-Saxon Cemeteries: Kinship, Community and Identity*, Manchester University Press, Manchester.
20. Institute for Name-Studies (2023), *Key to English Place-Names*, University of Nottingham, Key to English Place-names (nottingham.ac.uk), Accessed March 2, 2023.

21. Icknield Way Association (2023), 'Icknield Way Trail. History and Environment', *History and Environment* – Icknield Way Trail Accessed Mar 2 2023.
22. Institute for Name-Studies (2023), *Key to English Place-Names*, University of Nottingham, Key to English Place-names (nottingham.ac.uk), Accessed March 2, 2023.
23. ibid.
24. Giles, J.A; Ingram, J., trans. (1996), *The Anglo-Saxon Chronicles*, reproduced by the Gutenberg project.
25. Huntingdon, Henry of; Translated by Forester, T. (1853), *The Chronicle of Henry of Huntingdon*, London, Woodfall and Kinder, 1853.
26. Institute for Name-Studies (2023), *Key to English Place-Names*, University of Nottingham, Key to English Place-names (nottingham.ac.uk), Accessed March 2, 2023.
27. Woolf, Henry Bosley (1938), 'The Naming of Women in Old English Times', in *Modern Philology*, Vol. 36, No. 2, pp. 113–120.
28. Huntingdon, Henry of; Translated by Forester, T. (1853), *The Chronicle of Henry of Huntingdon*, London, Woodfall and Kinder, 1853.
29. Bede, St (673–735), *The Ecclesiastical History of England*, Christian Classics Ethereal Library.
30. Giles, J.A; Ingram, J., trans. (1996), *The Anglo-Saxon Chronicles*, reproduced by the Gutenberg project.
31. Institute for Name-Studies (2023), *Key to English Place-Names*, University of Nottingham, Key to English Place-names (nottingham.ac.uk), Accessed March 2, 2023.
32. Harte, Jeremy (2015), 'Language, Law, and Landscape in the Anglo-Saxon World', in *Time and Mind*, Vol. 8:1, pp. 51–67.
33. ibid.
34. Tacitus, Translated by C. W. Eliot ed. (1910), *Voyages and Travels: Ancient and Modern, with Introductions, Notes and Illustrations.* New York: P. F. Collier and Son, [c1910] The Harvard classics, [vol. XXXIII].
35. Harte, Jeremy (2015), 'Language, Law, and Landscape in the Anglo-Saxon World', in *Time and Mind*, Vol. 8:1, pp. 51–67.
36. Huntingdon, Henry of; Translated by Forester, T. (1853), *The Chronicle of Henry of Huntingdon*, London, Woodfall and Kinder, 1853.
37. ibid.
38. ibid.
39. Nennius, Translated by Giles, J.A. (2000), *Historia Brittonum*, In Parentheses Publications, Cambridge Ontario.
40. Institute for Name-Studies (2023), *Key to English Place-Names*, University of Nottingham, Key to English Place-names (nottingham.ac.uk), Accessed March 2, 2023.
41. Huntingdon, Henry of; Translated by Forester, T. (1853), *The Chronicle of Henry of Huntingdon*, London, Woodfall and Kinder, 1853.
42. Monmouth, Geoffrey of, Translated by Thompson, A. (1999), *Historia Regum Brittaniae*, In Parentheses Publications, Cambridge Ontario.
43. Institute for Name-Studies (2023), *Key to English Place-Names*, University of Nottingham, Key to English Place-names (nottingham.ac.uk), Accessed March 2, 2023.

Chapter 3

1. Büntgen, Ulf; Myglan, Vladimir; Charpentier Ljungqvist, Fredrik; McCormick, Michael; Di Cosmo, Nicola; Sig, Michael; Jungclaus, Johann; Wagner, Sebastian; Krusic, Paul; Esper, Jan; Kaplan, Jed; de Vaan, Michiel; Lyrerbacher, Jürg; Wacker, Lukas; Tegel, Willy

& Kirdyanov, Alexander (2016), 'Cooling and societal change during the Late Antique Little Ice Age (536 to around 660 CE)', in *Nature Geoscience*, Vol. 9.
2. Riechelmann, Dana & Gouw-Bouman, Marjolein (2018), 'A review of climate reconstructions from terrestrial climate archives covering the first millennium AD in northwestern Europe', in *Quaternary Research* (2019), Vol. 91, pp. 111–131
3. Helama, Samuli; Jones, Phil & Briffa, Keith (2017), 'Dark Ages Cold Period: A literature review and directions for future research', in *The Holocene* 2017, Vol. 27, pp.1600–1606.
4. Underwood, Richard (1999). *Anglo-Saxon Weapons and Warfare*. Stroud: Tempus. ISBN 0-7524-1412-7.
5. Tacitus, Translated by C. W. Eliot ed. (1910), *Voyages and Travels: Ancient and Modern, with Introductions, Notes and Illustrations.* New York: P. F. Collier and Son, [c1910] The Harvard classics, [vol. XXXIII].
6. ibid.
7. Jones, Prudence & Pennick, Nigel (2000), *A History of Pagan Europe*, Routledge, London.
8. Tacitus, Translated by C. W. Eliot ed. (1910), *Voyages and Travels: Ancient and Modern, with Introductions, Notes and Illustrations.* New York: P. F. Collier and Son, [c1910] The Harvard classics, [vol. XXXIII].
9. ibid.
10. Brady, Caroline (1983), 'Warriors' in Beowulf: an analysis of the nominal compounds and an evaluation of the poet's use of them', in *Anglo-Saxon England* Vol. 11, pp. 199–246.
11. Tyler, Damian (2007), 'Reluctant Kings and Christian Conversion in Seventh-Century England', in *History*, Vol. 92, No. 2, pp. 144–161.
12. Bates, Brian (2002), *The Real Middle Earth: Magic and Mystery in the Dark Ages*, Pan Books, Oxford.
13. Jones, Prudence & Pennick, Nigel (2000), *A History of Pagan Europe*, Routledge, London.
14. ibid.
15. Tacitus, Translated by C. W. Eliot ed. (1910), *Voyages and Travels: Ancient and Modern, with Introductions, Notes and Illustrations.* New York: P. F. Collier and Son, [c1910] The Harvard classics, [vol. XXXIII].
16. ibid.
17. Jones, Prudence & Pennick, Nigel (2000), *A History of Pagan Europe*, Routledge, London.
18. Bates, Brian (2002), *The Real Middle Earth: Magic and Mystery in the Dark Ages*, Pan Books, Oxford.
19. Bates, Brian (2002), *The Real Middle Earth: Magic and Mystery in the Dark Ages*, Pan Books, Oxford.
20. Bates, Brian (2012), *The Way of Wyrd*, Hay House Inc. London.
21. Orchard, Andy (1998), *Dictionary of Norse Myth and Legend*, Cassell, London.
22. ibid.
23. Thorpe, Benjamin (Trans) (1907). *Edda Sæmundar Hinns Frôoa The Edda of Sæmund the Learned. Part I.* London Trübner & Co.
24. Bates, Brian (2002), *The Real Middle Earth: Magic and Mystery in the Dark Ages*, Pan Books, Oxford.
25. Mackie, W.S, editor. *The Exeter Book: Part II: Poems IX-XXXII*. Oxford University Press, 1934, licensed under No Known Copyright.
26. ibid.
27. ibid.
28. Bcde, St, Translated by Wallis, Faith (1999), *The Reckoning of Time*, Liverpool University Press, Liverpool.

29. Bede, St (673–735), *The Ecclesiastical History of England*, Christian Classics Ethereal Library.
30. Tacitus, Translated by C. W. Eliot ed. (1910), *Voyages and Travels: Ancient and Modern, with Introductions, Notes and Illustrations.* New York: P. F. Collier and Son, [c1910] The Harvard classics, [vol. XXXIII].
31. Hooke, Della (2017), 'Groves in Anglo-Saxon England', L*andscape History*, Vol. 38:1, pp. 5–23.
32. Jones, Prudence & Pennick, Nigel (2000), *A History of Pagan Europe*, Routledge, London
33. Bede, St (673–735), *The Ecclesiastical History of England*, Christian Classics Ethereal Library
34. Wheeler, G.J. (2017), 'Witches, Odin, and the English state: the legal reception of a counter-cultural minority religious movement', in *Journal of Law and Religion*, Vol. 32, no. 3, pp. 449–469.
35. Bede, St (673–735), *The Ecclesiastical History of England*, Christian Classics Ethereal Library.
36. Jones, Prudence & Pennick, Nigel (2000), *A History of Pagan Europe*, Routledge, London.
37. ibid.
38. Tacitus, Translated by C. W. Eliot ed. (1910), *Voyages and Travels: Ancient and Modern, with Introductions, Notes and Illustrations.* New York: P. F. Collier and Son, [c1910] The Harvard classics, [vol. XXXIII].
39. Tyler, Damian (2007), 'Reluctant Kings and Christian Conversion in Seventh-Century England', in *History*, Vol. 92, No. 2, pp. 144–161.
40. Lancaster, Lorraine (1958), 'Kinship in Anglo-Saxon Society—I', in *The British Journal of Sociology*, Vol. 9, No. 3, pp. 230–250.
41. ibid.
42. Harte, Jeremy (2015), 'Language, Law, and Landscape in the Anglo-Saxon World', in *Time and Mind*, Vol. 8:1, pp. 51–67.
43. Lancaster, Lorraine (1958), 'Kinship in Anglo-Saxon Society—I', in *The British Journal of Sociology*, Vol. 9, No. 3, pp. 230–250.
44. Whitehead, Annie (2020), *Mercia: The Rise and Fall of a Kingdom*, Amberley Publishing, Stroud.
45. Baker, John (2014), 'Old English sæta and sætan names', in *Journal of the English Place-Name Society* Vol. 46, pp. 45–81.

Chapter 4
1. Breeze, Andrew (2006), 'Three Celtic Toponyms: Setantii, Blencathra, and Peny-Ghent', in *Northern History*, Vol. 43:1, pp. 161–165.
2. ibid.
3. ibid.
4. Tacitus, Translated by C. W. Eliot ed. (1910), *Voyages and Travels: Ancient and Modern, with Introductions, Notes and Illustrations.* New York: P. F. Collier and Son, [c1910] The Harvard classics, [vol. XXXIII].
5. Coates, Richard (2013), 'The name of the Hwicce: a discussion', in *Anglo-Saxon England*, Vol. 42 (2013), pp. 51–61.
6. ibid.
7. Dyer, Christopher, *Lords and Peasants in a Changing Society: The Estates of the Bishopric of Worcester, 680–1540*, 2008, Cambridge University Press.
8. Bede, St (673–735), *The Ecclesiastical History of England*, Christian Classics Ethereal Library.

9. Huntingdon, Henry of; Translated by Forester, T. (1853), *The Chronicle of Henry of Huntingdon*, London, Woodfall and Kinder, 1853.
10. ibid.
11. ibid.
12. Bede, St (673–735), *The Ecclesiastical History of England*, Christian Classics Ethereal Library.
13. Institute for Name-Studies (2023), *Key to English Place-Names*, University of Nottingham, Key to English Place-names (nottingham.ac.uk), Accessed March 2, 2023.
14. Harte, Jeremy (2015), 'Language, Law, and Landscape in the Anglo-Saxon World', in *Time and Mind*, Vol. 8:1, pp. 51–67.
15. Bede, St (673–735), *The Ecclesiastical History of England*, Christian Classics Ethereal Library.
16. ibid.
17. Huntingdon, Henry of; Translated by Forester, T. (1853), *The Chronicle of Henry of Huntingdon*, London, Woodfall and Kinder, 1853.
18. Bede, St (673–735), *The Ecclesiastical History of England*, Christian Classics Ethereal Library.
19. Nennius, Translated by Giles, J.A. (2000), *Historia Brittonum*, In Parentheses Publications, Cambridge Ontario.
20. Huntingdon, Henry of; Translated by Forester, T. (1853), *The Chronicle of Henry of Huntingdon*, London, Woodfall and Kinder, 1853.
21. Bede, St (673–735), *The Ecclesiastical History of England*, Christian Classics Ethereal Library.
22. Ingram, James (2008), *The Anglo-Saxon Chronicles*, project Gutenberg Ebook, https://www.gutenberg.org/cache/epub/657/pg657.html Accessed January 2022.
23. Bede, St (673–735), *The Ecclesiastical History of England*, Christian Classics Ethereal Library.

Chapter 5

1. Ingram, James (2008), *The Anglo-Saxon Chronicles*, project Gutenberg Ebook, https://www.gutenberg.org/cache/epub/657/pg657.html Accessed January 2022.
2. Breeze, Andrew (2004), 'the Anglo-Saxon Chronicle for 614 and Brean Down, Somerset', in: *Notes and Queries* Ser. NS, Vol. 51, pp. 234.
3. Huntingdon, Henry of; Translated by Forester, T. (1853), *The Chronicle of Henry of Huntingdon*, London, Woodfall and Kinder, 1853.
4. ibid.
5. Juranski, S & Oliver, L (2021), *The Laws of Alfred. The Domboc and the Making of Anglo-Saxon Law*, Cambridge University Press
6. Baker, John & Brookes, Stuart (2015), 'Explaining Anglo-Saxon military efficiency: the landscape of mobilization', in *Anglo-Saxon England*, Volume 44, pp. 221–258.
7. ibid.
8. Huntingdon, Henry of; Translated by Forester, T.(1853), *The Chronicle of Henry of Huntingdon*, London, Woodfall and Kinder, 1853.
9. Grammaticus, Saxo Translated by Elton, Oliver (1864) *Saxo Grammaticus. The First Nine Books of Danish History*, D. Nutt Collection, London.
10. ibid.

11. Brennan, Naomi & Hamerow, Helena (2015), 'An Anglo-Saxon Great Hall Complex at Sutton Courtenay/Drayton, Oxfordshire: A Royal Centre of Early Wessex?', in *Archaeological Journal*, Vol. 172, No.2, pp. 325–350.
12. ibid.
13. Baker, John & Brookes, Stuart (2015), 'Explaining Anglo-Saxon military efficiency: the landscape of mobilization', in *Anglo-Saxon England*, Volume 44, pp. 221–258.
14. Huntingdon, Henry of; Translated by Forester, T. (1853), *The Chronicle of Henry of Huntingdon*, London, Woodfall and Kinder, 1853.
15. ibid.
16. Davies, Sean (2010), 'The Battle of Chester and Warfare in Post-Roman Britain', in *History*, Vol. 95, No. 2, pp. 143–158.
17. Bede, St, Translated by Wallis, Faith (1999), *The Reckoning of Time*, Liverpool University Press, Liverpool.

Chapter 6
1. Ingram, James, translator. 'Annals Cambriae' found in *The Anglo-Saxon Chronicles*. London: Everyman Press, 1912.
2. Bede, St (673–735), *The Ecclesiastical History of England*, Christian Classics Ethereal Library.
3. ibid.
4. Huntingdon, Henry of; Translated by Forester, T. (1853), *The Chronicle of Henry of Huntingdon*, London, Woodfall and Kinder, 1853.
5. Ingram, James (2008), *The Anglo-Saxon Chronicle*, project Gutenberg Ebook, https://www.gutenberg.org/cache/epub/657/pg657.html Accessed January 2022.
6. Bede, St (673–735), *The Ecclesiastical History of England*, Christian Classics Ethereal Library.
7. Adams, Max (2013), *The King in the North*, Head of Zeus Ltd, Croydon.
8. Monmouth, Geoffrey of, Translated by Thompson, A. (1999), *Historia Regum Brittaniae* In Parentheses Publications, Cambridge Ontario.
9. Russell, M. (2014), 'Geoffrey of Monmouth: the lost voice of ancient Britain' in *BBC History Magazine*, December 2014.
10. Russell, M. (2014), 'Geoffrey of Monmouth: the lost voice of ancient Britain' in *BBC History Magazine*, December 2014.
11. Adams, Max (2013), *The King in the North*, Head of Zeus Ltd, Croydon.
12. Monmouth, Geoffrey of, Translated by Thompson, A. (1999), *Historia Regum Brittaniae* In Parentheses Publications, Cambridge Ontario.
13. ibid.
14. Rippon, S. (2021), 'Tracing the fluctuating fortunes of Roman and medieval Exeter', in *Current Archaeology*, March 31 2021.
15. Maltby, Mark (1979), *Faunal Studies on Urban Sites. The Animal Bones from Exeter*, Department of Prehistory and Archaeology, University of Sheffield.
16. ibid.
17. Allan, J.P. (1984), *Medieval and Post-Medieval Finds from Exeter 1971–1980*, Exeter City Council and The University of Exeter.
18. Monmouth, Geoffrey of, Translated by Thompson, A (1999), *Historia Regum Brittaniae* In Parentheses Publications, Cambridge Ontario.
19. Haldon, John (2011), 'Marching across Anatolia: Medieval Logistics and Modeling the Mantzikert Campaign', in *Dumbarton Oaks Papers*, Vol. 65/66, pp. 209–235.

20. Monmouth, Geoffrey of, Translated by Thompson, A. (1999), *Historia Regum Brittaniae* In Parentheses Publications, Cambridge Ontario.
21. ibid.
22. Pace, Edwin (2012), 'Geoffrey's 'Very Old Book' and Penda of Mercia', in *Arthuriana*, Vol. 22, No. 2, pp. 53–74.
23. ibid.
24. Wall, Martin (2017), *Warriors and Kings. The 1500-Year Battle for Celtic Britain*, Amberley Publishing, Gloucestershire.
25. ibid.
26. Breeze, Andrew (2001), 'Seventh-Century Northumbria and a Poem to Cadwallon', *Northern History*, Vol. 38:1, pp. 145–152.
27. Jones, Prudence & Pennick, Nigel (2000), *A History of Pagan Europe*, Routledge, London.
28. Bromwich, Rachel (1991), *Trioedd Ynys Prydein: The Welsh Triads*, [2nd edition, reprinted with corrections], Univ of Wales Press, Cardiff / Caerdydd.
29. Hankinson, R., 2018. Beacon Ring Hillfort: Archaeological Investigation, Unpublished CPAT Report No 1547.
30. Breeze, Andrew (2001), 'Seventh-Century Northumbria and a Poem to Cadwallon', *Northern History*, Vol. 38:1, pp. 145–152.
31. Monmouth, Geoffrey of, Translated by Thompson, A. (1999), *Historia Regum Brittaniae* In Parentheses Publications, Cambridge Ontario.

Chapter 7
1. Bede, St (673–735), *The Ecclesiastical History of England*, Christian Classics Ethereal Library.
2. Worcester, John of, Translated by Forester, T. (1854), *The Chronicle of John of Worcester* London.
3. Bede, St (673–735), *The Ecclesiastical History of England*, Christian Classics Ethereal Library.
4. ibid.
5. Adams, Max (2013), *The King in the North*, Head of Zeus Ltd, Croydon.
6. Hope-Taylor, Brian (1977), *Yeavering, An Anglo-British Centre of Early Northumbria*, Archaeological Report No 7 by Her Majesty's Stationery Office for the Department of the Environment Reprinted with corrections 2009.
7. Breeze, Andrew (2014), 'Communications 633 and the Battle of Hatfield Chase', in *Northern History*, Vol. 51, pp 77–182.
8. Huntingdon, Henry of; Translated by Forester, T. (1853), *The Chronicle of Henry of Huntingdon*, London, Woodfall and Kinder, 1853.
9. Bede, St (673–735), *The Ecclesiastical History of England*, Christian Classics Ethereal Library.
10. Huntingdon, Henry of; Translated by Forester, T. (1853), *The Chronicle of Henry of Huntingdon*, London, Woodfall and Kinder, 1853.
11. Bede, St (673–735), *The Ecclesiastical History of England*, Christian Classics Ethereal Library.
12. Martinon-Torres, Marcos, Fern, Chris; Dickinson, Tania; Webster, Leslie (2019), *The Staffordshire Hoard: An Anglo-Saxon Treasure*, Society of Antiquaries of London.
13. Bede, St (673–735), *The Ecclesiastical History of England*, Christian Classics Ethereal Library.
14. Leader, John (1897), *The Records of the Burgery of Sheffield*, Elliot Stock, London.

15. ibid.
16. ibid.
17. Bede, St (673–735), *The Ecclesiastical History of England*, Christian Classics Ethereal Library.
18. Huntingdon, Henry of; Translated by Forester, T. (1853), *The Chronicle of Henry of Huntingdon*, London, Woodfall and Kinder, 1853.
19. Bede, St (673–735), *The Ecclesiastical History of England*, Christian Classics Ethereal Library.
20. ibid.
21. ibid.

Chapter 8
1. Tacitus, Translated by C. W. Eliot ed. (1910), *Voyages and Travels: Ancient and Modern, with Introductions, Notes and Illustrations*. New York: P. F. Collier and Son, [c1910] The Harvard classics, [vol. XXXIII].
2. Paris, Mathew of; Trans Luard, Henry (1872), *Matthaei Parisiensis, Monachi Sancti Albani, Chronica Majora*, Longman & Co. London.
3. Bede, St (673–735), *The Ecclesiastical History of England*, Christian Classics Ethereal Library.
4. ibid.
5. Woolf, Alex (2004), 'Caedualla Rex Brettonum and the Passing of the Old North', *Northern History*, Vol 41:1, pp 5–24.
6. Hind, J.G.F. (1980), 'The Romano-British Name for Corbridge', in *Britannia*, 1980, Vol. 11 (1980), pp. 165–171.
7. ibid.
8. Tyrell, Henry (1911), *History of Bridge Engineering*, Published by the Author, Chicago 1911.
9. Archer, David; Leesch, Francois & Harwood, Kirsty (2007), 'Assessment of severity of the extreme River Tyne flood in January 2005 using gauged and historical information', in *Hydrological Sciences Journal*, Vol. 52, No.5, pp 992–1003.
10. Williams, A; Milner, N; O'keefe, N; Waterfall, R; Hubble, M; Webb, H (2008), *River Tyne Salmon Action Plan Review*, Scientific Report Environmental Agency 410230.
11. Hodgson, N. (2009), *Hadrian's Wall 1999–2009*, Cumberland and Westmorland Antiquarian and Archaeological Society.
12. ibid.
13. Kim, Hongnam (2020), 'A Study of Stone-joint Metal Clamps in China and Korea during the 6th-8th Centuries', in *The Silk Road. The Journal of the Silk Road House* Vol. 18.
14. Cramp, Rosemary (1999), 'The Place-name Hexham and its Interpretation', in *Notes and Queries*, Vol. 46.
15. Woolf, Alex (2004), 'Caedualla Rex Brettonum and the Passing of the Old North', *Northern History*, Vol 41:1, pp 5–24.
16. Bede, St (673–735), *The Ecclesiastical History of England*, Christian Classics Ethereal Library.
17. Stokes, Whitley trans. (1902) *Togail Bruidne Da Berga*, Librairie Emile Boullon, 1902.
18. Bede, St (673–735), *The Ecclesiastical History of England*, Christian Classics Ethereal Library.
19. ibid.
20. Adams, Max (2013), *The King in the North*, Head of Zeus Ltd, Croydon.
21. Albert, Edoardo & Gething, Paul (2020), *Warrior; A Life of War in Anglo-Saxon Britain*, Granta Publications, London.

22. Hodgson, N. (2009), *Hadrian's Wall 1999–2009*, Cumberland and Westmorland Antiquarian and Archaeological Society.
23. Bede, St (673–735), *The Ecclesiastical History of England*, Christian Classics Ethereal Library.
24. ibid.
25. ibid.
26. ibid.
27. Huntingdon, Henry of; Translated by Forester, T. (1853), *The Chronicle of Henry of Huntingdon*, London, Woodfall and Kinder, 1853.

Chapter 9
1. Whitehead, Annie (2020), *Mercia: The Rise and Fall of a Kingdom*, Amberley Publishing, Stroud.
2. Tacitus, Translated by C. W. Eliot ed. (1910), *Voyages and Travels: Ancient and Modern, with Introductions, Notes and Illustrations*. New York : P. F. Collier and Son, [c1910] The Harvard classics, [vol. XXXIII].
3. Helama, Samuli; Jones, Phil & Briffa, Keith (2017), 'Dark Ages Cold Period: A literature review and directions for future research', in *The Holocene* 2017, Vol. 27, pp.1600–1606.
4. Historic England Heritage Gateway, *Cambridgeshire HER, Devil's Dyke*, CHER No. 07801. https://www.heritagegateway.org.uk/Gateway/Results_Single.aspx?uid=MCB9420&resourceID=1000
5. Bede, St (673–735), *The Ecclesiastical History of England*, Christian Classics Ethereal Library.
6. ibid.
7. ibid.
8. ibid.
9. ibid.
10. ibid.
11. ibid.
12. ibid.
13. Bates, Brian (2002), *The Real Middle Earth: Magic and Mystery in the Dark Ages*, Pan Books, Oxford.
14. Martinon-Torres, Marcos, Fern, Chris; Dickinson, Tania; Webster, Leslie (2019), *The Staffordshire Hoard: An Anglo-Saxon Treasure*, Society of Antiquaries of London.
15. ibid.
16. ibid.
17. Bede, St (673–735), *The Ecclesiastical History of England*, Christian Classics Ethereal Library.
18. Martinon-Torres, Marcos, Fern, Chris; Dickinson, Tania; Webster, Leslie (2019), *The Staffordshire Hoard: An Anglo-Saxon Treasure*, Society of Antiquaries of London.

Chapter 10
1. Bede, St (673–735), *The Ecclesiastical History of England*, Christian Classics Ethereal Library.
2. Nennius, Translated by Giles, J.A. (2000), *Historia Brittonum*, In Parentheses Publications, Cambridge Ontario.
3. Clancy, Joseph (1970), *The Earliest Welsh Poetry*, Macmillan Publishing, London, pp. 87–89.

4. Shaw, Mike & Clark, Jo (2003), *Cheshire Historic Towns Survey: Warrington Archaeological Assessment*, Environmental Planning Cheshire County Council.
5. ibid.
6. Institute for Name-Studies (2023), *Key to English Place-Names*, University of Nottingham, Key to English Place-names (nottingham.ac.uk), Accessed March 2, 2023.
7. Paris, Mathew of; Trans Luard, Henry (1872), *Matthaei Parisiensis, Monachi Sancti Albani, Chronica Majora*, Longman & Co. London.
8. Bede, St, Translated by Wallis, Faith (1999), *The Reckoning of Time*, Liverpool University Press, Liverpool.
9. Bede, St (673–735), *The Ecclesiastical History of England*, Christian Classics Ethereal Library.
10. Nennius, Translated by Giles, J.A. (2000), *Historia Brittonum*, In Parentheses Publications, Cambridge Ontario.
11. ibid.
12. Bede, St (673–735), *The Ecclesiastical History of England*, Christian Classics Ethereal Library.
13. Orosius, Paulus; Translated by Woodworth, Raymond (1936), *Seven Books of History Against the Pagans: The Apology of Paulus Orosius*, Columbia Press, New York.
14. Rollason, D.W. (1978), '"Lists of saints" resting-places in Anglo-Saxon England', in *Anglo-Saxon England*, Vol. 7, pp. 61–93.
15. ibid.
16. ibid.
17. Bede, St (673–735), *The Ecclesiastical History of England*, Christian Classics Ethereal Library.
18. Hart, Cyril (1971), 'The Tribal Hidage', in *Transactions of the Royal Historical Society*, Vol. 21, pp. 133–157.
19. ibid.

Chapter 11

1. Bede, St (673–735), *The Ecclesiastical History of England*, Christian Classics Ethereal Library.
2. Bede, St (673–735), *The Ecclesiastical History of England*, Christian Classics Ethereal Library.
3. Huntingdon, Henry of; Translated by Forester, T. (1853), *The Chronicle of Henry of Huntingdon*, London, Woodfall and Kinder, 1853.
4. Ingram, James (2008), *The Anglo-Saxon Chronicles*, project Gutenberg Ebook, https://www.gutenberg.org/cache/epub/657/pg657.html Accessed January 2022.
5. ibid.
6. Bede, St (673–735), *The Ecclesiastical History of England*, Christian Classics Ethereal Library.
7. Ingram, James (2008), *The Anglo-Saxon Chronicles*, project Gutenberg Ebook, https://www.gutenberg.org/cache/epub/657/pg657.html Accessed January 2022.
8. Bede, St (673–735), *The Ecclesiastical History of England*, Christian Classics Ethereal Library.
9. Lyon, H.R. (1974) 'Kinship in Anglo-Saxon England', in *Anglo-Saxon England*, Vol. 3 pp. 197–209.
10. Woolf, Henry Bosley (1938), 'The Naming of Women in Old English Times', in *Modern Philology*, Vol. 36, No. 2, pp. 113–120.

11. Woolf, Henry Bosley (1938), 'The Naming of Women in Old English Times', in *Modern Philology*, Vol. 36, No. 2, pp. 113–120.
12. Lyon, H.R. (1974) 'Kinship in Anglo-Saxon England', in *Anglo-Saxon England*, Vol. 3 pp. 197–209.
13. Bede, St (673–735), *The Ecclesiastical History of England*, Christian Classics Ethereal Library.
14. Huntingdon, Henry of; Translated by Forester, T. (1853), *The Chronicle of Henry of Huntingdon*, London, Woodfall and Kinder, 1853.
15. ibid.
16. Bede, St (673–735), *The Ecclesiastical History of England*, Christian Classics Ethereal Library.
17. Huntingdon, Henry of; Translated by Forester, T. (1853), *The Chronicle of Henry of Huntingdon*, London, Woodfall and Kinder, 1853.
18. Ingram, James (2008), *The Anglo-Saxon Chronicles*, project Gutenberg Ebook, https://www.gutenberg.org/cache/epub/657/pg657.html Accessed January 2022.
19. Bede, St (673–735), *The Ecclesiastical History of England*, Christian Classics Ethereal Library.
20. Huntingdon, Henry of; Translated by Forester, T. (1853), *The Chronicle of Henry of Huntingdon*, London, Woodfall and Kinder, 1853.

Chapter 12

1. Clancy, Joseph (1970), *The Earliest Welsh Poetry*, Macmillan Publishing, London.
2. Ely, Thomas of, *Liber Eliensis, ad fidem codicum variorum*, Impensis Societatis (1848), London.
3. Bede, St (673–735), *The Ecclesiastical History of England*, Christian Classics Ethereal Library.
4. ibid.
5. ibid.
6. Roman Britain, *Burgh Caste (Gariannonum) Roman Fort*, https://www.roman-britain.co.uk/places/burgh-castle/, Accessed 30 May 2023.
7. English Heritage, *The History of Caister Roman Fort*, https://www.english-heritage.org.uk/visit/places/caister-roman-fort/history/, Accessed 5 January 2023.
8. Bede, St (673–735), *The Ecclesiastical History of England*, Christian Classics Ethereal Library.
9. Whitelock, Dorothy (1972), 'The pre-Viking age church in East Anglia', in *Anglo-Saxon England*, Vol. 1, pp. 1–22.
10. Feldman, Marian H. (2009), 'Hoarded Treasures: The Megiddo Ivories and the End of the Bronze Age', *Levant*, Vol. 41:2, pp. 175–194.
11. Levy, J. (1982), *Social and Religious Organisation in Bronze Age Denmark: An Analysis of Ritual Hoard Finds* in BAR International Series 124.

Chapter 13

1. Chaney, W. (1970), *The Cult of Kingship in Anglo-Saxon England*, University of California Press, Berkeley.
2. Adams, Max (2013), *The King in the North*, Head of Zeus Ltd, Croydon.
3. Bede, St (673–735), *The Ecclesiastical History of England*, Christian Classics Ethereal Library.
4. Breeze, Andrew (2005), 'Where Were Bede's Uilfaresdun and Paegnalaech?', *Northern History*, Vol 42:1, pp 189–191.

5. Bede, St (673–735), *The Ecclesiastical History of England*, Christian Classics Ethereal Library.
6. Hope-Taylor, Brian (1977), *Yeavering, An Anglo-British Centre of Early Northumbria*, Archaeological Report No 7 by Her Majesty's Stationery Office for the Department of the Environment. Reprinted with corrections 2009.
7. ibid.
8. ibid.
9. Ingram, James (2008), *The Anglo-Saxon Chronicles*, project Gutenberg Ebook, https://www.gutenberg.org/cache/epub/657/pg657.html Accessed January 2022.
10. Nennius, Translated by Giles, J.A. (2000), *Historia Brittonum*, In Parentheses Publications, Cambridge Ontario.
11. Bede, St (673–735), *The Ecclesiastical History of England*, Christian Classics Ethereal Library.
12. ibid.
13. ibid.
14. ibid.
15. ibid.
16. Ingram, James (2008), *The Anglo-Saxon Chronicles*, project Gutenberg Ebook, https://www.gutenberg.org/cache/epub/657/pg657.html Accessed January 2022.
17. Bede, St (673–735), *The Ecclesiastical History of England*, Christian Classics Ethereal Library.

Chapter 14

1. Bede, St (673–735), *The Ecclesiastical History of England*, Christian Classics Ethereal Library.
2. ibid.
3. ibid.
4. ibid.
5. ibid.
6. Huntingdon, Henry of; Translated by Forester, T. (1853), *The Chronicle of Henry of Huntingdon*, London, Woodfall and Kinder, 1853.
7. Paris, Mathew of; Trans Luard, Henry (1872), *Matthaei Parisiensis, Monachi Sancti Albani, Chronica Majora*, Longman & Co. London.
8. Huntingdon, Henry of; Translated by Forester, T. (1853), *The Chronicle of Henry of Huntingdon*, London, Woodfall and Kinder, 1853.
9. Ely, Thomas of, *Liber Eliensis, ad fidem codicum variorum*, Impensis Societatis (1848), London.
10. Leslie, Stephen; Winney, Bruce; Hellentha, Garrett; Davison, Dan; Boumertit, Abdelhamid; Day, Tammy; Hutnik, Katarzyna; Royrvik, Ellen C.; Cunliffe, Barry; Wellcome Trust Case Control Consortium International Multiple Sclerosis Genetics Consortium; Lawson, Daniel J.; Falush, Daniel; Freeman, Colin; Pirinen, Matti; Myers, Simon; Robinson, Mark; Donnelly, Peter & Bodme, Walter (2015), 'The fine-scale genetic structure of the British population', in *Nature*, Vol. 519, pp. 309–333.
11. Bede, St (673–735), *The Ecclesiastical History of England*, Christian Classics Ethereal Library.

Chapter 15

1. Bede, St (673–735), *The Ecclesiastical History of England*, Christian Classics Ethereal Library.

2. ibid.
3. ibid.
4. Fraser, James (2008), 'Bede, the Firth of Forth and the Location of Urbs Iudeu', *Scottish Historical Review*, Vol. 87, No. 1, pp. 1–25.
5. ibid.
6. ibid.
7. Bede, St (673–735), *The Ecclesiastical History of England*, Christian Classics Ethereal Library.
8. Nennius, Translated by Giles, J.A. (2000), *Historia Brittonum*, In Parentheses Publications, Cambridge Ontario.
9. ibid.
10. Institute for Name-Studies (2023), *Key to English Place-Names*, University of Nottingham, Key to English Place-names (nottingham.ac.uk), Accessed March 2, 2023.
11. Ordnance Map Office (1852), *Yorkshire, Sheet 250*. National Library of Scotland, View map: Ordnance Survey, Yorkshire 250 - Ordnance Survey Six-inch England and Wales, 1842-1952 (nls.uk)
12. Ordnance Map Office (1852), *Yorkshire, Sheet 249*. National Library of Scotland, View map: Ordnance Survey, Yorkshire 249 - Ordnance Survey Six-inch England and Wales, 1842–1952 (nls.uk).
13. Bede, St (673–735), *The Ecclesiastical History of England*, Christian Classics Ethereal Library.
14. ibid.
15. ibid.
16. ibid.
17. Ingram, James (2008), *The Anglo-Saxon Chronicles*, project Gutenberg Ebook, https://www.gutenberg.org/cache/epub/657/pg657.html Accessed January 2022.
18. Huntingdon, Henry of; Translated by Forester, T. (1853), *The Chronicle of Henry of Huntingdon*, London, Woodfall and Kinder, 1853.
19. Bede, St (673–735), *The Ecclesiastical History of England*, Christian Classics Ethereal Library.
20. ibid.

Epilogue
1. Meyer, Thomas (2012), *Beowulf, A Translation*, Punctum Books, New York.
2. Martinon-Torres, Marcos, Fern, Chris; Dickinson, Tania; Webster, Leslie (2019), *The Staffordshire Hoard: An Anglo-Saxon Treasure*, Society of Antiquaries of London.
3. Härke, Heinrich, (2004), *The Anglo-Saxon Weapon Burial Rite: An Interdisciplinary Analysis*, Opus (Moscow) vol. 3, 2004. 197–207.
4. ibid.
5. Von Clausewitz, General Carl, translated by Colonel J.J. Graham (1874), *On War*, Second Printing 1909 London.
6. Pattison, John (2003), 'Effect of the bubonic plague epidemic on inbreeding in 14th century Britain', American Journal of Human Biology.
7. Bede, St (673–735), *The Ecclesiastical History of England*, Christian Classics Ethereal Library.
8. ibid.
9. Jones, Prudence & Pennick, Nigel (2000), *A History of Pagan Europe*, Routledge, London.
10. Meyer, Thomas (2012), *Beowulf, A Translation*, Punctum Books, New York.

Bibliography

Adams, Max, *The King in the North* (Croydon: Head of Zeus Ltd, 2013)

Albert, Edoardo, & Gething, Paul, *Warrior: A Life of War in Anglo-Saxon Britain* (London: Granta Publications, 2020)

Allan, J.P., *Medieval and Post-Medieval Finds from Exeter 1971–1980* (Exeter City Council and The University of Exeter, 1984)

Annales Cambriae, Medieval Sourcebook, https://sourcebooks.fordham.edu/sbook.asp Accessed January 2022.

Apollinaris, Sidonius, trans. O.M. Dalton, Letters, Vol. 2, pp. 138–175; Book VIII, 1915.

Archer, David; Leesch, Francois & Harwood, Kirsty, 'Assessment of severity of the extreme River Tyne flood in January 2005 using gauged and historical information', in *Hydrological Sciences Journal*, Vol. 52, No.5, pp. 992–1003, 2007.

Baker, John, & Brookes, Stuart, 'Explaining Anglo-Saxon military efficiency: the landscape of mobilization', in *Anglo-Saxon England*, Vol. 44, pp. 221–258, 2015.

Baker, John, 'Old English sæta and sætan names', in *Journal of the English Place-Name Society*, Vol. 46, pp. 45–81, 2014.

Baker, John, 'Old English sæte and the historical significance of "folk" names', in *Early Medieval Europe*, Vol. 25, pp. 417–442, 2017.

Barney, Stephen, *Word-Hoard: An Introduction to Old English Vocabulary*, (New Haven: Yale University Press, 1985)

Bates, Brian, *The Real Middle Earth: Magic and Mystery in the Dark Ages* (Oxford: Pan Books, 2002)

Bates, Brian, *The Way of Wyrd* (London: Hay House Inc., 2012)

Bede, St (673–735), *The Ecclesiastical History of England* (Christian Classics Ethereal Library)

Bede, St, Translated by Wallis, Faith, *The Reckoning of Time* (Liverpool: Liverpool University Press, 1999)

Berge, R; Jasinski, M; Sognnes, K., *N-TAG TEN Proceedings of the 10th Nordic TAG conference at Stiklestad*, Norway 2009. Published by Archaeopress, Oxford, 2009.

Blakelock, E.S., *Scientific Analysis of the Staffordshire Hoard Seax Set*, British Museum, Department of Conservation and Scientific Research, 2014.

Blakelock, E.S., *Analysis of the Staffordshire Hoard Great Cross (K655, K657, K658, and K659), Gem Setting (K1314) and Inscribed Strip (K550)*, British Museum, Department of Conservation and Scientific Research, 2014.

Blakelock, Eleanor; La Niece, Susan; Fern, Chris, 'Secrets of the Anglo-Saxon goldsmiths: Analysis of gold objects from the Staffordshire Hoard', in *Journal of Archaeological Science*, Vol. 72, pp. 44–56, 2016.

Blakelock, E.S., 'Never Judge a Gold object By Its Surface Analysis: A Study of Surface Phenomena in a Selection of Gold Objects from the Staffordshire Hoard', *Archaeometry*, Vol. 58 pp. 912–929, 2016.

Blanton, Virginia, 'King Anna's Daughters: Genealogical Narrative and Cult Formation in the Liber Eliensis', in *Historical Reflections/Réflexions Historiques*, Spring 2004, Vol.

30, No.1, Historical Guineveres and Literary Eleanors: 'Narratizing' Medieval Women's Lives (Spring 2004), pp. 127–149, 2004.

Blenner-Hassett, Roland, 'Gernemuoe: A Place-Name Puzzle in Lawman's Brut', in *Modern Language Notes*, Vol. 57, No. 3, pp. 179–181, 1942.

Brady, Caroline, 'Warriors' in Beowulf: an analysis of the nominal compounds and an evaluation of the poet's use of them', in *Anglo-Saxon England* Vol. 11, pp. 199–246, 1983.

Brady, Lindy, 'Echoes of Britons on a Fenland Frontier in the Old English 'Andreas', in *The Review of English Studies*, Vol. 61, No. 252, pp. 669–689, 2010.

Breeze, Andrew, 'Seventh-Century Northumbria and a Poem to Cadwallon', *Northern History*, Vol. 38:1, pp. 145–152, 2001.

Breeze, Andrew, 'The Battle of the Uinued and the River Went, Yorkshire', *Northern History*, Vol 41:2, pp. 377–383, 2004.

Breeze, Andrew, 'The Anglo-Saxon Chronicles for 614 and Brean Down, Somerset', in: *Notes and Queries* Ser. NS, Vol. 51, pp. 234, 2004.

Breeze, Andrew, 'Where Were Bede's Uilfaresdun and Paegnalaech?', *Northern History*, Vol. 42:1, pp 189–191, 2005.

Breeze, Andrew, 'Three Celtic Toponyms: Setantii, Blencathra, and Peny-Ghent', in *Northern History*, Vol. 43:1, pp. 161–165, 2006.

Breeze, Andrew, 'Bede's Hefenfeld and the Campaign of 633', in *Northern History*, Vol 44:2, pp. 193–197, 2007.

Breeze, Andrew, 'Communications 633 and the Battle of Hatfield Chase', in *Northern History*, Vol. 51, pp. 77–182, 2014.

Brennan, Naomi & Hamerow, Helena, 'An Anglo-Saxon Great Hall Complex at Sutton Courtenay/Drayton, Oxfordshire: A Royal Centre of Early Wessex?', in *Archaeological Journal*, Vol. 172, No.2, pp. 325–350, 2015.

Bromwich, Rachel, *Trioedd Ynys Prydein: The Welsh Triads*, [2nd edition, reprinted with corrections] Univ of Wales Press, Cardiff /Caerdydd, 1991.

Brooks, Nicholas, 'Why is the "Anglo-Saxon Chronicles" about kings?', in *Anglo-Saxon England*, Vol. 39, pp. 43–70, 2011.

Budge, David, *Archaeological Investigation at Cuckney, Nottinghamshire*, Mercian Archaeological Services CIC, Report MAS049, 2019.

Büntgen, Ulf; Myglan, Vladimir; Charpentier Ljungqvist, Fredrik; McCormick, Michael; Di Cosmo, Nicola; Sig, Michael; Jungclaus, Johann; Wagner, Sebastian; Krusic, Paul; Esper, Jan; Kaplan, Jed; de Vaan, Michiel; Lyrerbacher, Jürg; Wacker, Lukas; Tegel, Willy & Kirdyanov, Alexander (2016), 'Cooling and societal change during the Late Antique Little Ice Age (536 to around 660 CE)', in *Nature Geoscience*, Vol. 9.

Burns, M.L. & Harvey, K.M., *Post-Excavation Assessment: Land at Land Gate, Ashton-in-Makerfield, Wigan, Greater Manchester*, University of Salford, 2019.

Capper, Morn & Scully, Marc, 'Ancient objects with modern meanings: museums, volunteers, and the Anglo-Saxon 'Staffordshire Hoard' as a marker of twenty-first century regional identity', *Ethnic and Racial Studies*, 39:2, 181–203, 2016. DOI:10.1080/01419870.2016.1105996

Carroll, Jayne, & Baker, John, 'The afterlives of Bede's tribal names in English place-names' In L. Alexander James, & L. Ryan (Eds.), *Land of the English Kin*: Studies of Wessex and *Anglo-Saxon England* in Honour of Barbara Yorke (112–153) (Leiden, Netherlands: Brill Academic Publishers, 2020)

Chaney, W., *The Cult of Kingship in Anglo-Saxon England* (Berkeley: University of California Press, 1970)

Chapman, Henry, *The Staffordshire Hoard Surveys an Assessment*, Barbican Research Associates Ltd, 2017.

Charpentier Ljungqvist, 'A new Reconstruction of Temperature Variability in the Extra-Tropical Northern Hemisphere during the Last Two Millennia', in Geografiska Annaler. Series A, *Physical Geography*, 2010, Vol. 92, No. 3, pp. 339–351, 2010.

Chenard, Marianne Malo, 'King Oswald's Holy Hands: Metonymy and the Making of a Saint in Bede's Ecclesiastical History', in *Exemplaria*, Vol. 17, No.1, pp.33–56, 2005.

Church, S.D., 'Paganism in Conversion-Age *Anglo-Saxon England*: The Evidence of Bede's "Ecclesiastical History" Reconsidered', in *History*, Vol. 93, No. 2, pp. 162–180, 2008.

Clancy, Joseph, *The Earliest Welsh Poetry*, Macmillan Publishing, London, pp. 87–89

Clwyd-Powys Archaeological Trust (2008), 'Newsletter Autumn 2008', The Clwyd-Powys Archaeological Trust Welshpool, Powys, 1970.

Coates, Richard, 'The name of the Hwicce: a discussion', in *Anglo-Saxon England*, Vol. 42, pp. 51–61, 2013.

Cook, Albert, *Select Translations from Old English Poetry* (Boston: Glinn and Company, 1902)

Cool, H.E.M., *The Development and Progress of the Staffordshire Hoard Research Project*, Barbican Research Associates Ltd, 2014.

Corning, Caitlin, 'The Baptism of Edwin, King of Northumbria: A New Analysis of the British Tradition', in *Northern History*, Vol. 36:1, pp. 5–15, 2000.

Cramp, Rosemary, 'The Place-name Hexham and its Interpretation', in *Notes and Queries*, Vol. 46, 1999.

Crowland, Felix of, Translated by Goodwin, Charles, *Life of St. Guthlac* (London: John Russell Smith, 1848)

Davies, Sean, 'The Battle of Chester and Warfare in Post-Roman Britain', in *History*, Vol. 95, No. 2, pp. 143–158, 2010.

Davis, Kathleen, *Periodization and Sovereignty: How Ideas of Feudalism and Secularization Govern the Politics of Time* (University of Pennsylvania Press, 2008)

Davis, Kathleen, 'Timelines: Feudalism, Secularity and Early Modernity', in South Asia: *Journal of South Asian Studies*, Vol. 38, No.1, pp. 69–83, 2015.

Davis, Kathleen, 'From periodization to the autoimmune secular state', *Griffith Law Review*, 27:4, pp. 411–425, 2018.

Deegan, Alison, *Air Photo Mapping and Interpretation For Contextualising Metal-Detected Discoveries: Staffordshire Anglo-Saxon Hoard*, Barbican Research Associates Limited, 2013.

Diamond, Robert E., *Old English Grammar and Reader* (Detroit: Wayne State University Press, 1989)

Dumville, David, 'The Anglian collection of royal genealogies and regnal lists', in *Anglo-Saxon England*, Vol. 5, pp. 23–50, 1976.

Dumville, David, 'The aetheling: a study in Anglo-Saxon constitutional history', in *Anglo-Saxon England*, Vol. 8, pp. 1–33, 1979.

Dunshea, Philip, 'The road to Winwæd? Penda's wars against Oswiu of Bernicia, c. 642 to c. 655', in *Anglo-Saxon England*, Vol. 44, pp. 1–16, 2016.

Edmonds, Fiona, 'The expansion of the kingdom of Strathclyde', in *Early Medieval Europe*, Vol. 23, No.1, pp. 43–66, 2015.

Edwards, K.J., 'Recent Developments in the Study of Place-names and the Anglo-Saxon Settlement', in *Kent Archaeology Society*, 2017.

Ejstrud, B; Hunnicke, T; Husum, C; Korre, A; Maarleveld, T; Vafeiadou, K., *The migration period, Southern Denmark and the North Sea: A workbook in relation to the Gredstedbro find*, Maritime Archaeology Programme, University of Southern Denmark, 2008.

Ellard, Donna, 'Anglo-Saxon(ist) Pasts, Postsaxon Futures', Punctum Books
Ely, Thomas of, 'Liber Eliensis, ad fidem codicum variorum', Impensis Societatis (1848), London, 2019.
Erlewine, Robert, 'Hermann Cohen and the Humane Intolerance of Ethical Monotheism', in *Jewish Studies Quarterly*, Vol. 15, No. 2, pp. 148–173, 2008.
Estes, Heide, *Anglo-Saxon Literary Landscapes: Ecotheory and the Environmental Imagination* (Amsterdam University Press, 2017)
Feldman, Marian H., 'Hoarded Treasures: The Megiddo Ivories and the End of the Bronze Age', *Levant*, Vol. 41:2, pp. 175–194, 2009.
Fern, Chris; Martinon-Torres, Marcos; Dickinson, Tania; Webster, Leslie, *The Staffordshire Hoard: An Anglo-Saxon Treasure*, Society of Antiquaries of London, 2019.
Finlayson, Rhona & Hardie, Caroline, 'Corbridge Northumberland Extensive Urban Survey', Northumberland County Council and English Heritage, 2008.
Flood, Victoria, 'Arthur's Return from Avalon: Geoffrey of Monmouth and the Development of the Legend', in *Arthuriana*, Summer 2015, Vol. 25, No. 2, pp. 84–110, 2015.
Fraser, James, 'Bede, the Firth of Forth and the Location of Urbs Iudeu', *Scottish Historical Review*, Vol. 87, No. 1, pp. 1–25, 2008.
Gaiman, Neil, *Norse Mythology* (New York: W.W. Norton & Company, 2018)
Gebühr, M., 'Angulus desertus?' In: Hans- Jürgen Hässler (eds.): Die Wanderung der Angeln nach England. Studien zur Sachsenforschung, 1996.
Gildas, Translated by Giles, J.A., *On the Ruin of Britain*, Project Gutenberg Ebook.
Giles, J.A., *The British History of Geoffrey of Monmouth in twelve books* (London: James Bohn Publishing, 1892)
Goodwin, Jon, 'A Survey of the Sources for Possible Contemporary Activity in the Vicinity of the Hoard Find Spot', Heritage and Design Department of Stoke-on-Trent City Council, 2016.
Gover, J.E.B.; Mawer, A. & Stenton, F.M., *The Place-Names of Warwickshire* (Cambridge University Press, 1970)
Graham-Campbell, James & Sheehan, John (2009), 'Viking Age gold and silver from Irish crannogs and other watery places', in *The Journal of Irish Archaeology*, Vol. 18, pp. 77–93.
Grammaticus, Saxo, Translated by Elton, Oliver, *Saxo Grammaticus: The First Nine Books of Danish History* (London: D. Nutt Collection, 1864)
Greenfield, Stanley, 'The Formulaic Expression of the Theme of "Exile" in Anglo-Saxon Poetry', in *Speculum*, Vol. 30, No. 2, pp. 200–206, 1955.
Grierson, P., 'Election and Inheritance in Early Germanic Kingship', in *The Cambridge Historical Journal*, 1941, Vol. 7, No. 1, pp. 1–22, 1941.
Haldon, John, 'Marching across Anatolia: Medieval Logistics and Modeling the Mantzikert Campaign', in *Dumbarton Oaks Papers*, Vol. 65/66, pp. 209–235, 2011.
Hamann, Stefanie, 'St Fursa, the genealogy of an Irish saint – the historical person and his cult', in Proceedings of the Royal Irish Academy: Archaeology, Culture, History, Literature, Vol. 112C (2012), pp. 147–187, 2012.
Hammon, Andy, 'Understanding the Romano-British-Early Medieval Transition: A Zooarchaeological Perspective from Wroxeter (Viroconium Cornoviorum)', in *Britannia*, Vol. 42, pp. 275–305, 2011.
Hankinson, R., 'Beacon Ring Hillfort: Archaeological Investigation', Unpublished CPAT Report No 1547, 2018.
Härke, Heinrich, *The Anglo-Saxon weapon burial rite: an interdisciplinary analysis*, Opus (Moscow) Vol. 3, pp. 197–207, 2004.

Hart, Cyril, 'The Tribal Hidage', in *Transactions of the Royal Historical Society*, Vol. 21, pp. 133–157, 1971.

Harte, Jeremy, 'Language, Law, and Landscape in the Anglo-Saxon World', in *Time and Mind*, Vol. 8:1, pp. 51–67, 2015.

Helama, Samuli; Jones, Phil & Briffa, Keith, 'Dark Ages Cold Period: A literature review and directions for future research', in *The Holocene*, Vol. 27, pp. 1600–1606, 2017.

Hicks, Carola, 'The birds on the Sutton Hoo purse', in *Anglo-Saxon England*, Vol. 15, pp. 153–165, 1986.

Higham, Nick, 'Northumbria's southern frontier: a review', in *Early Medieval Europe*, Vol. 14, No. 4, pp. 391–418, 2006.

Hind, J.G.F., 'The Romano-British Name for Corbridge', in *Britannia*, Vol. 11, pp. 165–171, 1980.

Historic England Heritage Gateway, *Cambridgeshire HER, Devil's Dyke*, CHER No. 07801. https://www.heritagegateway.org.uk/Gateway/Results_Single.aspx?uid=MCB9420&resourceID=1000

Hodgson, N., *Hadrian's Wall 1999–2009*, Cumberland and Westmorland Antiquarian and Archaeological Society, 2009.

Holmes, Matilda, *Animals in Saxon & Scandinavian England: Backbones of Economy and Society* (Leiden: Sidestone Press, 2014)

Hooke, Della, 'Groves in *Anglo-Saxon England*', *Landscape History*, Vol. 38:1, pp. 5–23, 2017.

Hope-Taylor, Brian (1977), *Yeavering, An Anglo-British Centre of Early Northumbria*, Archaeological Report No 7 by Her Majesty's Stationery Office for the Department of the Environment Reprinted with corrections 2009.

Hostetter, Dr. Aaron Translated (2017), 'Maxim I', in Olde English Poetry Project, Rutgers, The State University of New Jersey, https://oldenglishpoetry.camden.rutgers.edu/maxims-i/

Howorth, Henry, 'The Beginnings of Wessex', in *The English Historical Review*, Vol. 13, No. 52, pp. 667–671, October 1898.

Hume, Kathryn, 'The concept of the hall in Old English poetry', in *Anglo-Saxon England* Vol. 3, pp. 63–74, 1974.

Hunter-Mann, Kurt, 'When (and What) Was the End of Roman Britain?' in *Theoretical Roman Archaeology: First Conference Proceedings. Worldwide Archaeology Series*, Vol. 4. Aldershot: Avebury/Ashgate, 1993.

Huntingdon, Henry of; Translated by Forester, T., *The Chronicle of Henry of Huntingdon* (London: Woodfall and Kinder, 1853)

Ingram, James (2008), *The Anglo-Saxon Chronicles*, project Gutenberg Ebook, https://www.gutenberg.org/cache/epub/657/pg657.html Accessed January 2022.

Ingram, James, translator. 'Annals Cambriae' found in *The Anglo-Saxon Chronicles* (London: Everyman Press, 1912)

Institute for Name-Studies, *Key to English Place-Names*, University of Nottingham, Key to English Place-names (nottingham.ac.uk), Accessed 2 March, 2023.

Johnson, Flint, 'The Gwynedd Dynasty from Padarn to Maelgwn', *International Journal of Regional and Local History*, Vol. 15:2, pp 75–88, 2020.

Jones, Alex & Baldwin, Eamonn, *The Staffordshire Hoard Fieldwork 2009–2010*, Barbican Research Associates Ltd, 2017.

Jones, Michael & Casey, John, 'The Gallic Chronicle Restored: A Chronology for the Anglo-Saxon Invasions and the End of Roman Britain', in *Britannia*, Vol. 19, pp. 367–398, 1988.

Jones, Prudence & Pennick, Nigel, *A History of Pagan Europe* (London: Routledge, 2000).

Juranski, S. & Oliver, L., *The Laws of Alfred: The Domboc and the Making of Anglo-Saxon Law* (Cambridge University Press, 2021)

Kim, Hongnam, 'A Study of Stone-joint Metal Clamps in China and Korea during the 6th-8th Centuries', in *The Silk Road: The Journal of the Silk Road House* Vol. 18, 2020.

Lancaster, Lorraine, 'Kinship in Anglo-Saxon Society – I', in *The British Journal of Sociology*, Vol. 9, No. 3, pp. 230–250, 1958.

Lancaster, Lorraine, 'Kinship in Anglo-Saxon Society – II', in *The British Journal of Sociology*, Vol. 9, No. 4, pp. 359–377.

Lane, Alan, 'Wroxeter and the end of Roman Britain', in *Antiquity*, Vol. 88, pp. 501–515, 2014.

Lapidge, Michael, 'The career of Aldhelm', *Anglo-Saxon England*, Vol. 36, pp. 15–69, 2007.

Leader, John, *The Records of the Burgery of Sheffield* (London: Elliot Stock, 1897)

Leneghan, Francis, 'Royal wisdom and the Alfredian context of Cynewulf and Cyneheard', in *Anglo-Saxon England*, Vol. 39, pp. 71–10, 2010.

Leslie, Stephen; Winney, Bruce; Hellentha, Garrett; Davison, Dan; Boumertit, Abdelhamid; Day, Tammy; Hutnik, Katarzyna; Royrvik, Ellen C.; Cunliffe, Barry; Wellcome Trust Case Control Consortium International Multiple Sclerosis Genetics Consortium; Lawson, Daniel J.; Falush, Daniel; Freeman, Colin; Pirinen, Matti; Myers, Simon; Robinson, Mark; Donnelly, Peter & Bodme, Walter, 'The fine-scale genetic structure of the British population', in *Nature*, Vol. 519, pp. 309–333, 2015.

Levy, J., *Social and Religious Organisation in Bronze Age Denmark: An Analysis of Ritual Hoard Finds*, in BAR International Series 124, 1892.

Lyon, H.R., 'Kinship in *Anglo-Saxon England*', in *Anglo-Saxon England*, Vol. 3 pp. 197–209, 1974.

Mackie, W.S (ed.), *The Exeter Book: Part II: Poems IX-XXXII* (Oxford University Press, 1934, licensed under No Known Copyright)

Mackinlay, J.M., 'Celtic Relations of St. Oswald of Northumbria', in *The Celtic Review*, Vol. 5, No. 20, pp. 304–309, 1909.

Maltby, Mark, *Faunal Studies on Urban Sites: The Animal Bones from Exeter*, Department of Prehistory and Archaeology, University of Sheffield, 1979.

Manco, Jean, *The Origins of The Anglo-Saxons* (London: Thames & Hudson Ltd, 2018)

McCarthy, Mike, 'The Kingdom of Rheged: A Landscape Perspective', in *Northern History*, Vol. 48, No.1, pp. 9–22, 2011.

McCarthy, Mike, 'Carlisle: Function and Change between the First and Seventh Centuries AD', *Archaeological Journal*, Vol. 175:2, pp. 292–314, 2018.

Meyer, Thomas, *Beowulf, A translation* (New York: Punctum Books, 2012)

Miket, Roger & Semple, Sarah (2009), *Yeavering, Rediscovering the Landscape of the Northumbrian Kings*, Published by Northumberland County Council, ISBN: 978-1-873402-29-5

Miller, Molly, 'The Dates of Deira', in *Anglo-Saxon England*, Vol. 8, pp. 35–61, 1979.

Minter, Faye; Plouviez, Jude; Scull, Christopher, *Rendlesham Survey 2008–2014: Assessment Report*, Suffolk County Council Archaeology Service, 2016.

Monmouth, Geoffrey of, Translated by Thompson, A., *Historia Regum Brittaniae* (Cambridge, Ontario: Parentheses Publications, 1999)

Myhre, B. & I. Øye 2002. *Norges landbrukshistorie I. 4000 f. Kr. – 1350 e. Kr.*, Oslo, Det norske samlaget.

Neidorf, Leonard, 'Beowulf Before "Beowulf": Anglo-Saxon Anthroponymy and Heroic Legend', in *The Review of English Studies*, Vol. 64, No. 266, pp. 553–573, 2013.

Nennius, Translated by Giles, J.A., *Historia Brittonum* (Cambridge, Ontario: Parentheses Publications, 2000)

Oosthuizen, Susan, 'Archaeology, common rights and the origins of Anglo-Saxon identity', in *Early Medieval Europe*, Vol. 19 (2), pp. 153–181, 2011.

Orchard, Andy, *Dictionary of Norse Myth and Legend* (London: Cassell, 1998)

Ordnance Map Office (1852), *Yorkshire, Sheet 249*. National Library of Scotland, View map: Ordnance Survey, Yorkshire 249 – Ordnance Survey Six-inch England and Wales, 1842–1952 (nls.uk)

Orosius, Paulus; Translated by Woodworth, Raymond, *Seven Books of History Against the Pagans: The Apology of Paulus Orosius* (New York: Columbia Press, 1936)

Pace, Edwin, 'Geoffrey's "Very Old Book" and Penda of Mercia', in *Arthuriana*, Vol. 22, No. 2, pp. 53–74, 2012.

Parisiensis, Matthew Edited by Luard, Henry, *Chronica Majora*, Published by the Authority of the Lords Commissioners, London, 1872.

Pattison, John, 'Effect of the bubonic plague epidemic on inbreeding in 14th century Britain', *American Journal of Human Biology*, 2003.

Pattison, John (2008), 'Is it necessary to assume an apartheid-like social structure in Early Anglo-Saxon England?' in Proceedings of the Royal Society 275(1650):2423–9

Peregrine, Peter N., 'Social resilience to Climate Change during the Late Antique Little Ice Age: A Replication Study', in *Weather, Climate and Society*, Vol. 12, pp. 561–575, 2020.

Pfeffer, Georg, 'The Vocabulary of Anglo-Saxon Kinship', in *L'Homme*, Vol. 27, No. 103, pp. 113–128, 1987.

Platts, Calum, *The Annals of Ulster and the Anglo-Saxon Kingship: a Preliminary Discourse*, Proceedings of the Harvard Celtic Colloquium, Vol. 38 pp. 173–200, 2018.

Prestwich, J.O., 'King Æthelhere and the Battle of the Winwaed', in *The English Historical Review*, Vol. 83, No. 326, pp. 89–95, 1968.

Procopius, Translated by H.B. Dewing, *History of the Wars*, book VIII, chapter XX, section 31'(London: Harvard Press, 1962)

Riechelmann, Dana & Gouw-Bouman, Marjolein, 'A review of climate reconstructions from terrestrial climate archives covering the first millennium AD in northwestern Europe', in *Quaternary Research*, Vol. 91, pp. 111–131, 2018.

Rippon, S., 'Tracing the fluctuating fortunes of Roman and medieval Exeter', in *Current Archaeology*, 31 March 2021.

Rollason, D.W., 'Lists of saints' resting-places in *Anglo-Saxon England*', in *Anglo-Saxon England*, Vol. 7, pp. 61–93, 1978.

Roman Britain, *Burgh Castle (Gariannonum) Roman Fort*, https://www.roman-britain.co.uk/places/burgh-castle/, Accessed 30 May 2023.

Sayer, Duncan, *Early Anglo-Saxon cemeteries: Kinship, community and identity* (Manchester: Manchester University Press, 2020)

Shaw, Mike & Clark, Jo, *Cheshire Historic Towns Survey; Warrington Archaeological Assessment*, Environmental Planning Cheshire County Council, 2003.

Smith, A.H., *English Place-Name Elements*, Part 1 (A-Iw) [hereafter EPNE] (Cambridge: Cambridge University Press, 1956)

Spear, David, 'Christianizing Kinship: Ritual Sponsorship in *Anglo-Saxon England*', *History: Reviews of New Books*, 27:3, p. 121, 1999.

Stapleton, Paul, 'The Cross Cult, King Oswald, and Elizabethan Historiography', in *Catholic History*, Vol. 33, No. 1, pp. 32–57, 2016.

Stokes, Whitley trans., *Togail Bruidne Da Berga*, Librairie Emile Boullon, 1902.

Symonds, Matthew, 'Fords and the frontier: waging counter-mobility on Hadrian's Wall', in *Antiquity*, Vol. 94, pp. 92–109, 2020.

Tacitus, Translated by C.W. Eliot ed. (1910), *Voyages and Travels: Ancient and Modern, with Introductions, Notes and Illustrations.* New York: P.F. Collier and Son, [c1910] The Harvard classics, [vol. XXXIII]

Tacitus, Translated by Jackson, J. (1937), *The Annals of Tacitus*, Published in Vol V. of the Loeb Classical Library edition of Tacitus.

Tacitus, edited by Rives, James, *Agricola and the Germania* (New York: Penguin Classics, 2010)

Talbot, J., 'The Die is Cast: Investigating Icenian Coinage', in *Current Archaeology*, Vol 341, 16 July 2018.

Tarzia, Wade, 'The Hoarding Ritual in Germanic Epic Tradition', in *Journal of Folklore Research*, Vol. 26, No. 2, pp. 99–121, 1989.

Thorpe, Benjamin (Trans.), *Edda Sæmundar Hinns Fróða The Edda of Sæmund the Learned. Part I* (London: Trubner & Co, 1907)

Toswell, M.J., 'Quid Tacitus . . . ? The Germania and the Study of *Anglo-Saxon England*', in *Florilegium*, Vol. 27, pp. 27–62, 2010.

Tremblay, M; Vezina, H., 'New Estimates of Intergenerational Time Intervals for the Calculation of Age and Origins of Mutations'. In *American Journal of Human Genetics* Vol. 66 Iss. 2 pp. 651–658, 2000.

Tyler, Damian, 'Reluctant Kings and Christian Conversion in Seventh-Century England', in *History*, Vol. 92, No. 2, pp. 144–161, 2007.

Tyrell, Henry, *History of Bridge Engineering* (Chicago: Published by the Author, 1911)

Von Clausewitz, General Carl, translated by Colonel J.J. Graham (1874), *On War*, Second Printing 1909 London. Project Gutenberg Ebook, https://www.gutenberg.org/files/1946/1946-h/1946-h.htm, Accessed December 2021.

Wade-Evans, A.W., 'The Saxones in the "Excidium Britanniæ"', in *The Celtic Review*, Vol. 10, No. 40 (June, 1916), pp. 322–333, 1916.

Walker, H.E., 'Bede and the Gewissae: The Political Evolution of the Heptarchy and Its Nomenclature', in *The Cambridge Historical Journal*, Vol. 12, No. 2, pp. 174–186, 1956.

Wall, Martin, *Warriors and Kings: The 1500-Year Battle for Celtic Britain* (Gloucestershire: Amberley Publishing, 2017)

Ward, Richard (2006), 'Newton Park. Location of the field named "Gallows Croft" battlefield restoration archaeological survey', St Helens Council, PINS Reference 3253194; 3253230; and 3253232

Weldrake, Dave, *Grim's Ditch*, West Yorkshire Archaeology Advisory Service, 2011.

Wentersdorf, Karl, 'Beowulf: The Paganism of Hrothgar's Danes', in *Studies in Philology*, winter, Vol. 78, No. 5, Texts and Studies, 1981. *Eight Anglo-Saxon Studies*, pp. 91–119, Winter 1981.

Wentersdorf, Karl, 'Beowulf – Poet's Vision of Heorot', in *Studies in Philology*, Vol. 104, No. 4, pp. 409–426, 2007.

Wheeler, G.J., 'Witches, Odin, and the English state: the legal reception of a counter-cultural minority religious movement', in *Journal of Law and Religion*, Vol. 32, No. 3, pp. 449–469, 2017.

White, Roger, 'Managing Transition: Western Britain from the End of Empire to the Rise of Penda', in *History Compass*, Vol. 11, No. 8, pp. 584–596, 2013.

Whitehead, Annie, *Mercia: The Rise and Fall of a Kingdom* (Stroud: Amberley Publishing, 2020)

Whitelock, Dorothy, 'The pre-Viking age church in East Anglia', in *Anglo-Saxon England*, Vol. 1, pp. 1–22, 1972.

Woolf, Alex, 'Caedualla Rex Brettonum and the Passing of the Old North', *Northern History*, Vol 41:1, pp. 5–24, 2004.

Woolf, Henry Bosley, 'The Naming of Women in Old English Times', in *Modern Philology*, Vol. 36, No. 2, pp. 113–120, 1938.

Worcester, John of, Translated by Forester, T., *The Chronicle of John of Worcester*, London, 1854.

Index

Abbot of Pertaneu, 58
Abingdon, 66, 151
Ackworth, 197
Adam of Bremmen, 135
Æthelburg, 89
Æthelfrith, King, 54–6
Æthelhere, King, 188
Æthelwald, King, 179
Aidan, St, 176–7
Alfred the Great, 72
Alhflaed, 183, 190
Alhfrith, 178
   Rheged, 190
Alkham, 39
Alliteration, naming convention, 23, 70, 145, 148
Angelthew, 16
Angles, Origin, 5–11
Anglesey, 39, 75, 87
Angln, 6, 14–16
Anglo-sphere, 41
Angul, 65
Anna, King, 126–7
   Christianity, 156–7
   Cnobheresburg, 160–3
   death, 187
   exile of Cenwalh, 152–3, 156, 192
   River Blyth, 186–7
Annales Cambriae, 73, 108, 113, 135
Annales Tigernach, 108–109
Armorica, 76, 79, 82, 89
Arosæta, 43
Arthurian legend, 76, 81
Arwald, King, 208
Ascott-under-Wychwood, 139
Ashton-in-Makerfield, 133, 136
Athelred, 144
Augustine mission, 77
Augustine, St, 75
Aurelius, 81

Aviones, 15
Aylesford, 18

Bates, Brian, 35
Bawtry, 54, 95
Beacon Ring, 83–4
Beandun, Battle of, *see* Brean Down
Bebba, 174
Bebbanburg, 12, 90–1
   siege of, 175–6, 178
Beodericsworth, 123, 125, 127, 157, 159
Beowulf, 2, 21, 205
Berkshire, 38
Bernicia,
   attack on Cadwallon, 109–11
   conflict in Gwynedd, 82–4
   etymology, 45
   origins, 12, 16, 46
   unification with Deira, 54–6
Berserker, 118
Bilateral kinship, 41–2
Birmingham, 20, 139
Blackness, 195
Blyth,
   estuary, 186–7
   river, 186–7
Blythburg, 187
Boar's Head, 55
Boars Hill, 150–1
Boudicca, 19
Brean Down, 52, 61–4, 75, 85
Bretton, town of, 199
Bretwalda, 153, 163
Bridgnorth, 52, 82
Brien, 77–8, 81
Bristol, 28, 52
Bristol Channel, 61, 64
Brittany, 7, 76
Brittonic,
   etymology of Maserfield, 132–3
   Hwicce, 53

Iclingas descent, 26, 42
languages, 7, 13, 19
relationship with Penda, 60, 86, 116, 179, 183, 189, 202, 207
tactics, 63, 94, 133, 195
Bronze Age, 9, 61, 167
Brycheiniog, 52, 89, 183
Buffer states, 43–4
Bulcamp,
  battle of, 186–7
  oddity, 187
Bury St Edmonds, 123
Buxton, 93
Byzantium, 121

Cadafael, 104–105
Cadwaladr, 202
Cadwallader, 86
Cadwallon, 73, 105
  Armorica, 76
  Arthurian legend, 81
  assassination of Pellitus, 77–8
  battle of Hatfield Chase, 94–7
  battle of Heavenfield, 110–12
  death, 112
  death of Eanfrith, 108–109
  defeat of Osric, 102–104
  Exeter, 78–80
  exile, 75–6
  invasion of Deira, 91, 102–105
  liberation of Gwynedd, 82–6
  rebellion against Edwin, 74–5
Caedwalla, 208
Caertrick, 196
Caesar, 9
Caister, 158
Calais, 10
Calendar, Angle, 37–8
Caletum, 10
Cambridge, 119, 148, 159, 185–6, 188
Campodonum, 74, 90–1, 98–9
Camulodunum, 19
Canada, 41, 46
Canterbury, 125
Cantscaul, 108
Canu Llywarch Hen Saga, 84
Caradog's fort, 82
Carlingnose Battery, 195

Carlisle, 172
Carolingian, 46–7
Castrum, 157–8, 160–1
Cataract, 170
Catraeth, 12
Catterick, 46
Cefn Digoll, 82–5, 87–8, 91, 95, 101, 131
Cenwalh, 70
  exile to East Anglia, 149, 152–6
  king, 147
  Penda's sister, 143–4
Ceols, 7–8, 10–11, 13–14, 17–18
Ceorl, King, 27–8, 42, 44, 54, 58, 138
Cerdic, 13, 23, 62
Charford, 23
Charlemagne, 46
Chester, Battle of, 74–5
Chester's Bridge, 111
Churn, River, 67
Cimbri, 135
Cirencester, 4, 52, 64, 69–70, 72–3, 78, 104, 115, 142, 144, 149–51
  battle of, 65–7
Clun, 82
Cnebba, 16, 23–4
Cnobheresburg, 156–7
  Penda's attack, 161–2
Codex Amiatinus, 124
Colchester, 19
Coleshill, 25–7
Colles Hyl, 25
Collesæta, 25
Cor Burn, 107
Corbridge, 106–108, 111
Corioritum, 106
Cornwall, 7, 13, 46, 52, 73
Corporeal relics, 136
Cramond Island, 195–6
Craven Arms, 82
Crayford, 18
Credenhill, 26
Creoda, 16, 25–7
Cuckney, 95
Cultural Bias, 3, 32
Curdworth, 25, 27
Cwenburg, 56
Cwichelm, King, 61
  assassination attempt, 56–9

Cynddylan, 131, 134
Cyneburh, 23, 73, 144, 178
Cynegils, King, 61
   conversion, 112–13, 142
   death, 144
Cyneswith, 23, 73, 144
Cynewald, 16, 23–5
Cynewise, 23, 70–2
   after Penda's death, 202–203
Cynric, 13, 23

Dal Riata, 110, 189, 200
Dan, 65
Danelaw, 11, 179
Danes, 7, 16, 101
Dark Ages Cooling Period (DACP), 29, 119
Deheubarth, 52, 89
Deira,
   battle of Cefn Digoll, *see* Cefn Digoll
   conflict in Gwynedd, 82–4
   origins, 12
   unification with Bernicia, 54–6
Denisesburna, 112
Denmark, 5, 7, 15, 46, 65, 167
Derby, 93–4
Derwent, River, 56–7
Devil's Dyke, 119–21, 125–6
   Penda's first invasion, 122–3
Devil's Water, 111
Devon, 52, 73
Diddersley Hill, 170
Ditton Green, 119
DNA, 7
Domnall Brecc, king, 110
Doncaster, 93–6, 98, 129, 197
Dorchester-on-Thames, 143
Dornsæta, 43
Dorset, 22, 46
Dovetail clamp, 107
Dryhten, 6, 22, 30, 32
Dumonia, 46, 61
Dunwich, 18
Durham, 136
Durham *Liber Vitae*, 169
Dyfed, 73
Dynguoaroy, 174

Eadbald, King, 99
Eadfrid, 97
Eahl, 39
Eanfrith, king, 99, 108–10
East Anglia,
   geography, 119
   origins, 9, 13–14, 18
   political instability, 121–3
East Saxons, 6, 13
Easter, 38
Eastleigh, 39
Ebbsfleet, 6, 11, 18
Ecgric, King,
   conflict with Penda, 123–7
   death, 124
Edwin, King, 54–9, 61
   Cefn Digoll, 84
   control of Gwynedd, 76
   conversion, 74, 89
   death, 96–7
   Hatfield Chase, 94–6
   retreat from Gwynedd, 85
   Staffordshire Hoard Helmet, 98
Edwinstowe, 94–5
Egfrid, 202
Elham, 39
Ella, 13
Elmet, 13, 45–8, 56, 88, 101, 182
Ely, Isle of, 119, 155
English Channel, 10
Eni, 188
Eoforwic, 90
   see also York
Eomer Iclingas, 14–18, 20, 21
Eomer the Assassin, 56–8
Eorpwald, 121–2, 157, 188
Eostre, 33, 37–8, 64, 71, 159
Eowa, 54
   allegiance to Deira and Bernicia, 75, 92, 100, 113
   death, 135
   king, 58–9
   relationship with Penda, 88
Equinox, 91, 159
Erconbert, King, 149
Ermine Street, 93, 130
Esc, 18, 23
Esk, river, 168

Ethilwin, 170
Exe, River, 78–9
Exeter, 4, 77
  book, 37
  Cadwallon's counter-attack, 79–81
  siege by Penda, 78
Exning, 125, 156
Ezra, Prophet, 124

Farne Islands, 176
Felix, Bishop, 125
Felixstowe, 18
Fenlands, 119–20
Fens, 119
Finan, Bishop, 184
Fingecester, 58
Firth of Forth, 13, 109, 195–6
Foederati, 12–14, 31, 63, 90, 102, 158
Foillan, 157, 161
Forden, 83–4
Foss Cross, 67
Fosterage, 42–3, 56, 86, 145
France, 7, 46, 76
Frankia, 47, 163
Franks, 10, 46–7, 148, 185
Freya, 33
Frigg, 33
Frisians, 7–8, 10, 13
Frothhere, 57
Fursa, 157–8, 161
Fyrd, 30

Gallic Chronicle, 11, 18
Gallows Croft, 135
Gaul, 11, 121–2, 125, 157
  aftermath of Penda's attack on Cnobheresburg, 161–3
Geoffrey of Monmouth, 28, 76–8, 80–1, 86, 102
Germania,
  book by Tacitus, 101
  region of, 15
Gewisse, 23
  etymology, 45
  expansion, 52
  origins, 13, 21
Gewissians, 28, 86
Gildas Sapien, 5–8, 11

Glannauc, 73, 103
Glen, river, 44, 90, 173–5, 194
Gloucester, 52, 136
Gododdin, 12, 46, 48, 101, 189, 194, 196
Gotland, 8
Grange Castle, 170
Gregory, Pope, 39, 89
Groves, 34, 39, 82
Gwent, 52, 89, 183
Gwych, 53
Gwynedd, 43, 51–2
  conflict with King Edwin, 74–7
  King Edwin's retreat, 84–6
Gypsy Hill, 79

Hades, 34
Hadrian's Wall, 5, 12, 93, 110, 120
  Turret 25B, 111
Haegstaldtham, 108
Haida, 9
Halesworth, 186–7
Halloween, 38
Hatfield Chase, Battle of, 94–8
Heathenry, 21, 32–7, 71, 118, 208–209
Heathfield, 46, 48, 59
Heavenfield, 110–11
Hel, 34
Hengist, 6, 11–12, 18, 65, 89, 102, 148
Henry of Huntingdon, 23–4, 26, 27
  Brittonic tactics, 62
  Cirencester, 68–9
  death of King Anna, 187
  death of King Edwin, 96
  death of Penda, 201
  King Cenwalh, 143–4, 146–7, 149, 152
  River Idle, 55
  sons of Pybba, 28, 30
Herbert, Terry, 1–2
Hercules, 33
Hereford, 26, 52, 139
Herewulf, 83, 123
Herne the Hunter, 38
Hexham, 108, 110–11
Hide, Measurement, 139
High Cross, 20, 24
High Warden, 111
Historia Brittonum, *see* Nennius

Historia Regum Brittaniae, see Geoffrey of Monmouth
Historium Anglorum, see Henry of Huntingdon
Holy-Island, *see* Lindisfarne
Honorius, Archbishop, 99
Hope-Taylor, Brian, 91, 173
Horsa, 6, 11–12, 18, 65, 89, 102, 148
Hostage exchange, 97, 202
Hretha, 37
Huginn, 36
Humber, River, 6, 12–13
 migration route, 20
Humble, King, 65
Hunwald, 170
Hwicce, 139–40
 battle of Cirencester, 64–70
 etymology, 53
 origins, 27, 45, 52

Icel, 14, 16–23, 27, 115, 118
Iceni, 18–20, 119, 125
 etymology, 19
Ickford, 21–2
Ickleford, 21–4
Ickleton, 21–2, 118–19
Icklingham, 21–2
Icknield Way, 22, 116, 118–20, 122, 188
Iclingas 16–21
Ida, King, 174
Ingas, suffix, 16
Ingestre, 39
Iona, 110, 177
Ireland,
 Cadwallon, 75–7, 79
 migration to the east, 7, 13
 Oswald, 109–10
Irish Chronicles, 87, 105
Irish Sea, 77, 102
Isle of Ely, 155
Isle of Man, 75
Isle of Wight, 6, 208
Iudeu, 195–7, 203–204
 restitution of, 196, 204

Jarrow-Wearmouth, 124
John of Worcester, 893
Jurmin, 187

Jutes, 5–7, 11–12, 15, 135
Jutland, 8, 135

Kaer-legion, 74
Kenric, 62
Kent, 89–90, 99, 148
 origin, 6, 9, 18
 river, 168
King's Lane, 186
Kinship, 16, 29, 40–3, 146
 Penda, 42–4
Kinwalsey Farm, 24–5, 27
Knebworth, 23–4, 27

Læccford, 132, 198
Land Hill, 186
Latin, 13, 32, 45–6, 73, 195
Ledwyche, 139
Leeds, 92, 103, 133, 197
Lege-cester, 74
Leicester, 159
Liber Eliensis, 155–6, 169, 183
Lichfield, 100, 155
Lilla, 57
Lilla's Cross, 57
Lincoln, 96, 129–30
Lincolnshire, 88
Lindisfarne, 176–8, 195
Lindsey, 16, 45–6
Little Ice Age, 29
Llong, 85
London, 18, 93
Lutwyche Hall, 139

Mæthel, 25, 57, 64, 167
Magonsæta, 43, 48, 162, 183–4, 203–204
Manchester, 92, 103
Maniple system, 26, 63
March, boundary, 46–50
Marcomanni, 46–7
Market Harborough, 20
Mars, 33
Marwnad Cynddylan, 131, 155
Maserfield, Battle of, 130–5
Mathew of Paris, 102
Matlock, 167
Maxims I, 37
Mayfield, 167

Mearc, 46
  see also March, boundary
Mediterranean Sea, 9
Mellitus, Abbot, 39
Menai Straight, 75
Mercia:
  etymology, 46–50
  supremacy, 25, 71
  migration, 20
Mercury, 33
Merewalh, King, 181–5
  parentage, 144–5
Mersey, River, 49–50
Mesolithic, 18
Meteia, 49
Mevanian Islands, 75
Middle Angles, 116–17, 167, 182, 184, 189, 204
Middle-Earth, 100, 164, 201
Migration:
  Celtic, 3
  early, 3
  Germanic, 7, 10–13, 16, 21, 29, 45, 189
  modern, 41
Mirce, 49
Modranecht, 71
Morgannwg, 52, 89
Muninn, 36
Mustering, 64, 173

Natanleod, 23
Nef, 145
Nennius, 26, 58–9, 131, 135, 196, 199
Neolithic, 22, 24, 173
Nerthus, 15, 33–4, 37
Netley, 23
Newmarket, 122
Newton Brook, 134
Normans, 23, 33, 47, 53, 145
Norns, 36, 80, 141
North Tyne, 111
North Yorkshire, 56–7
Northumbria, 12, 47–8, 87, 98, 178
Northwich, 93
Norway, 10, 46
Norwich, 21
Nottingham, 93
Nydam, 7–8

Oaths, 55, 79, 101, 168, 192, 201
  Æthelwald, 200
  Alhfrith, 190
  Cenwalh, 153
  Eanfrith, 108
  Eowa, 126
  Oswiu, 178
  Peada, 203
  Penda, 80, 86, 91, 97, 102, 116, 127, 142, 146
  Rædwald, 54, 121
  Rings, 167
Offa, 16
Onnenau Meigion, 81
Osbrit Longhand, 109
Osfrid, 96
Osric, King, 99, 103–105, 109
Oswald, King, 112–13, 128
  baptism, 87, 142
  Christianity, 112, 122, 127, 176–7
  death, 137, 147
  exile, 76, 109–10
  godfather, 112–13, 142
  Heavenfield, 111, 172
  Maserfield, 133–5
  River Mersey, 130–1
  sacrifice of, 135–6
  St Oswald's Well, 133
Oswestry, 137
Oswine, King, 137
  conflict with Oswiu, 169–72
Oswiu, King, 137, 138
  baptism, 184
  Bebbanburg, 175–7
  Iudeu, 195–6
  Rheged, 169
  Winwaed, 200–204
Ouse, River, 56
Oxford, 21–2, 48, 52, 56, 64, 150–1

Paulinus, 58, 98
  background, 77, 89
  flees, 99
  Imperial Rome, 90–1, 98
Peada, 20, 73, 144–5, 152–3, 179
  conversion, 183–4, 190
  death, 203
  King, 180–1, 185, 189, 191–2, 204

Peak District, 93
Pebworth, 27, 51–3, 64, 66, 70, 150
Pecsæta, 25, 43
Peddimore, 25, 27
Pellitus, 76–7
Penda's monikers,
    Penda ap Pyd, 43, 85, 89, 92, 131
    Penda the Strong, 31, 89, 96, 97, 191
Penda's sister, 70–1, 86, 142–7, 149–51
Pengwern, 131
Peterborough, 139
Picts, 5, 7, 13, 99, 189
    exile with, 99, 109–10
Plutarch, 83
Polytheism, 33–4, 40
Port Gate, 110
Porta, 14
Portsmouth, 14, 21
Powys, 26, 43, 50–2, 137
    campaign against King Edwin, 81–4
Prasutagus, King, 19
Preston, 92
Procopius, 9
Publow, 28
Pybba, 16, 26–8
    etymology, 20
    wife of, 42

Quatford, 82

Rædwald,
    battle at the River Idle, 54–6, 95, 132
    Christianity, 38, 157
    King, 98, 118–21, 127, 148, 153, 163
    oath to Edwin, 54, 121
Reach, 119
Red Bank, 132–4, 137–8
Reeve, 170, 173, 194
Reginald of Durham, 138
Rendlesham, 18, 126, 162
Rheged, 12, 48, 168
    Alhfrith, 190
    Mevanian Islands, 75
    Oswiu, 169
    western route north, 170–2
Rheinmelth, 168–9
Ricbert, 121, 188
Ridgeway, 66, 150

Rigg Lane, 199
Ritual Hoard, 164
River Idle, Battle of, 28, 54–5, 120
Roman Britain,
    fortifications,
        Bawtry, 54
        Caister, 158
        Corbridge, 106–107
        Exeter, 67–77
        Gariannonum, 157–8
            see also Cnobheresburg
        Wigan, 132
        Wilfar's Hill, 170
    invasion of Britain, 3, 207
    roads, 24, 48–9
    Romano-Celtic, 3, 5, 7, 11, 62, 102
    tactics, 31, 62–4
    withdrawal from Britain, 4, 11–12, 40, 43

Sæta, 43–4
Sailing, 8, 10
Samhain, 38
Saxo Grammaticus, 65
Saxon Shore, 5, 10, 158
Saxons, origin, 5–11
Saxony, 5–6, 155
Scandinavia, 8, 33, 121
Schlei estuary, 15
Scoti, 7, 13, 46, 48, 88, 129
Scotland, 7, 13
Scots, 5, 99, 112, 114
Scots' Dyke, 170
Scrobsæta, 43
Scyldburh, 30
    see also Shield-wall
Seaxburg, 147–9, 156
Seaxburh, 147–9, 156
Seaxnat, 33
Severn River, 52, 61, 71, 82, 183
    estuary, 61, 70, 78
    river valley, 23, 51, 70
Shaman, 34–5
Sherwood Forest, 94–7
Shield-Fortress, 30
    see also Shield-wall
Shield-wall, 31, 55, 62–3
Ships, 9, 161

Nydam, 7–9
Sutton Hoo, 7–9, 121, 162
Shrewsbury, 24, 82, 131
Sidonius Apollinaris, 8–10, 162
Sigbert, King of East Anglia,
  abdication, 122
  death, 124, 126
  exile in Gaul, 121–2
  monastic retirement, 123
  Staffordshire hoard priest's head mount, 124–5
Sigbert, King of the East Saxons, 184–5
Six Mile Bottom, 159
Six-Ashes, 81–2, 91
Snorri Sturluson, 209
Solstice, Summer, 38
Solstice, Winter, 38
Somerset, 46, 52, 61, 73
South Tyne, 111
South-Humbrians, 92, 167
South-Saxons, 6, 13, 23, 45, 47, 155, 188, 192, 202
Southwell, 58
Southwold, 185–6
St Albans, 19
Staffordshire Hoard, 1, 138, 163, 165, 205–206
  contents, 2, 165
  discovery, 1–3
  helmet, 98
  priest's head mount, 124–5
Stangate Road, 107
Stirling, 195
Stoke-on-Trent, 93
Strathclyde, 12, 46, 48
Sutton Courtenay, 66, 91, 150–2, 156, 173
Sutton Hoo, 7, 205
  helmet, 98, 118
  ship, 7–9, 121, 162
Swindon, 21

Tacitus, 15
  Germanic dances, 118
  Germanic religion, 15, 33–4, 39–40
  Iceni, 18–19
  kingship, 17, 40
  sailing, 9
  shields, 30–1

Tartarus, 34
Templeborough, 99
Thames,
  estuary, 18
  river, 23, 52, 64, 66, 150–1
Thetford, 21
  forest, 122
þing, 25
Thundersley, 39
Thunor, 33, 89
Thurleigh, 39
Thursley, 39
Thuuf, 90
Tiw, 33, 207
Tjängvide, 8
Togail Bruidne Da Derga, Irish Saga, 109
Tomsæta, 20, 25, 43, 48, 138
Tondhere, 170
Træf, 39
Trent, River, 20, 48, 58, 203
Tribal Hidage, 48, 114, 139
Tuck Hill, 82
Tuesley, 39
Tuesnoad, 39
Tufa, 90
Tumuli, 2, 39, 57, 66–7, 166
Tweed, river, 194
Tyne, River, 106–108, 129, 172, 193
  floods, 106–107

Ulster Chronicle, 135
Ultan, 157
Uppsala, 39, 135
Uther Pendragon, 81

Variation, naming convention, 23, 145
Varinians, 15
Varni, 9
Venerable Bede, 5–7
Verulamium, 19
Vikings, 10–11, 178
Vita Sancti Oswaldi, 137
Von Clausewitz, Carl, 7
Vortigern, 5, 12, 17–18, 102

Wade, 10, 33
Wales, 7, 13, 39, 45, 48, 51–2, 73–4
Warrington, 132

Index 241

Warrior dance, 118
Washington, 9
Watling Street, 20, 24
Wayland-The-Smith, 10
Wearmund, 16
Weedon, 39
Weeley, 39
Welland, River, 20
Welsh Triads, 84
Wensley, 39
Went, river, *see* Winwaed
Wergild, 42
Wessex, 21, 23, 71–2, 143, 147–8, 188
West-Saxons, 6, 24–45
Whissendine, 139
Whiston, 139
Whitley, 16
Whyly, 39
Wic, suffix, 90
Wigan, 132, 134
Wih, 39
Wihtwara, 13, 208
Wilderspool, 132
Wilfaraesdun, *see* Diddersley Hill
Wilfar's Hill, *See* Diddersley Hill
Willey, 39
Winchester, 143
Wing, 39

Winwaed,
 battle of, 200–201
 river, 197
Winwick, 132
Wippidsfleet, 17
Witan, 197
Witchley Hundred, 139
Woden, 16, 33–6
Wodensburh, 26
 battle of, 28
Worsted Lodge, 120, 159
Wreocensæta, 43
Wroxeter, 4, 131
Wuffingas, 125
Wulfhere, 144, 190
Wych Brook, 139
Wychavon, 139
Wychbol, 139
Wychbury Hill, 139
Wychnor, 139
Wychwood, 70, 139
Wye, 39
Wyrd, 35–7

Yeavering, 66, 91, 173–6
 bell, 173
 Paulinus, 90
Yggdrasil, 135
York, 57, 74, 77, 90–3, 95, 98–9, 102–105

Dear Reader,

We hope you have enjoyed this book, but why not share your views on social media? You can also follow our pages to see more about our other products: facebook.com/penandswordbooks or follow us on Twitter @penswordbooks

You can also view our products at www.pen-and-sword.co.uk (UK and ROW) or www.penandswordbooks.com (North America).

To keep up to date with our latest releases and online catalogues, please sign up to our newsletter at: www.pen-and-sword.co.uk/newsletter

If you would like a printed catalogue with our latest books, then please email: enquiries@pen-and-sword.co.uk or telephone: 01226 734555 (UK and ROW) or email: uspen-and-sword@casematepublishers.com or telephone: (610) 853-9131 (North America).

We respect your privacy and we will only use personal information to send you information about our products.

Thank you!